MARVELS OF INDIAN IRON THROUGH THE AGES

MARVELS OF INDIAN IRON THROUGH THE AGES

R. BALASUBRAMANIAM

Introduction by
M.G.K. MENON

Rupa & Co

in association with

INFINITY FOUNDATION

Published 2008 by

Rupa . Co

7/16, Ansari Road, Daryaganj,
New Delhi 110 002

Sales Centres:

Allahabad Bengalooru Chandigarh
Chennai Hyderabad Jaipur Kathmandu
Kolkata Mumbai Pune

Typeset in 12 pt. Weiss BT by
Mindways.Design
1410 Chiranjiv Tower,
43 Nehru Place
New Delhi 110 019

Printed in India by
Gopsons Papers Ltd.
A-2&3, Sector-64,
Noida 201 301

To my dear *Guruji*, Professor Tanjore R. Anantharaman, on his eightieth birthday

sabbapāpassa akaraṇam kusalassa upasampadā
sacittapariyodapanam etam budhāna sāsanam

The eschewing of all evil, the perfecting of good deeds, the purifying of one's mind, this is the teaching of the Buddhas (the awakened)

Buddha (*Dhammapada* 183)

CONTENTS

INTRODUCTION TO THE SERIES

IT SEEMS THAT HISTORY OF SCIENCE AND TECHNOLOGY IN INDIA HAS SO FAR NOT been accorded the significance it deserves. Both laymen and students need to know and feel proud about the great achievements that were made in the past. This exercise should also help us to find out the causes which pushed us back and the West overtook us in its Industrial Revolution. In the western accounts of history of science and technology most of the important achievements are traced back to Greece thus giving these studies a Eurocentric bias.

In recent years several laudable efforts have been made in compiling the Indian History of Science and Technology. As is to be expected, these efforts had their own biases and perspectives. It was, however, felt that detailed accounts of individual technologies need to be reconstructed and not mere short descriptions. The History of Science and Technology Book Project was launched by Infinity Foundation keeping in view the need to correct the Eurocentric distortions as also to provide authentic and detailed summaries of the main technologies and how they evolved through history.

There is a vast amount of literature on these subjects but literary evidence is often prone to a variety of interpretations. It is therefore wise on the part of the organisers to place more reliance on material evidence available through archaeological excavations and museum exhibits. It was soon realised that the Indus civilisation, vast as it is in its expanse both in time and space, itself required a number of volumes to cover its achievements in the fields of metallurgy, architecture, hydraulics and a variety of other technologies. Under this series they have already commissioned a general book on Harappan Technology and its legacy to be written by Prof. D.P. Agrawal. Prof. J.P. Joshi has already completed a monograph on the Harappan architecture and engineering.

Probably, a few more volumes covering Harappan metallurgy and hydraulics etc. will be useful. It seems that Infinity Foundation has already commissioned about a dozen volumes covering iron technology, Himalayan architecture, zinc technology, traditional hydraulics, chalcolithic technology, archaeometallurgy of eastern India, traditional hydraulics of Uttaranchal etc. The future volumes may cover history of agriculture and animal husbandry, glass technology, ceramic and textile technologies etc.

Iron Technology is in itself a vast theme covering more than 3000 years. Prof. Vibha Tripathi has prepared a volume covering in brief all the aspects of Iron Technology right from its beginnings to pre-modern period. Prof. R. Balasubramaniam has produced a volume on the much neglected class of iron objects including pillars, beams and cannons. Unlike China, Indians preferred wrought iron technology in India. During the medieval period India attained some of its peaks in wrought iron forging technology in the manufacture of forge welded cannons. The skill required to fabricate the barrels of cannons by the use of forge-welded iron rings is a technological feat because it required good understanding of properties of iron. The excellent skills of the medieval Indian smiths become evident when one considers the enormous number of rings used in the construction of each cannon.

The Harappans built massive cities over huge platforms defying the annual inundations of the mighty Indus. In Mohenjodaro they dug 700-odd wells with burnt bricks to get clean potable water. In towns like Dholavira in Kachchh, they built elaborate reservoirs covering almost ten percent of the town to store rain harvested water. In the Harappan towns we see for the first time a gridiron layout of the streets. At Dholavira they have drains for potable water, sullage as also for run-off of the storm water but they have been constructed in such a manner that no mixing of dirty water with potable water ever takes place. The Harappans used a binary system of weights with high accuracy. Their linear unit of 17 mm seems to have led to the *angula* width mentioned in the *Arthasastra.*

Indians mastered the technology of making extremely tough steel known as the Wootz. It was such a famous and a precious commodity that it was considered a fitting gift to be presented to an emperor like Alexander and also to the Persian kings in the fifth century BC.

Thus, a series of book series on History of Science and Technology of India as sponsored by the Infinity Foundation covers a very important but so far neglected area and we do hope soon we will have an authentic history of science and technology of India and its role in a global history.

M.G.K. Menon

NOTE ON INFINITY FOUNDATION

Facilitating Research, Publishing and Education in: History of Indian Contributions to Science & Technology (HIST)

"In 1750 China accounted for almost one-third, ***India for almost one-quarter*** *and the West for less than a fifth of the world's manufacturing output... In the following decades...the industrialization of the West led to the de-industrialization of the rest of the world".*

— Samuel Huntington, *Clash of Civilizations*, pp.86-87

It has become largely forgotten that India held its prominent economic position referenced above because of its accomplishments in science and technology. The commonly taught history of India emphasises mostly kings, invasions and conflicts. The history of Indian ideas, if taught at all, is limited to religion, philosophy and popular culture. What is being often ignored is the well-documented evidence of India's significant contributions in metallurgy, civil engineering and architecture, water harvesting, shipping and ship building, textiles, medicinal plants, medicine, agriculture, forest management, management, astronomy and linguistics, among other disciplines.

By way of comparison, Joseph Needham's 30+ volumes on Chinese history of science and technology have made a monumental impact in the academic repositioning of China as having a rational and progressive civilisation. This work is a premier reference in China studies worldwide. But nothing equivalent exists for India, as explained below:

"Fear of elitism did not, happily, deter Joseph Needham from writing his authoritative account of the history of science and technology in China, and to dismiss that work as elitist history would be a serious neglect of China's past..."

> "***A similar history of India's science and technology has not yet been attempted, though many of the elements have been well discussed in particular studies.*** *The absence of a general study like Needham's is influenced by an attitudinal dichotomy. On the one hand, those who take a rather spiritual — even perhaps a religious — view of India's history do not have a great interest in the analytical and scientific parts of India's past, except to use it as a piece of propaganda about India's greatness (as in the bloated account of what is imaginatively called 'Vedic mathematics', missing the really creative period in Indian mathematics by many centuries). On the other hand, many who oppose religious and communal politics are particularly suspicious of what may even look like a 'glorification' of India's past.* ***The need for a work like Needham's has remained unmet.***"
>
> — Amartya Sen, 1997

HIST is an important part of India's story because it has been the substratum of its civilisation's rationality and secular progress, the basis for pre-colonial Indian Ocean global trade, the foundation for building India's future knowledge society, and a key element in projecting *Brand India*.

Infinity Foundation, a private non-profit foundation based in Princeton, USA, launched its HIST project with the following objectives:

- Document and discuss the history of scientific and technological achievements in the Indian subcontinent until the end of the nineteenth century, because the period after that has already been well documented.
- Inspire creativity and self-confidence among our youth, refuting the popular notion that Indians were irrational and mystical. Replace colonial notions of intellectual dependency and revive India as a premier knowledge exporter.
- Bridge the socio-economic divide: It is often the rural and the underprivileged in India who have preserved key aspects of traditional knowledge, such as in medicinal plants, or traditional civil engineering and home building. By restoring legitimacy to traditional knowledge, which is decentralised and less capital intensive, we empower local/rural cultures, lifestyles and economies. If India hopes to create genuine alternatives to rural migration and the burden of high-density metro lifestyles, we need to re-engage with, and build upon, the strengths of traditional knowledge systems.
- Build India's brand, cultural capital and soft power: Ancient India's higher education and technological genius attracted the cream of Asian students to Nalanda, Taxila

and other Indian centers of learning. The alumni and visiting scholars spread India's cultural capital across Asia. Today, USA has a strategy to educate the future leaders of the world to gain influence globally. China has also embarked upon a strategy to export its higher education for geopolitical influence. If India hopes to preserve and expand its role in the information economy or in engineering design, she needs a civilizational or "cultural brand" in the same sense as the following culture specific brands:

Japanese-ness	Quality
French-ness	Beauty/aesthetics: cosmetics, fashion, wine, Cannes, tourism
Italian-ness	Design, art, cuisine
British-ness	Justice, law, rationality
German-ness	Precision, manufacturing
Chinese-ness	Efficiency

In each of these cases, the soft power wielded by the country's brand has fueled economic expansion using its civilisational advantages. It is important to restore a realistic counterbalance to India's negative branding brought about by some of the thrusts of the social sciences until now. The following table is not intended as a generalisation but merely as indicative of some differences between two ways of seeking Indian culture – the one by social scientists and the other by technocrats such as those pursuing HIST research.

Social Sciences on Indian-ness	HIST on Indian-ness
Mystical and otherworldly	Rational, innovative and creative
Frozen in time and backward	Pragmatic and progressive
"Caste, dowry, sati, conflicts"	Multicultural and interdependent
Knowledge came from invaders	Indian knowledge systems
British made us a nation	Many prior nations existed
Lacking self-esteem and afraid of future	Confident and competitive
Defensive and closed	Open and globalised

Once again, Indians are increasingly being acknowledged worldwide for their brainpower, but the *civilisational brand* is dominated by "caste, cows, curry" images from anthropology.

Furthermore, many Indians have distanced themselves from what they see as "baggage", bringing about disconnects with their own past. HIST is a secular and all-encompassing shared past for nation-building.

It is important to bring scientists and technologists into this historical research so as to stay focused on the evidence and not the politics. The goal is to not glorify but analyse objectively, in order use the knowledge for present and future growth and to learn from past mistakes.

INFINITY FOUNDATION'S HIST PROJECT

Although Infinity's vision is to implement this unprecedented, composite and inclusive series, we would like to acknowledge and applaud many pioneering research and contributions made in this field, such as the following, and work with them to expand the discipline:

- 5 volume series on traditional agricultural practices by Indian Council for Agricultural Research;
- 2 volume series on History of Science by Dr D.P. Chattopadhyay;
- History of Indian Medicine by Dr. S. Valliathan;
- Works of Indian National Science Academy; and
- many others.

The HIST project was started in 2002, after being conceived at the Foundation's Colloquium in Woodstock that was jointly convened by Infinity Foundation and Columbia University. So far, only the series on Materials and Technologies has been started. Two other series, one on Life Sciences and another on Theoretical Sciences, are envisioned for the future.

Annual project meetings have been held all over India to review progress, share research and foster collaboration. These meetings — in places as varied as Indian Institute of Technology, Kanpur, India International Center (Delhi), Kumaon University (Nainital) and Banaras Hindu University (Varanasi) — have also served as outreach to local colleges and to the general public by giving them a chance to interact with our academic scholars. Each volume takes approximately three years to develop the final manuscript, and involves a team of scholars in addition to the author(s).

TOPIC SELECTION CRITERIA

The following criteria were applied in selected topics for the series:

- Time period of focus should be sciences and technologies developed until the end of the nineteenth century.
- Topics must have empirically verifiable and significant Indian contributions.
- Subject matter experts should be available, *especially within India.* This helps the growth of research communities invested in such investigations and secures the roots of this work in India over time.
- Religion and "stories" should be avoided as evidence, i.e. no "Pushpak Viman" to be included. The goal is an honest exploration, not glorification.
- The sources and scholar must be internationally credible.

Infinity thanks Sashi Kejriwal, Arjun Bhagat and Navin Doshi for their generous financial contributions to support this volume. Infinity also thanks Shruti (India Head of Infinity Foundation) for her valuable contributions in creative and strategic areas of this project.

About Infinity Foundation (IF)

Infinity Foundation is a 501 (c)(3) non-profit tax-exempt private foundation that was started in 1995 as a vehicle for its founder to give back to the Indian and American societies. For further information, please contact:

Project: http://www.indianscience.org/
Foundation: www.infinityfoundation.com
Address: 53 White Oak Drive, Princeton NJ 08540, USA
Email: infinityfoundation@gmail.com

Rajiv Malhotra
President, Infinity Foundation

FOREWORD

THE GLORIOUS TRADITION OF IRON AND STEEL TECHNOLOGY OF THE INDIAN subcontinent is the subject of study of this book in the series on India's contribution to the history of science and technology. India's history of science and technology is yet to be written and the available data does not expose its full potential. The presentation of some wonderful examples of Indian metallurgical skill in this book presents only the tip of the iceberg of the knowledge and skill of the ancient Indian craftsmen.

The tradition of making iron and steel by indigenous craftsmen continued widely in India till the end of the nineteenth century. It is almost extinct now, except perhaps among some isolated groups in Madhya Pradesh, Bihar, Jharkhand and Chattisgarh. The long and glorious tradition of iron and steel in the subcontinent has merited serious attention from the historians of Indian technology in the recent past. The iron making origin and processes have been explained by rigorous analysis of archaeological data. In this context, when reference is made of examples revealing the Indian blacksmith's skill in the art of working with iron, usually some important examples are cited like the Delhi iron pillar and wootz steel. In this book, Balasubramaniam has explored and placed on record some of the wonders of the Indian blacksmith skills, from a different perspective. The objects themselves are the subject of attention. Balasubramaniam analyses the objects with engineering precision. Detailed discussions on the Delhi and Dhar iron pillars have added value to the book. These are based on the original work of the author. In this manner, the author draws most of the material for this book from his original publications. This is a unique aspect of this book. Balasubramaniam's original work on the Delhi Iron Pillar, considered by many to be *the* metallurgical wonder of India, has earned him international attention. One notable feature of this work is the great detail in which forge welded cannons have been discussed apart from visually presenting some of the massive forge welded cannons of the subcontinent. It is a visual pleasure to view these pieces presented in this richly illustrated volume. When one considers that such large numbers of forge welded cannons are not present any where else in the world, the skill of the Indian blacksmith in the working of iron must be appreciated. Apart from this, there is also a useful documentation angle because this is one of the first time that massive forge welded cannons have been collected and catalogued in one book. The author also discusses at length the wonder material of the Orient – wootz steel. The examples presented by the author are excellent testimonies to the history of iron and steel in the subcontinent.

The volume is a seminal contribution to the history of iron and steel of the subcontinent. It will accomplish the task of creating a sense of awe among the reader after viewing first hand the glorious examples of Indian iron and steel making skills. I am sure/sincerely hope that the marvels of Indian iron and steel making skill presented in this volume will excite both the learned scholar and common reader and would serve as a standard reference in libraries for time to come.

M.G.K. Menon
New Delhi, January 2008

EDITOR'S NOTE

IRON TECHNOLOGY IN INDIA SEEMS TO HAVE MADE A BEGINNING MORE THAN THREE thousand years ago. High quality steel was made in the first millennium BCE. During the medieval period, it attained some of its peaks in wrought iron forging technology. For example, the skill required to manufacture the barrel by the use of forge welded iron rings is a technological feat because it required close dimensional tolerances besides a good understanding of the thermal expansion and contraction properties of the material. When one considers the enormous number of rings used in the construction of each cannon, the excellent skills of the medieval Indian smiths become evident. Another example was of the superb skill demonstrated in shrink fitting. Tensile stresses usually cause damage, while compressive stresses are beneficial because they must first be overcome to cause any damage. The process of shrink fitting was very beneficial as it helped in producing tight joints as well as lent toughness to the wall. This is why the Indian blacksmiths preferred forge-welded cannons because they were far superior to the cast iron cannons in terms of their strength and toughness. The Delhi Iron Pillar is not only famous for its corrosion resistance all through these sixteen hundred years but is also an example of the amazing feat of handling such a massive structure (weighing six tonnes!) through forge welding of wrought iron.

The numerous massive cannons scattered all over the forts of India are begging for attention. There is an urgent need for scholars from different disciplines to study these wonderful pieces and unravel their metallurgical excellence. Prof. Balasubramaniam has drawn attention to these requirements in this comprehensive volume and given us a glimpse of the technological prowess of the Indian smiths in forging massive pillars, beams, cannons and guns. He also gives a summary of the wonder metal of India, the wootz steel, which was in great demand all over the world. Prof. Balasubramaniam, a leading metallurgist and science historian of the country, has specialised in forge welded monumental structures between the Gupta period and the British rule, and has written numerous papers and books on these themes. This book is a summary of his wide-ranging contributions to highlight the achievements of our iron smiths of yore. Wootz steel will be discussed in greater detail in another forthcoming volume under this series.

Unfortunately, such technological achievements are conspicuous by their absence in the Western version of the global history of science and technology. The Western history of science and technology suffers from Eurocentric distortions in which all major innovations are traced back to Greece. It needs to be recognised that both India and China were world leaders in technology and industry right from the third millennium BCE till as late as the eighteenth century CE. To correct such distortions and to produce a balanced and an unbiased history of science and technology, which gives due recognition to the contributions made by India and the other nations of the world, the Infinity Foundation has sponsored the present series of books.

We are aware that even to highlight the evolution of science and technology during the past five thousand years, in a vast country like India, is an immense undertaking. Inspired by the enthusiastic cooperation of the authors and the publishers, and in the fond hope of getting a warm response from the readers, the Infinity Foundation has launched this ambitious project. We will cover the histories of metal technologies (zinc, iron, copper, etc.), architecture and engineering, hydraulics, textiles, agriculture, husbandry, navigation, maths, ceramics, lapidary crafts, glass and faience, and so on, in twenty-four volumes.

D.P. Agrawal
Chief Editor

PREFACE

THE GLORIOUS TRADITION OF IRON-MAKING IN INDIA HAS BEEN WELL-RESEARCHED and documented in the recent past. Several excellent publications dealing with the primacy of iron in the Indian subcontinent, its local origin as opposed to Western diffusion, archaeological and literary perspectives are available. These books deal with several aspects of iron technology relating to the Indian subcontinent and provide a strong foundation for studies the subject. The wonderful examples of Indian iron technology have not been dealt with exclusively, although there are stray references.

One of the main aims of our research into India's rich metallurgical past is to excite young readers about the exalted status of India's metallurgical knowledge in ancient and medieval times.. A related aim is to inform the eager and interested non-Indian reader about the wonders of Indian metallurgical skills. In this regard, the Infinity Foundation of USA has pioneered the study and diffusion of Indian traditional knowledge systems and the documentation of the history of science and technology in India. Vibha Tripathi's book in this series provides a complete overview of iron in the Indian subcontinent. The present book deals with wonderful examples of Indian blacksmithy skills. A third book in this series will delve into wootz steel.

Once it was decided to focus attention on the marvels of Indian metallurgical knowledge and skills, with particular reference to iron technology, the task of putting together this book became much easier. For the book dealing with the wonders of Indian blacksmithy skills, there was a ready source of reference, namely, our original works dealing with iron pillars and forge welded cannons. Therefore, this book draws inspiration and major material from my original publications on this subject. In this manner, most of the material presented and discussed in this book are my original researches. I am presently researching the wonder material of the Orient – wootz steel. In order to complete the fourth chapter devoted to wootz steel, material has been collected and reviewed from the vast existing literature. The topic of wootz steel will be dealt in greater detail in a complimentary volume.

This book is divided into four major sections. In the first introductory chapter, some basic ideas of iron metallurgy, with special reference to the Indian subcontinent, are presented. The discussion does not call for detailed knowledge of science and metallurgy. A basic highschool background in science would be sufficient to understand most of the material presented in this chapter and in the subsequent ones. The aim of writing this chapter was not to review the entire gamut of metallurgy of ancient Indian iron, but to provide the reader a glimpse of the intricate knowledge that Indians possessed in producing marvellous iron objects, which are discussed in great detail in this book.

The second chapter deals with massive iron objects, with special reference to pillars and beams. The most famous example, of course, is the Delhi Iron Pillar, and most of the material presented on this metallurgical wonder is based on my personal research. The other well-known iron pillar that is located at Dhar has also been described in some detail and its story makes for a fascinating reading. The massive iron beams in the Orissa temples have been described next. The chapter ends with a short discussion on the Iron Pillar at Kodachadri Hill.

Some of the less-known wonders of Indian blacksmithy skills are forge welded iron cannons, available all across the subcontinent in different historical locations. We shall specifically address forge welded iron cannons and not cast iron cannons in Chapter 3 because cast iron technology did not originate in India. It is difficult to understand, in the present context, why Indians were not ready to adopt cast iron technology from Europe, when it first made its large-scale appearance in the sixteenth century. One possible reason for the same could be the proficiency of Indian blacksmiths in the science and engineering of handling wrought iron so that they never felt the need to adopt cast iron technology. Some wonderful examples of forge welded iron cannons in the Indian subcontinent will be outlined. The forge welded iron cannons of India are truly the neglected gems of Indian blacksmithy skills. While only a handful can be counted in the whole of Europe, India possesses hundreds of massive forge welded iron cannons, totally uncared for and standing as mute spectators to the glorious heights attained by the Indian blacksmiths before the advent of mechanisation and large-scale industrial production of iron.

The fourth chapter reviews the famous wootz steel of the Indian subcontinent. Wootz steel was a prized commodity during the medieval period for its wonderful ability to be wrought into tough swords. These swords wrought from wootz steel exhibited typical patterns on their surface. Wootz steel was highly regarded all over the world. It was truly an engineering material with a large geographical spread – one that originated from the Indian subcontinent. This chapter will highlight the properties of wootz steel, the method of its production, the forging of tough blades from wootz pancakes and finally, the European fascination with this wonderful material. This chapter is brief in nature because this subject will be dealt in greater detail in a complimentary volume.

The book ends with a bibliography which has been presented in a detailed manner in order to assist readers to the original sources of publications where some of the issues have been discussed in much greater depth.

The book aims to review and present the wonderful iron objects of the Indian subcontinent. All these objects have been placed in a historical perspective in order to highlight the continuous achievements of Indians' mastery over iron and steel technology. The care required in conserving and preserving these wonderful objects needs to be thought about. There are several possible modern-day applications for the technologies that went into the making of these iron objects. The immense potential and value of traditional technologies for producing objects of high value been has somehow neglected in modern India. One must understand that traditionally produced iron craft objects can be gainfully sold at a premium for their artistic as well as technical value. It is the traditional art industry of India that has earned the country world recognition and fame in the past. It is the traditional art industry of India that would pave the way for India to obtain her exalted position in the world community of nations again.

I must thank several people for inspiring me to write this book. Professor Anantharaman has always been a great source of inspiration for all my academic endeavours and I owe all my skills and knowledge to his inspirational guidance and charismatic leadership. In fact, this book is my offering to my beloved *Guruji* on his eightieth birthday. The constant encouragement and support provided by Rajiv Malhotra and D.P. Agrawal formed the bedrock on which this work rests. They have always been there to provide valuable criticisms and constructive comments over the last three years. Professor Ranganathan has been a well-wisher and an intelligent critic. He has fired my imagination with several of his keen observations and queries. It is always a pleasure to discuss science and technology with him. Professor Rama Rao has been like a guide-in-the-background.

He has provided valuable comments on my work and has guided me in improving my writing and presentation skills. I thank him for all the valuable advice on my work on Indian archaoemetallurgy. I must also thank Professor Bhanu Prakash, who first introduced me to the wonders of ancient Indian metallurgy during my undergraduate days at the Benaras Hindu University. It was also a great privilege to interact and work with a renowned scholar, specialising in the historical and archaeological aspects of iron in the Indian subcontinent, Professor Vibha Tripathi of Benaras Hindu University. Her well-meaning critical comments have always helped improve the quality of my work. Dr Sharada Srinivasan has provided me valuable feedback at several critical junctures and I thank her for all her insightful comments. I cherish the continuing interaction with Dr S. Jaikishan, Dr Pranab Chattopadhyaya, Robert D. Smith and Ruth Rhynas Brown on the subject of cannons in general. I must also thank and place on record the excellent discussions that I have had on the subject of archaeometallurgy, in general, with Professors A.K. Biswas, A. Ghosh, P. Ramachandra Rao, K. Chatttopadhyay, C.V. Sundaram, A.K. Bhatnagar, R.K. Dube, and Drs M.N. Mungole, Placid Rodriguez, Baldev Raj, K. Roessler, K. Igaki, Ellen M. Raven, A.V. Ramesh Kumar, P. Dillmann, Paolo Piccardo, Delphine Neff and A.K. Bag. Finally, I remember that all that I do is because of the wonderful support and affection of my parents, (late) Rasipuram Subramaniam Ramamoorthi and Dr. R. Savithri, my children Gargi and Gowri, and my wife Gaitri.

R. Balasubramaniam
Kanpur, January 2008

1

INTRODUCTION

IN THIS CHAPTER, WE SHALL INTRODUCE SOME BASIC CONCEPTS RELATED TO THE metallurgy of iron. Appreciation of these aspects will provide a sound background to understanding the complexities and skills involved in manufacturing the metallurgical marvels that are dealt with in detail in the book. After discussing various aspects related to the working of iron, the extraction of iron practised by Indians through the ages (till the advent of the modern process of extracting iron using blast furnaces) will be briefly reviewed. Salient features of ancient Indian iron would then be described to provide the necessary background to help the understanding of the material (iron) that went into the manufacture of the marvels discussed in this book.

METAL EXTRACTION

We shall begin by briefly addressing the method by which iron was extracted in ancient and medieval India. It appears that the direct reduction method of iron extraction continued for a fairly long period in Indian history, showing that the ancient Indian metallurgists had mastered this method of iron extraction. We shall also compare the ancient method of iron extraction with the modern method using the blast furnace.

The extraction of iron by ancient Indians needs to be understood because iron lumps were the starting material for the fabrication of most objects. There are excellent articles and books dealing with ancient Indian iron making furnaces and processes, and these are provided in the bibliography. Here, we shall only provide a broad overview.

Iron melts at 1540°C and the ancient Indian furnaces were incapable of attaining such a high temperature. The various aspects of construction and operation of ancient Indian iron furnaces (called bloomery furnaces because the end product was an iron bloom) have been studied and discussed in literature. The ore for extracting iron was carefully collected by ironsmiths. Interestingly, the specific ore was collected depending on the end application. Preheating facilitated breaking of the ores, and the fine dust separated by washing or by wind. The preheated iron ore and charcoal were charged in alternating layers, the furnace ignited and slowly heated to the reduction temperature (1000°C-1200°C). Different designs of iron extraction furnaces have been described in literature. Their heights ranged between roughly 2m and 6m. A typical ancient Indian bloomery furnace has been schematically compared with a modern blast furnace in **Figure 1.1**. The illustration in **Figure 1.2** shows the steps involved in the manufacture of large objects, for example, the Delhi Iron Pillar.

Bellows placed at the bottom of the furnaces were operated at a controlled rate. Iron ore had to be reduced in order to obtain iron. Iron ore is essentially oxide of iron, and it is reduced by the carbon monoxide (CO) that is produced by the burning of charcoal in the bloomery furnace (or coking coal in a modern blast furnace, see **Figure 1.1**). The other unwanted oxides, like SiO_2, which are commonly found in iron ores, have to be removed and this was possible by the creation of a liquid slag called fayalite of composition Fe_2SiO_4 or $2FeO.SiO_2$. While some of the liquid slag flowed out of the bloomery furnace during the reduction of iron ore to iron, some of it still remained when the hot iron lumps were taken out of the furnace. Therefore, the hot lumps that were extracted from the bloomery furnace at the end of the heat (typically lasting for about six to eight hours) were immediately hammered. In this process, most of the entrapped liquid fayalitic slag flowed out of the solid reduced iron mass. However, it was not possible to remove all the entrapped liquid slag and therefore, ancient irons produced by the direct reduction process always contained entrapped inclusions. The inclusions are essentially composed of fayalite, some iron oxides (for instance, wüstite, FeO) and glassy phases (due to calcium silico-phosphates). As a result of entrapped slag particles and iron oxides in the structure, the specific gravity of ancient irons is lower than that of the purest form of Fe.

The slag present in ancient irons is generally microscopic in nature, with a few pieces of larger size. These were not of uniform size and also not strictly uniform in composition.

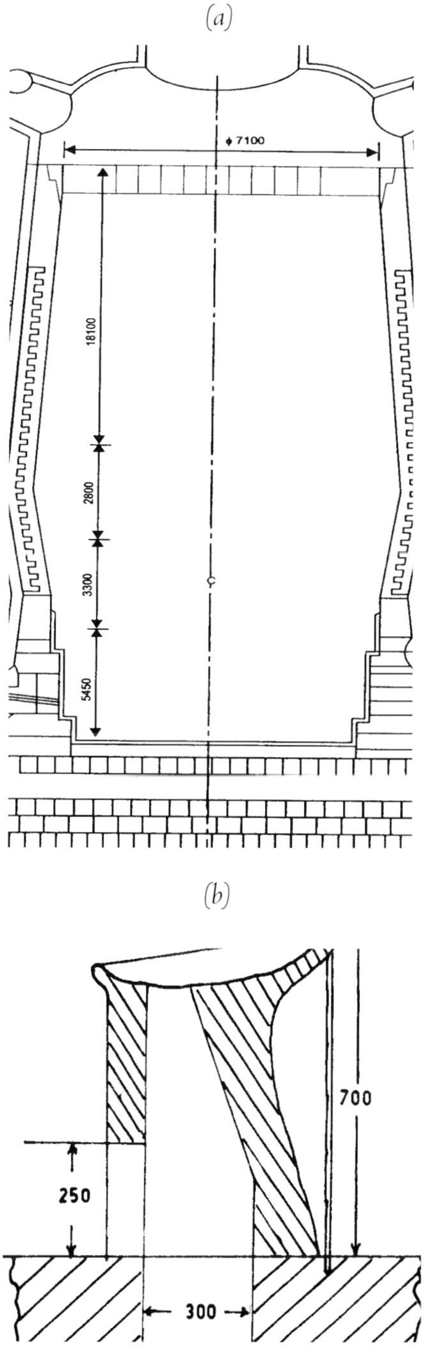

Fig. 1.1. *Comparison of (a) modern and (b) ancient furnaces for extracting iron from ore.*

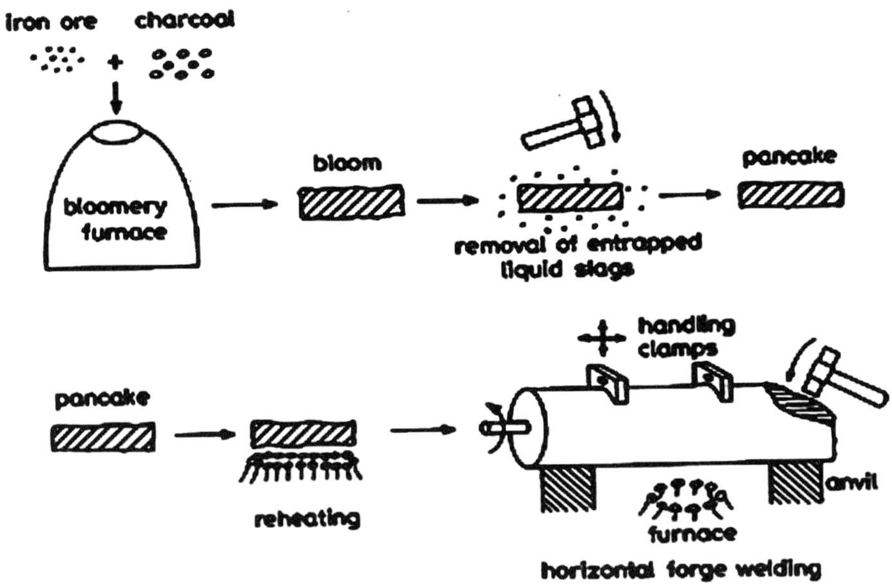

Fig. 1.2: *Schematic illustration of steps involved in the manufacture of large iron objects, like the Delhi Iron Pillar.*

Viewing the production of iron lumps from a powder metallurgical viewpoint, it has been noted that the ancient Indians produced iron 'pre-forms' directly from iron ore, which implied that the powder production, powder consolidation and sintering processes were combined into one operation.

The end product of the extraction process was a lump of iron that was subsequently used for a wide variety of applications, either directly or after further heat treatments depending upon the application. One important heat treatment that was successfully conducted was controlled carburisation of iron in specially designed crucibles. The carbon content of steel (which is an alloy of iron and carbon) was carefully controlled by subsequent decarburisation treatment. It is important to control the carbon content in steel because the mechanical properties of steel are critically dependent on the carbon content. As a thumb rule, the higher the carbon content, the higher the strength of steel.

The relatively small iron lumps produced in the bloomery furnace were the starting materials for the manufacture of large iron objects, in general. The lumps were also used, after suitable heat treatments, for manufacturing agricultural tools (hoes, spades, sickles and weeding forks), household items (knives, ladles, spoons, sieves, saucepans, cauldrons, bowls, dishes, saucers and tripod), building tools (nails, clamps, staples, sheets, door handles and spikes), other artefacts (anvils, hammers, scissors, saws, chains and smithy tools) and warfare weapons (swords, javelins, armour, helmets and shield bases).

CLASSIFICATION

It must be remembered that ancient Indians were masters in the production of steel. The iron and steel manufactured were as per pre-determined quality, and the ancient Indians had mastered the art of quality steel making. The method of production of wrought iron directly from the ore by the process of direct reduction continued for a fairly long time in the Indian subcontinent, all the way up to the end of the eighteenth century AD. The Indians knew fairly early in history about the benefits of carburising iron, so as to increase its strength. The Second Urbanisation of India (that is, settlements along the Ganga) was strongly influenced by the steeling of iron.

Three principal varieties of iron were recognised based on the carbon content. Each of these principal varieties was further sub-divided into other varieties depending on their composition and properties (Prakash 1991: 351-371). Sanskrit literary sources (for instance, the *Rasa Ratna Samuchchaya* dated to the eighth to the twelfth century AD) classify iron into three basic categories: wrought iron (*kanta loha*), carbon steel (*tikshna loha*) and cast iron (*munda loha*). The *Rasendrashâr Samgraha* again mentions these three classifications and also states that '*munda* is ten times better than iron rust, *tikshna* hundred times better than *munda*, and *kanta* million times better than *tikshna* iron'. These three basic categories were further classified according to the carbon content, heat treatment and end use. *Munda* was again of three varieties: *mridu* that which melts easily and does not break and is glossy; *kuntha* that which expands with difficulty when struck with hammer; *kadâra* that which breaks when struck with a hammer and has a black fractured surface. Six varieties of *tikshna* have been provided: *khara, sâra, hrinnâla, târâbatta, bâjira* and *kâlaauha* (black metal). One variety is rough and free from hair-like lines and has a quicksilver-like fractured surface, while another variety breaks with difficulty and presents a sharp edge. Five different varieties of *kanta* were recognised: *bhrâmaka, chumbaka, karshaka, dvâvaka* and *romakântâ*. The variety of iron which makes all kinds of iron move about was called *bhrâmaka*, that which kisses iron was called *chumbaka*, that which attracts iron was called *karshaka*, that which at once melts iron was called *drâvaka*, and *romakântâ* was the kind which, when broken, shoots forth hair-like filaments.

Literary evidence suggests that the ancient Indian iron furnaces were capable of producing iron of consistent (low) carbon content containing entrapped slag inclusions. Iron meant for corrosion-resistant applications contained higher phosphorous (P) contents. Therefore it is reasonable to conclude that the ancient Indian metallurgists possessed the skill of manufacturing iron and steel according to the desired application, and corrosion-resistant iron was one amongst them. The excellent corrosion resistance of ancient Indian iron can be attributed to the relatively high phosphorus (P) content in ancient Indian iron. The process of protection against corrosion will be described later in this book.

Interestingly, in nearly all published ancient Indian iron compositions, a relatively larger percentage of P can be noted. Modern steels cannot tolerate such high P contents, as they would be susceptible to cracking during the process of mechanical working due to the presence of P in steel. While it was earlier believed that P in ancient steels comes from slag inclusions, recent developments in slag chemistry help in understanding the probable reason. The relatively higher P content in ancient iron is attributed to the kind of slag that was created in the extraction process by solid-state reduction. Slag is the product formed between the flux and gangue in the mineral. This aids the extraction of metal from the ore. Lime was not added in the ancient Indian furnaces. In modern blast furnaces lime is added as a flux along with iron ore and coking coal. Therefore, the slag generated in the ancient Indian furnaces was essentially fayalitic slag (that is consisting of iron orthosilicates Fe_2SiO_4). This is also corroborated by available compositions of ancient Indian iron-making slag from archaeological excavation sites. The slag does not contain lime. The removal of P from the metal into the slag is facilitated by the basic components (for instance, FeO and CaO) in the slag. The efficiency of removal of P from the metal is much higher for CaO compared to FeO in the slag. These facts are well-established in slag chemistry. Therefore, the absence of CaO in the slag leads to a lower efficiency of removal of P from the metal, which invariably must have resulted in higher P contents in ancient Indian irons. Rigorous thermodynamic analysis of P removal from iron, in the absence of CaO in the slag, also provides the same answer. As the entrapped slag seen in the ancient Indian iron is generally fayalitic with insignificant CaO contents, thermodynamics dictates that a higher amount of P should remain in solid solution in iron. This is the reason for the presence of higher P in ancient Indian irons. We shall note later the excellent state of preservation of massive Indian iron objects exposed to the atmosphere. This is related to the high P content of iron.

It must also be noted that there are indications that P addition in some cases was intentional. For instance, a British explorer named Buchanan (1807) travelled extensively throughout South India in the eighteenth century and carefully recorded all the activities of the people he encountered. In his detailed description of steel making in Karnataka in the eighteenth century, he describes one furnace operated at Devaraya Durga. In this furnace, conical clay crucibles were filled with a specific amount of wood, from the barks of a plant, *Cassia auriculata*, and pieces of wrought iron, then sealed and fired. Interestingly, the bark of this plant contains a high content of P, extracted by osmosis from the ground. Further research is required to throw light on this aspect of the use of the specific plant and tree species in the extraction of iron and the subsequent manufacture of steel.

MICROSTRUCTURES

In material engineering, the close co-relation between structure and properties is well-known. Structure indicates arrangement of the material. When one views the arrangement of electrons, neutrons and protons, we term it atomic structure. The ordered (or disordered) arrangement of atoms is called atomic structure. On a microscopic scale, in the order of micrometres, the grain structure of engineering materials is understood. Finally, the macrostructure refers to observations made in the range of millimetres. Structure affects the properties of engineering materials. We shall concentrate on the microstructure of ancient Indian iron, that is, the arrangement of the constituent phases and grain sizes.

Some important aspects of the underlying microstructure of ancient Indian iron would be presented. In fact, the microstructures of ancient irons are highly heterogeneous. The irons normally possess non-uniform grain structures.

A typical microstructure of ancient Indian iron in the unetched condition is shown in Figure 1.3. In the unetched condition, the specimens generally reveal slag inclusions irregularly distributed in the microstructure.

The end product of the bloomery furnace was a lump of direct reduced iron, which contained phosphorous as the major alloying element. Therefore the end product of the ancient Indian direct process of extracting iron can be termed as phosphoric irons. On the other hand, the end product of modern blast furnaces is pig iron, in which carbon is the major alloying element. In contrast to macrosegregation of P in pig iron, microsegregation of P is realised in ancient phosphoric irons. Figure 1.4 is an optical metallograph obtained after polishing the sample to mirror-like finish and etching with

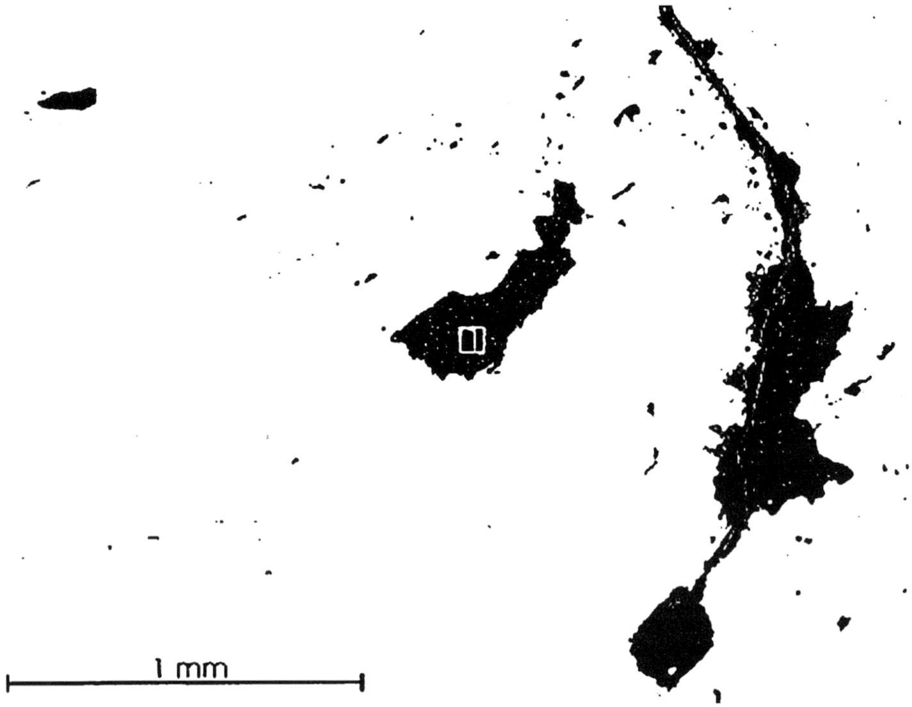

Fig. 1.3: *Typical microstructure of ancient Indian iron in the unetched condition. Notice the presence of entrapped slag inclusions.*

an etchant. Two etchants were used to reveal the microstructure. In **Figure 1.4a**, the etchant used is Nital, and typical ghosting features are observed. These features are due to differences in P contents. In **Figure 1.4b**, the etchant used is Oberhoffer etchant. The particular etchant used reveals the distribution of P in the microstructure. The dark areas are the regions where the P content is less, while the bright areas are indicative of higher P contents. Notice that P is depleted from the grain boundaries and from the regions surrounding the entrapped slag particles. There are several fascinating insights that can be obtained from the study of microstructures, but those are beyond the scope of the present book.

Addressing the microstructures in metallurgical parlance, etched specimens generally reveal medium to coarse grains of ferrite. The presence of carbon leads to another phase called pearlite, which consists of alternating layers of ferrite and cementite. Ferrite can be considered as almost pure iron and cementite as a compound having the formula Fe_3C.

(a)

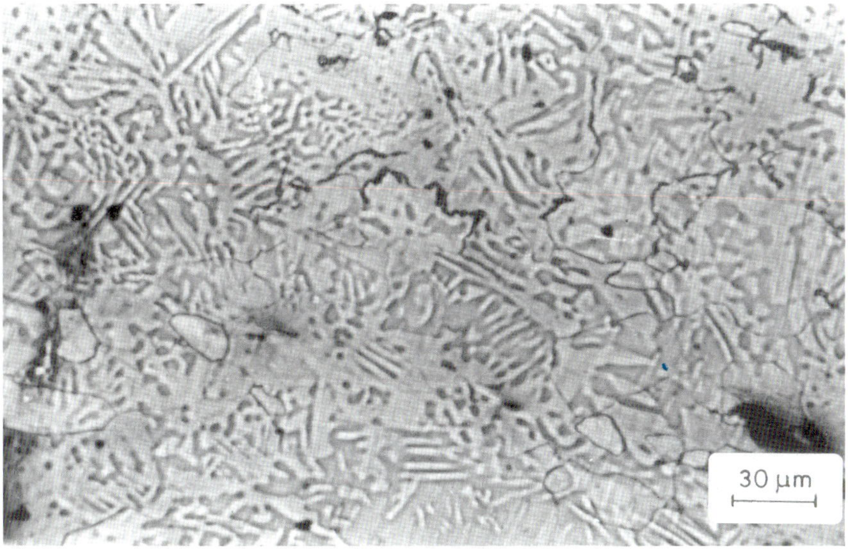

(b)

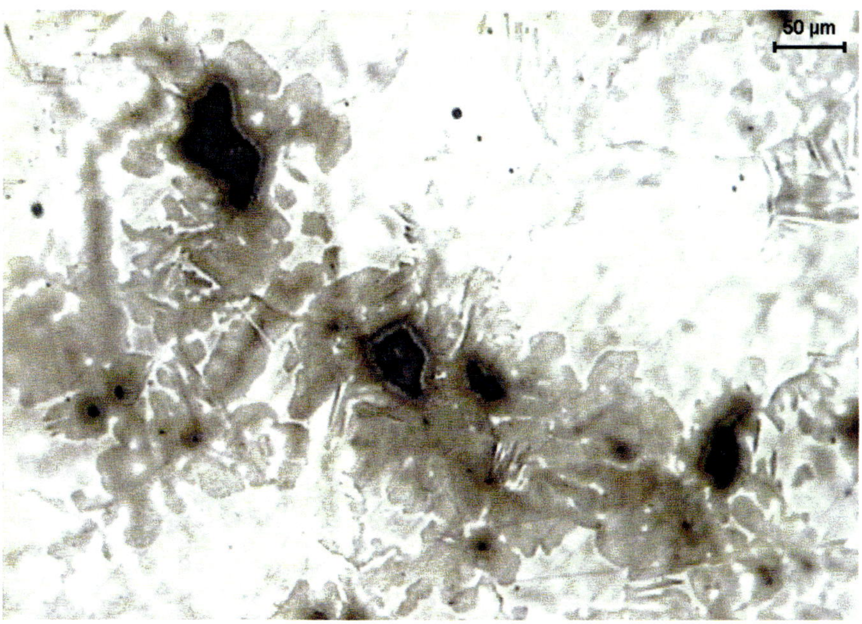

Fig. 1.4: *Typical microstructure of ancient Indian iron in the etched condition using (a) Nital and (b) Oberhoffer etchant.*

The pearlite phase is generally observed where the carbon contents are higher. The irregular distribution of pearlite is generally noted in ancient irons. In case the material is worked, there are straight-line features that are called slip bands, which can also be seen in the microstructures. The absence of a uniform distribution of pearlite is indicative of removal or segregation of P because, in such areas of P segregation, C diffuses out and the material becomes poorer in C content. Therefore, pearlite can generally be observed near entrapped inclusions as P has been depleted in these regions due to the action of slag in removing P (see **Figure 1.5**).

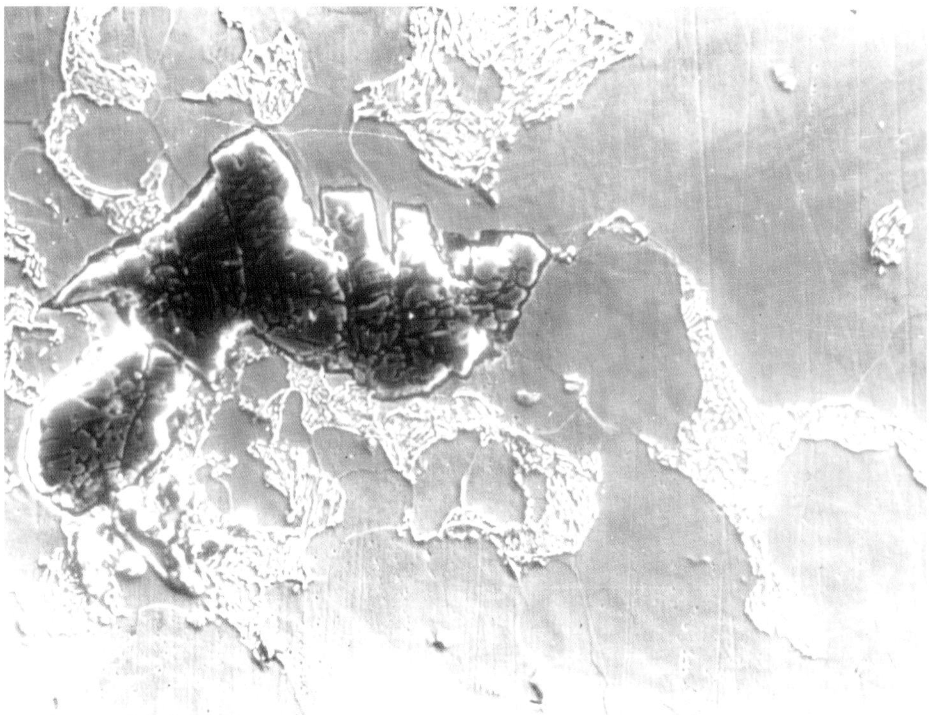

Fig. 1.5: *Pearlite found near entrapped slag inclusions (in Dhar pillar iron) indicating that carbon segregates to regions where phosphorous is depleted.*

The non-uniform structure of ancient irons is one reason for observed differences in chemical analyses of samples taken from different locations of the same structure. This must be borne in mind.

WORKING IRON

We shall now appreciate some simple facts about handling and working with iron. As stated earlier, iron melts at a temperature of 1540°C, which is quite high. One way to produce an engineered structure is to melt iron and then cast the molten iron into prefabricated moulds, so that after the metal solidifies, it takes the shape of the mould. This material manufacturing process is called casting. We shall discount the casting technique in the Indian context because the ancient Indian furnaces were not capable of reaching such a high temperature. It is also well-established that ancient Indians did not really work with liquid iron. However, the process of manufacturing wootz steel required a high carbon content and the way in which this was achieved will be addressed in the chapter on wootz. One of the interesting features of casting of iron is that when carbon is present in relatively large amounts (greater than two weight per cent) in the iron (the material being called cast iron), then the melting point of the material is significantly lowered. However, as the ancient Indian iron-making furnaces produced iron with very low carbon contents, it was not possible to obtain iron in the liquid form. Therefore, ancient Indians did not employ the casting technology for manufacturing large objects. This is validated by microstructural observations of ancient Indian large iron objects which do not indicate any sign of melting and subsequent solidification.

Let us address a related issue, namely the mechanical property of iron. One important mechanical property is ductility. Metals typically exhibit ductility or malleability, which is simply defined as the ability of the material to undergo permanent deformation. A necessary requirement for imparting permanent deformation is the application of force to the material. Permanent deformation must be contrasted with elastic deformation, wherein the material, on removal of the applying force, returns to the shape it was in prior to the application of force. A simple example of this kind of deformation is noticed in the stretching of elastic rubber bands. You must have noticed that when you remove the force on the rubber band, it returns to its original shape. The ability and the extent of an engineering material to undergo elastic or permanent deformation is dictated by the atomic as well as the electronic structure of the material.

Metals are by definition ductile. In contrast, ceramic materials (a good example being glass) are quite brittle. Ceramic materials constitute an important class of engineering materials and they have become quite important in modern technology. They can be defined as compounds formed between metals and non-metals (such as oxygen, boron, carbon, nitrogen, etc.). A typical example of a ceramic material is silicon nitride. Brittleness implies lack of ductility and therefore, brittle materials fail without any permanent deformation under the application of sufficient load.

There is another important mechanical property and this is the strength of the material. It is indicative of the load-carrying capacity of the metal. The higher the load the material can carry, the stronger it is. Of course when we are comparing different metals, we should implicitly assume that the same cross-section of the material is being addressed because only then can we compare. Otherwise, a less strong material of larger cross-section area can carry a higher load than a stronger material of smaller cross-section. In order to overcome this difficulty, strength is usually expressed in terms of engineering stress, which is the force applied per unit initial area of cross-section. Two kinds of strength are to be understood while addressing the mechanical properties of a typical metal. Yield strength defines the stress at which the material begins to deform permanently or undergoes plastic deformation. The ultimate tensile strength refers to the maximum stress that the material can withstand. If the material is loaded beyond the ultimate tensile strength, permanent deformation is no longer uniform and it becomes localised. With the onset of localised plastic deformation, conditions causing failure of the material are initiated and the engineering material fractures. Therefore, engineering materials used for structural applications (such as bridges, buildings, transportation vehicles, etc.) are generally not loaded beyond the yield strength in actual practice, otherwise, they will be subject to dimensional changes during their functioning.

A complimentary material property that is dependent on both ductility and strength is toughness. A tough material is one that is both strong as well as ductile and will not fail easily under impact loading. Some typical examples of impact loading are hammering and impact with a fast moving object. You must have noticed that glass breaks into pieces when struck with a piece of stone, whereas a typical metal will not fracture, but will be dented at the location of the impact. In this example, the metal is tougher compared to glass. One of the biggest drawbacks of ceramic materials when compared with metallic materials is their poor toughness. Materials engineers, however, have recently devised several methods to render ceramic materials tougher.

Having understood some important mechanical properties, we shall turn our attention back to iron and consider the change in mechanical properties with the increase in temperature. When iron is heated, it becomes more ductile, thereby making it more pliable and workable. In metallurgical parlance, the ductility of iron increases with increasing temperature. Therefore at higher temperatures, iron can be deformed to produce the desired shape much more easily. This is called hot working in metallurgical engineering. While there is a more rigorous definition of hot working, we shall simply note here that any deformation processing operation conducted above 650°C can be called hot working, in the case of iron. As a corollary, any shaping operation performed at temperatures lower than this is called cold working.

There are different techniques available to deform engineering materials in order to obtain the desired shape and size of the engineering product. Each method is referred to by a particular name. One simple operation that we are quite familiar with, at home, is the process of rolling. You must have noticed *rotis* being rolled. In this case, a large lump of the well-kneaded dough, that is plastic in nature, is placed on a smooth surface and is rolled down by successive rolling operation using a rolling stick (called *belan*) in order to produce the flat thin *roti*, which is later baked and, of course, consumed! In a similar fashion, it is possible for a metal to be rolled down to smaller thickness, by passing the metal through a pair of rolls. The operation of rolling can be done with the starting material either in hot or cold condition and accordingly, we can term the process as hot or cold rolling.

Another deformation operation that is commonly used in the industry is extrusion. This process has its counterpart in the preparation of *murukku* in our kitchens. You must have noticed that pliable dough is placed in a cylindrical holder, which contains small openings with the desired cross-section at the bottom. A piston is then plunged so as to force the dough through these well-defined openings. In this manner, the dough ball is extruded into long strips possessing a cross-section similar to the cross-section of the opening. These extruded dough strips are later fried in oil to produce the sumptuous *murukkus* (noodles)!

A related operation that is used to shape metallic objects is forging. In one variation of this process, the hot mass of material, say iron, is placed on a hard object possessing the contours of the required finished product. This is called a die. The hot mass is subject to repeated impact loading using a heavy hammer, for example, by dropping it from a height. As a result, the hot metal deforms permanently and takes the shape of the contour that has been cut out in the die. This operation is known as forging. Instead of using a die, imagine what will happen if the hot mass of metal is placed on another hot mass of metal and impact force is applied. It is easy to visualise that both these masses of metal will be joined together. This process is known as forge welding. This was precisely the metallurgical operation by which large iron objects were manufactured in ancient and medieval India. The ancient Indian engineers were the masters in the art of forge welding. They were able to manufacture large iron objects, which would have certainly required patience, skill and intelligence. We, therefore, first understand that the process used to construct large iron objects was forge welding. Of course, it is easy to visualize the joining of two hot lumps of iron. However, you can very well imagine the additional complexities involved in the addition of a hot iron lump to a large-sized object. Indian blacksmiths were well versed in forge welding methodology. It should be borne in mind that the massive iron objects, to be discussed later in the book, were manufactured by forge welding.

Bhanu Prakash (1997) rightly concludes that, "from the study of the archaeological iron objects there remains no doubt that ancient black-smiths had attained a very high level of skill in cold and hot working and sheet metal forming of wrought iron and iron-carbon alloys. They were also aware of the better metal workability of Fe-C alloys in hot condition that is greater than 900°C, and that two pieces of iron could be forge welded in the white hot condition (–1100°C)".

METALLURGICAL OPERATIONS

Apart from the major shaping operations performed usually in hot conditions, there were other techniques used for metal working, in general, and iron working, in particular. Let us briefly look at these techniques.

Joining

There were several applications where the objects had to be manufactured by joining parts that were separately manufactured. The techniques used for making mechanical joints were crimping, overlapping seam, overlapping sheets, riveting, and tab-and-slot methods. These kinds of techniques are termed mechanical because the joining action is due to mechanical forces. On the other hand, much better joint strength is obtained when a metallurgical bond is produced between the objects to be joined. The techniques for making metallurgical joints were soldering, brazing, fusion-welding, and welding using filler of similar composition (both in liquid and solid state). Lead-based solders were particularly utilised for producing metallurgically strong joints in the case of iron objects. A classic example of the use of lead-based solders is available in the joining of the individual parts that make the decorative bell capital of the Delhi Iron Pillar (see **Figure 1.6**).

Fig. 1.6: *Use of lead based solder seen in this picture as a black filling between the individual parts that make up the decorative bell capital of the Delhi Iron Pillar.*

Firm evidence for the use of lead-based solder during the Gupta period is available from ancient Indian texts. The *Brahatsamhita* gives an account of compositions of adhesive materials like *vajra-lepa* and *vajra-samghata* (Subbarayappa 1971: 274-349). The former was a glutinous material made from extracts of certain types of plants, fruits, seeds and barks, etc. This was used for application in roofs and walls of temples and mansions. *Vajra-samghata* was a metal cement consisting of eight parts of lead, two of bell metal and one of iron rust or brass. It was melted and poured hot as desired. The small amount of tin in *vajra-samghata* must have come from the bell metal. It is interesting to further note the addition of iron rust to the soldering alloy. It is well-known in corrosion that lead, with a few per cent tin, greatly aids the bonding of iron and steel and also the pores in the alloy are filled up with rust (from the process of corrosion) and this prevents further corrosion.

Casting

Casting is a process where the molten metal is poured into moulds such that after solidification, the metal takes the shape and form of the mould. We must bear in mind an important fact that casting was not utilized for the manufacture of iron objects. One of the reasons cited for this is the inefficient method of blowing air into the iron-making furnaces using human-operated bellows, which did not produce sufficiently high temperatures required for melting iron. Moreover, the Indian blacksmiths were very conversant with forge welding of direct reduced iron that they did not really bother about producing liquid iron. The Chinese learnt the production of cast iron quite early in history because of their efficient furnaces. In contrast, the Europeans discovered cast iron only by the sixteenth century, with the revolutionary adoption of iron extraction using the *stuckhoven*, the forerunner of today's blast furnace.

We must note that the casting method was very skilfully employed to manufacture objects using metals and alloys of lower melting point compared to iron. The ancient Indian furnaces were capable of melting a range of brasses (alloys of copper and zinc) and bronzes (alloys of copper and tin). It is clear that apart from making and working iron, Indian metal workers were equally skilled in handling other metallic materials. The Indians can rightfully be called masters in metals, while the Chinese, masters in ceramics. The idea of shaping metal by handling it in molten condition is supposed to have originated from the observation of the flow characteristic of molten gold, silver or copper and their capacity to take the shape of the channel on re-solidification. The copper objects discovered from the Harappan Civilisation and the Chalcolithic sites clearly indicate casting, based on the observation of typical dendritic microstructures.

The Indians knew several different casting methods. These were: casting in a mould; casting over a core from a master matrix; die-casting; and lost-wax process.

The beautiful bronze statue of the Harappan dancing girl reveals that metal casting technology was well-understood during the Harappan period (2600 to 1900 BCE). It has been hypothesized that the idea of making metal statues probably arose from the manufacture of terracotta toys. This method was adopted for mass manufacture of cast metal objects using a baked clay die, made of two halves. Archaeological evidence indicates that the process of melting metal into crucibles and its casting into earthen channels may have originated using pre-shaped moulds of clay or cavities made in sandstone or soapstone pieces. This, incidentally, applies to the basic concept of modern die-casting. The casting skills were later upgraded with the knowledge of preparing clay or wooden patterns. These patterns were used to produce a replica of the final object in consumable moulds using sand and clay mixtures. This resulted in the development of modern moulding methods and foundry technology.

An advanced casting method followed was the so-called lost-wax (also called *cire perdue*) process. This was known as *madhuchchist* (or lost-wax) in ancient Sanskrit literature. The dancing girl of Mohenjodaro was produced by this method. So were the wonderful bronze castings right through Indian history, like the Gupta, Pala and Chola bronzes. The lost-wax process is a refined technique wherein the model of the desired shape is made from bees wax and a mould is prepared by applying coatings of prepared clay slurry on it. After the drying of the refractory clay slurry, the wax was removed by baking the refractory shell. Only one casting could be made from one wax pattern. The refractory shell was first embedded in a box filled with the sand clay mixture to support the refractory wall. Molten metal was poured into the mould thus prepared. After solidification of the molten metal, the mould was carefully broken to remove the metal casting.

Study of ancient brass and bronze icons has also revealed that the craftsmen were capable of producing solid as well as hollow castings. The latter were probably produced by pouring out the remaining liquid metal after partial solidification had taken place near the mould wall or by the use of cores. There are several ancient literary sources that provide detailed accounts of the method of preparation of wax pattern, slurry coating, spruce, riser and runner. The clay slurry coating consisted of clay mixed with charred rice husk and sodium chloride, all mixed in a definite proportion and finely ground.

Several finishing operations were employed to provide the finishing touch. These operations included chiselling, filing, engraving, polishing, etc. In some cases, parts of an object that were cast separately were joined together to produce the final object. The wonderful bronze statues originally produced in the Indian subcontinent adorn almost all the major museums of the world and they rightly attest to the high quality of workmanship and skill in producing castings by the lost-wax process. A typical bronze icon produced by the Indian metal-casting masters is shown in **Figure 1.7**.

Another class of large objects produced by casting methodology is the medieval bronze cannons. The details of casting bronze cannons and composite iron-bronze cannons will be briefly described in the chapter on cannons. It must be realized that most of the massive cannons were large artillery pieces weighing more than ten tonnes. When we understand that heavy crane and machinery was not available for handling such objects when they were manufactured and also realize the large amount of molten metal that was needed for casting each cannon, the skill of the master *recktagars* (workers in bronze and copper) must be appreciated. Remember that a large amount of bronze (possessing

Fig. 1.7: *A typical Chola bronze icon of Nataraja produced by the lost-wax process. This object is currently on display at the Rijksvijik Museum, Amsterdam.*

the desired composition and fluidity) had to be first melted, possibly in several furnaces, and then the molten metal taken from the furnaces and poured into the mould. The engineering skill required for such an operation must have been fairly advanced.

Mechanical Working

Any engineering or decorative object had to be worked upon in order to give it the final shape. The mechanical working skill of the Indians is evident from the time of the Indus Valley Civilisation. Indian craftsmen had gained a high level of knowledge regarding the effect of cold working of metals and their recovery on annealing. It is possible that they also knew the improvements achieved by hot working of metals. Another important aspect of ancient Indian metal forming technologies was that properties were altered and controlled by suitable thermal treatments such as quenching, annealing, hardening and tempering of metals. This is known in today's parlance as thermomechanical treatments. The processes for mechanical working of metals were improved upon with time. The Indian metal smiths were able to apply a wide variety of thermomechanical operations that provided materials with the desired mechanical properties.

Ancient Indians knew several different mechanical working techniques. These included chasing, drawing, engraving, filing, machining, turning, drilling, boring and milling. Other related techniques included piercing, punching, raising, *repousse*, spinning, stamping and tempering. Let us just briefly look at some of these techniques.

The arts of embossing and engraving were utilised to provide an artistic touch to both ferrous and non-ferrous objects. These methods were also used to make jewellery. It has been hypothesized that the art of engraving on metals to produce beautiful designs of flora and fauna might have been a continuation of the tradition of wood carving and painting. In many cases, wooden panels and carvings have been inlayed with fine gold and silver wires, pearls, shells and pieces of mirrors to produce masterpieces. Wooden panels were covered with gold, silver, copper and brass sheets and beautiful designs were carved on them by embossing and engraving techniques. The artisans must have used very fine and precisely designed tools mostly made of iron and steel. The thrones on which the Indian monarchs sat and crowns worn by them typically exemplified the skill of the metal craftsmen. There are several examples of this in literature. Interestingly, the metal working skills were usually passed from one generation to another. The skilled people who produced and manufactured engineering objects were known as *Vishwakarmas*. Included in this classification were the carpenters, blacksmiths, potters, weavers, etc. These were the gems of India and their practical skills are what we note in the samples that are available. Several of the methods used and the techniques applied were closely guarded family secrets. Therefore, there was a socio-economic pattern to the use and application of metal working technologies in ancient India. Disciples were trained from their very childhood in their traditional craft. Blacksmiths made iron and steel tools, gold and silver work was done by *sonars* and sheet metal work by *thatheras*. The skill was passed on from one generation to the other and sometimes lost due to natural calamities or other causes.

In the particular case of iron-making, it is interesting to note that this was not practised by the higher castes but rather by tribals and lower castes who lived on the fringes of society. Therefore we note that some of the brightest and brilliant minds who took part in the development of iron metallurgy belonged to the so-called lower strata of Indian society. The inability of the nobility and higher castes to inculcate in them the modern developments taking part in other parts of the world, or to enhance their skill level, was one of the reasons for the stagnation of technology and science towards the end of the Mughal period. This was the same time that scientific inquiry and experimentation were revolutionising critical thinking in Europe.

A related working operation was wire drawing. Wire drawing craft has been well known in India for the manufacture of gold and silver *jari*. It was also utilized for manufacturing fine wires of bronze, brass, iron and steel, which were used in stringed musical instruments such as *sitar, sarangi, veena,* etc. The Indian crafts of *jari*-making and the production of sarees are famous all over the world. The process of manufacture of *jari* thread consists of making a fine wire of gold, silver or their alloys. They were then flattened to obtain thin strips. These strips were then wound around silk and cotton threads to produce the *jari* thread, which was then used to weave clothes. The technique of wire drawing required the use of hardened steel dies or die plates possessing hair-like fine holes. The wire manufacturers were also well-versed in the metallurgy of work hardening and annealing. As it was difficult to continuously work the material, it had to be made soft by annealing. Therefore, the wire manufacturers annealed the wires in between the process of wiredrawing. The process of intermittent annealing was usually performed in a slow heat produced by burning cow dung cakes. The final thin wire was flattened by rolling it between a set of highly polished rolls (50 to 100mm diameter) possessing a mirror-like surface finish. As these rolls flattened the thin wire, the shining surface finish was transferred to the gold and silver strip which was finally wound around cotton or silk thread.

The manufacture of a variety of stringed musical instruments of Indian origin required wires of various diameters. The material used in manufacturing these wires was carefully extracted so that they were free of non-metallic inclusions. This was important to ensure that a long wire could be drawn without fracturing it during the drawing operation. This also implied that the Indian ironsmiths were skilled smelters producing steel free from micron-sized non-metallic inclusions. Needless to say, the manufacture of steel wire required skill of a very high level and precise knowledge about the thermomechanical behaviour of steel. It required the understanding of work hardening properties as well as of annealing behaviour. All this knowledge was learnt empirically through experience and was transferred by the master craftsman to his chosen disciples, usually his progeny.

The thermomechanical response of steel, particularly those containing high carbon, was well-understood by ancient Indians as revealed in their mastery of producing tough swords from wootz steel cakes. These aspects will be addressed while discussing wootz steel. While considering the history of the Indian subcontinent and the numerous wars fought on this land, it is obvious that an enormous amount of skill went into the production of arms and armour made of steel. India was one of the largest manufacturers of arms in the world till the eighteenth century. There was a wide variety of arms and armour used through the ages in the Indian subcontinent and, needless to say, all this required a thorough knowledge of iron metallurgy. A wonderful collection of magnificent arms and armour pieces is available in the National Museum at New Delhi and these have also been catalogued in a wonderful publication (Pant and Sharma 2001). There are other excellent references that describe the wonderful arms and armour produced in the Indian subcontinent. One typical blade from the Indian subcontinent is seen in **Figure 1.8**. The huge collection of arms and armour in Indian museums and foreign collections rightly attest to the high level of skill of the Indian blacksmiths and provide visual evidence for the glorious metallurgical tradition of the country.

The basic raw material used in the manufacture of arms and armour was ultra-high carbon steel and a complete chapter is devoted in this book to understanding this wonder material of the Orient – wootz steel. The important role played by the metalworker in the fabrication of large iron cannons by forge welding would be dealt with in detail in the chapter on cannons. Before we reach there, let us take a careful look at some of the massive ancient iron structures in the Indian subcontinent that continue to fascinate the world. In the next chapter, we are going to take a closer look at iron pillars and beams.

Fig. 1.8: *One blade from the Indian subcontinent. The arms and armour of the country are a living testimony to the high skill levels of the Indian blacksmiths.*

2

PILLARS AND BEAMS

THIS CHAPTER WILL HIGHLIGHT SOME OF THE MOST SIGNIFICANT EXAMPLES OF Indian metallurgical skill. The first object that we shall discuss is the Delhi Iron Pillar. This stands as a symbol not only of Indian iron heritage but of the entire metallurgical heritage of India. The other significant monuments that will be discussed are the iron pillars at Dhar and Kodachadri Hill, and the iron beams in the temples of Orissa.

DELHI IRON PILLAR

The Delhi Iron Pillar (**Figure 2.1**) is testimony to the high level of skill achieved by the ancient Indian ironsmiths in the extraction and processing of iron. It has attracted the attention of archaeologists and corrosion technologists as it has withstood corrosion for the last sixteen hundred years. Extensive studies on the Iron Pillar by the author indicate that the excellent atmospheric corrosion resistance is because of the formation of a protective passive film on the surface of the pillar. The high phosphorus content in the iron of the pillar aids the formation of the protective passive film. The theories outlining the excellent corrosion resistance of the pillar will be described in detail later.

It is singularly featured on the emblems of several Indian institutions (for instance, the National Metallurgical Laboratory), thereby signifying its prime identity as the country's metallurgical pride and heritage. Hadfield (1912) undertook the first systematic scientific study of the Delhi Iron Pillar. Ever since, there have been a growing number

Fig. 2.1: *The Delhi Iron Pillar located in the Quwwat-ul-Islam mosque in the Qutub Complex in New Delhi.*

of studies where several aspects of the Delhi Iron Pillar have been discussed. In the centenary year of the Archaeological Survey of India in 1961, the Delhi Iron Pillar was studied in detail with the co-operation of the National Metallurgical Laboratory (NML)at Jamshedpur. The buried underground region of the pillar was examined by archaeological excavation. Moreover, a relatively large iron sample was sectioned from the pillar and subjected to several metallurgical analyses at the NML. The results of these scientific studies have been summarized in a special issue of the *NML Technical Journal* (Volume 5, 1963). These studies provide the firm foundation on which future scientific studies of the pillar were based. A review of the pillar's corrosion resistance later appeared

(Wranglen 1970) and recently, Anantharaman (1996) has published the known scientific facts about the Delhi Iron Pillar in a book. Balasubramaniam (2002a, 2005h) has compiled several new insights on the historical, scientific and technical aspects of the Delhi Iron Pillar in two recent books. The present review will focus attention on the new research insights obtained on the Delhi Iron Pillar.

History

Among the several inscriptions on the pillar, the oldest (and also the largest) is a three-stanza six-line Sanskrit inscription (**Figure 2.2**), at a level of about 2m from the stone platform. This inscription records that the pillar was set up by *Chandra* ("having in faith fixed his mind upon Vishnu") as a standard of Vishnu ("*Vishnuordhvajah*") at Vishnupadagiri. The monarch's conquests have also been poetically described in the inscription. It must be noted that three directions are referred to in the inscription (that is, east, south and west), and also Vishnu's name appears three times in the inscription, although in different contexts. On palaeographic grounds (that is, based on the nature of the characters of the Brahmi script of Sanskrit), the inscription can be dated between 400 and 450 CE.

Fig. 2.2: *The 6-line 3-stanza Brahmi-Sanskrit inscription on the Delhi pillar, the oldest and largest of all the inscriptions on the pillar. This inscription is at a level of about 2m from the stone platform. Notice that the first line is shorter than the other five lines and that the letters exhibit minimal corrosion damage.*

Another interesting detail concerning the inscription is the fact that the characters of the inscription were created by die striking operation and not by inscribing or by gouging out metal from the surface. Some characters are seen in **Figure 2.3**. Careful analysis has further revealed that certain specific die shapes were used to create all the characters that appear in the inscription. Die striking is an operation in which a die of the required shape and size is placed on the surface of the pillar and struck with force. The image of the die is thus transferred as a depression on to the surface.

Fig. 2.3: *Close-up view of some of the characters of the Brahmi inscription indicates that the characters were created by die striking and not by inscribing.*

Chandra is Chandragupta II Vikramaditya

Who do we give the credit for this masterpiece was a subject of debate among scholars. The name of the monarch *Chandra* appears on the oldest inscription on the pillar. Therefore, the identification of this person is important for appreciating the history of the Delhi Iron Pillar.

Chandra has been identified unambiguously with Chandragupta II Vikramaditya (375 CE-414 CE) based on a detailed analysis (Balasubramaniam 2000a) of the archer-type gold coins of the imperial Guptas (320 CE-600 CE). The most popular gold coin type, which was issued by the Gupta monarchs was the archer-type gold coin. In fact, the archer coin type seems to have been the only type issued by the later Gupta monarchs. The obverse in these coins depicts the king with a bow and an arrow (**Figure 2.4**). The Garuda emblem is another regular feature of these coins. Garuda is a mythological bird, who serves as the *vâhana* (vehicle) of Lord Vishnu. The Guptas, especially Chandragupta II Vikramaditya, were ardent devotees of Vishnu. The most interesting aspect of the archer coin type is that the king's short name is inscribed in the obverse field (that is, region of the issuing monarch's figure) with the full name and title of the monarch provided in the circular legend. The short name of the issuing king is inscribed in vertical fashion (**Figure 2.4**).

Let us analyse the king's full name in the circular legend and the short name written in vertical fashion in all the archer-type coins of the Guptas. The results of the analysis are presented in **Table 2.1**. In all the different archer type gold coins of Chandragupta II, the short name of the king is inscribed as *Chandra* while the king's complete title and name is provided in the circular legend. Therefore, it is amply clear that Chandragupta II Vikramaditya was called in short as *Chandra* and this is attested firmly by his most popular coin-type.

Fig. 2.4: *Archer-type gold coin of Chandragupta II Vikramaditya. In the obverse, the short name* (Chandra) *of the king is provided below his left arm while his full name appears in the circular legend. (Photograph courtesy: Ellen M. Raven).*

TABLE 2.1

Short names of Gupta monarchs inscribed in vertical direction in archer-type gold coins

Gupta Monarch	Short Name
Samudragupta	*Samudra*
Chandragupta II Vikramaditya	*Chandra*
Kumaragupta I Mahendraditya	*Kumara/Ku*
Skandagupta	*Skanda*
Purugupta	*Puru*
Ghatotkachagupta	*Ghato*
Narasimhagupta I Baladitya	*Nara*
Kumaragupta II Kramaditya	*Ku+kramaditya*
Budhagupta Vikramaditya	*Budha*
Vainyagupta Dvadasaditya	*Va(in)ya*
Vishnugupta Chandraditya	*Vishnu*

Detailed arguments regarding the identification problem have been presented in the author's books (Balasubramaniam 2002a, 2005h, 2005i).

It is interesting, at this point, to understand briefly the Gupta period in Ancient India, considered by many as the Golden Age of India. The Guptas rose to power from the first half of the fourth century CE. The first Gupta monarch to declare his sovereignty and call himself a *Maharajadhiraja* (that is, Great King of Kings) was Chandragupta I. The Gupta Era (GE) commences with the date of his coronation as *Maharajadhiraja* in 319-320 CE. His son and successor, Samudragupta, expanded the Gupta dominion significantly. Recent research has shown that Samudragupta's rule was followed by the short reign of his son, Ramagupta. Owing to his weakness, the people replaced him with his brother Chandragupta II who ascended the throne in 375 CE. Chandragupta II also took on the title of "Vikramaditya", which was appended to his name. Interestingly, he is the first "Vikramaditya" in Indian history based on firm archaeological evidence. He affected further conquests and added large territories to the Gupta Empire. His son, Kumaragupta I whose known dates are between 415 and 455 CE, succeeded him. The Gupta Empire attained its zenith during the rule of Chandragupta II Vikramaditya and Kumaragupta I. Kumaragupta I was succeeded by his son, Skandagupta and after his demise in 467 CE, the Gupta empire slowly lost its pre-eminence in Indian politics.

Iron technology reached significant heights during the Gupta period, which also saw the flowering of many other technologies such as bronze casting, coin making, stone sculpting, painting, etc. The excellent Buddha bronze castings from Mathura and the famous Iron Pillar amply exemplify the Gupta metallurgists' skill in the art of working with metals. Moreover, there were several other significant advances made in science, technology, medicine, literature, etc. during the Gupta period. It has been, therefore, rightly called as the Golden Age of India. Therefore, the Iron Pillar, that is currently in the courtyard of the mosque, is at least sixteen hundred years old and one of the finest examples of metallurgical skill and knowledge that existed in India during the Gupta period.

A possible image of how Chandragupta II Vikramaditya would have looked like can be hypothesised. The Ajanta cave paintings were executed during the Gupta period by the Vakatakas. In one of the Ajanta paintings, the king is seen having his royal bath (**Figure 2.5**). It is reasonable to propose that the Gupta monarch must have appeared similar to the person seen in this picture, having his royal bath. The excellent correlation of the stool seen in this plate with the stools that appear in several Gupta gold coins (for instance, the couch-type gold coin of Chandragupta II Vikramaditya) indicate that

Fig. 2.5: *Ajanta painting showing the king having a royal bath. It is reasonable to assume that Chandragupta II Vikramaditya must have appeared similar to this image of the king in this painting which was executed during the Gupta period.*

similar artistic ideas were represented in different mediums. The appearance of the Gupta and Vakataka monarchs must have been similar. Hence, we do have a rough idea about what Chandragupta II Vikramaditya must have looked like.

Udayagiri, near Sanchi, is Vishnupadagiri

The Delhi Iron Pillar is currently located in the courtyard of the Quwwat-ul-Islam mosque in New Delhi (Balasubramaniam 2005i). This mosque was erected as a monument to the "Might of Islam" as its name "Quwwat-ul-Islam" denotes. It was constructed by Qutubuddin Aibak, the Turkish slave army commander and viceroy of the Afghan monarch Muhammad Ghori, to commemorate the significant victory of Afghans over the Rajput forces led by Prithiviraj Chauhan in 1192 CE, and the subsequent capture of Qila Rai Pithora (the fortified bastion within the fortified Lal Kot city). The inscription on the eastern gateway of the mosque specifically mentions that materials from twenty-seven pre-existing temples at this location were used in its construction. This mosque is one of the earliest and finest examples of Indo-Islamic architecture, namely Hindu temple elements which were used in the construction of a mosque. However, Qila Rai Pithora was not the original erection site of the pillar.

Several earlier commentators have stated that the pillar was originally present at the site when the temples in the vicinity were destroyed to construct the mosque. They based their conclusion on an inscription on the pillar, which Cunningham in 1864 read as "*Samvat Dihali 1109 Ang Pal bahi*" (translated by Cunningham as "In Samvat 1109 (1052 CE) Ang (or Anang) Pal peopled Dilli") In true Indian fashion (that is, to believe whatever is told by a foreigner as being the truth), most commentators accepted Cunningham's translation. Learned Indian scholars have properly read this inscription recently as "*Samvat Kinlli 1109 Angapala badi*", which means "Anangapala tightened the nail (Iron Pillar) in Samvat 1109 (1052 CE)'. This is also logical because the last word '*badi*' meaning 'tightened'is related to "*kinlli*" (iron nail). Moreover, this particular inscription is of a later date than 1052 CE because, as we shall see shortly, Iltutmish transported the Iron Pillar to its current location from Udayagiri in central India. The inscription referring to the tightening of the loosened iron nail is related to an interesting local story. It goes something like this. A Brahmin assured the founder of the Tomar dynasty that, the pillar having been firmly driven into the head of Shesh Nag, the serpent king, his empire would be as permanent as the pillar. The Raja, however, was incredulous and anxious to test a prophecy of such deep importance to his dynasty. He ordered the pillar to be removed, when, to his horror, the foot of the pillar, which had pierced the serpent's head, was found wet with blood. All attempts again to fix the pillar proved of no avail: it stood loose on the ground, the serpent was gone, and the event is remembered in the well known verse: *"Killi to dhilli bhai, Tomar bhaya mat hin"* meaning "The pillar has become loose, the Tomar's wish will not be fulfilled." Incidentally, several sources claim that the name Delhi is derived from the concept of lose pillar, *i.e. "dhilli"*.

The original location of the pillar, Vishnupadagiri (meaning "Hill with footprint of Vishnu"), has been identified as modern Udayagiri, in the close vicinity of Besnagar, Vidisha and Sanchi. These towns are located about 50km east of Bhopal, in central India, the region that is traditionally called Malwa. It must be noted that the short form of "a" is used in the word *"pada"* which means "footprint". Had the long form of "a" been used, then *"pâda"* would translate as "foot". Therefore, the correct translation for the term Vishnupadagiri is "hill with footprint of Vishnu".

There are literary, archaeological, numismatic and geographical evidences for the identification of modern Udayagiri as ancient Vishnupadagiri. If there was one location that Chandragupta II Vikramaditya was personally associated with, it must have been Udayagiri because it is here that we find two datable inscriptions specifically mentioning Chandragupta II, and, moreover, nineteen of the twenty cave temples at this location are from his reign. The antiquity of *pada* (that is, footprint) worship is well-established in the region near Udayagiri as indicated by several evidences (Dass 2001): worship of an inscribed Vishnupada (footprint of Vishnu) at a place called Charan Tirth situated at the confluence of rivers Bes and Betwa at the foot of Udayagiri hill, the presence of the Heliodorous pillar at Besnagar, worship of the tenth Jain Tirthankara Sheetalnath's footmarks in Cave 20 in Udayagiri (dated by an inscription in this cave to 426 CE) and the discovery of a Kushan-period brick with partial marking of a foot at Udayagiri. A later-day inscription from 1036 CE in Cave 19 specifically identifies Chandragupta II as having built the temples at Udayagiri. In order to further emphasise Udayagiri's positive identification as Vishnupadagiri, and hence the original location of the Iron Pillar, Meera Dass (2001) provided several evidences for the iron-making tradition in the Udayagiri-Vidisha-Besnagar-Sanchi region (iron wedges from Sanchi and Heliodorous pillars, iron slags from several sites near Vidisha, remains of iron-making furnaces, names of nearby places like Lohangi ("Iron-Body") and Lohapura ("Iron-City").

The astronomical significance and importance of Udayagiri, that is, Vishnupadagiri during the Gupta period has also been established for the first time, from several archaeological evidences by Meera Dass (2001). The most significant aspect of the location of Udayagiri is that it is situated at 23°31' latitude, almost on the Tropic of Cancer. There are several evidences to show that Udayagiri was a major centre for astronomical observations in Ancient India and an important centre for Surya (that is, Sun God) worship. Astronomical studies were being conducted at this location, even in times prior to the Gupta period. The relationship between Surya (that is, Sun God) and Vishnu was emphasised, especially at Udayagiri, during the Gupta period. During the reign of Chandragupta II, this connection was symbolically extended to a greater length by the invocation of Chandragupta's epithet Vikramaditya, meaning "valorous sun". The adoption of the title Vikramaditya by Chandragupta II appears to signify several different meanings. The word is a combination of Vikrama and Aditya. As the term Vikrama is connected with Vishnu and Aditya means Surya, the term Vikramaditya embodies the oneness of Vishnu and Surya. In Vaishnava mythology, Vishnu is often associated with Surya.

The complete layout of Udayagiri is provided in **Figure 2.6a.** The general observation of the overall hill site is that it is shaped like a foot. A saddle connects the northern and southern hills. A specially cut passageway is located at the place where the northern hill meets the saddle. The Gupta period embellishment, modification and construction at Udayagiri were concentrated around this passage (shown hatched in **Figure 2.6a**). The passage is very important because it is the only path leading to the west of the hill, and it is the main approach to the temple on the northern hilltop enroute to it. The discovery of an ancient elephant path (see **Figure 2.6a**) further reinforces the importance of the passageway. Most of the cave temples are located around the passageway. The locations of the cave temples around the passage are provided in **Figure 2.6b**, which is the detailed map of the hatched region in **Figure 2.6a**. All the carvings and the caves are cut into the south wall of this passage and also on the east face abutting it (**Figure 2.6b**). In this figure, the cave temples have been numbered within circles, as per the existing classification system, and the most important ones are the *Varaha* panel in Cave 5 and the *Anantasayin Vishnu* panel in Cave 13. The astronomical aspects of the iconography of images that appear at Udayagiri have been addressed and analysed in detail elsewhere (Dass and Balasubramaniam 2004: 54-71).

As the Udayagiri site was astronomically significant, the Iron Pillar was located at a calculated position with respect to the important caves. It has been shown elsewhere (Balasubramaniam *et al.* 2004b: 177-203) that the decorative bell capital of the Delhi Iron

(a)

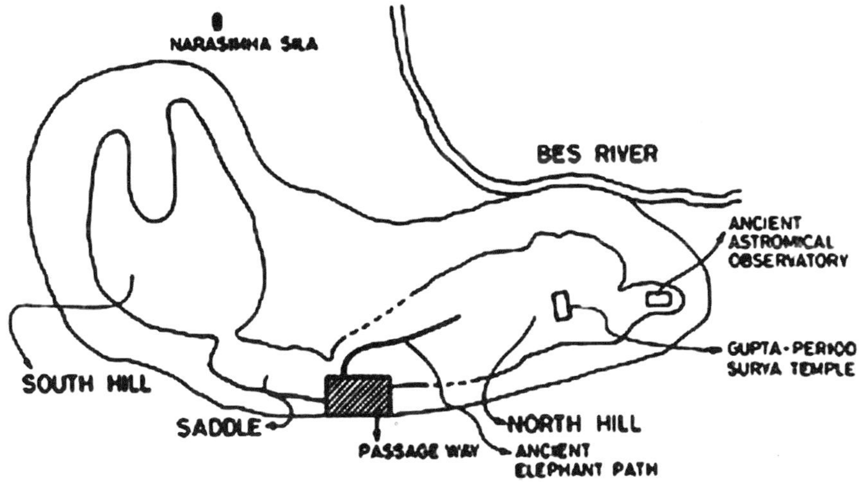

(b)

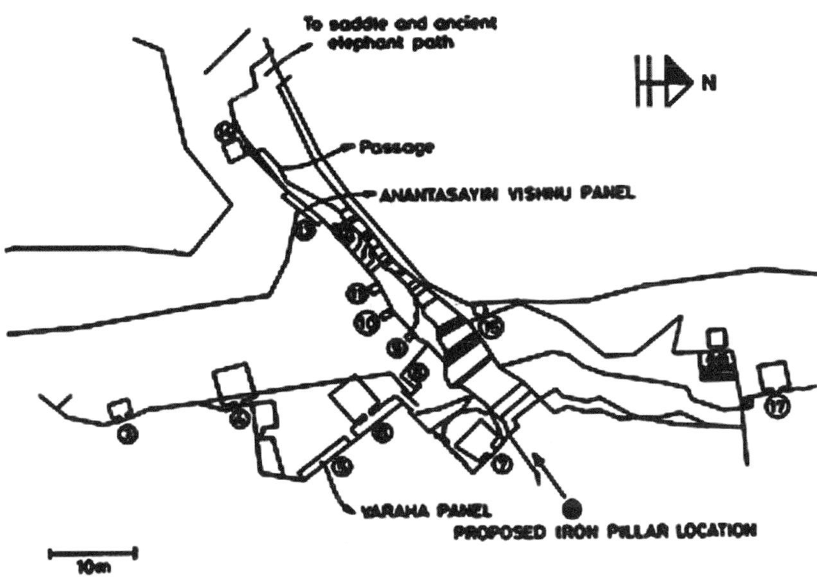

Fig. 2.6: *The layout of (a) Udayagiri hill, and (b) of the important caves around the passageway.*

Pillar was originally topped with a *chakra* image (**Figure 2.7**). This is also in tune with the Iron Pillar inscription that the pillar was meant to be the standard of Vishnu (*Vishnuordhvajah*). The pillar topped with *chakra,* symbolising the greatness of the *Chakravartin,* is a constant recurring theme in Indian iconography. Interestingly, the image of the Delhi Iron Pillar capital's box pedestal along with the *chakra* image is depicted in one of the Vishnu panels in Cave 6 at Udayagiri itself (**Figure 2.8**) and this is the

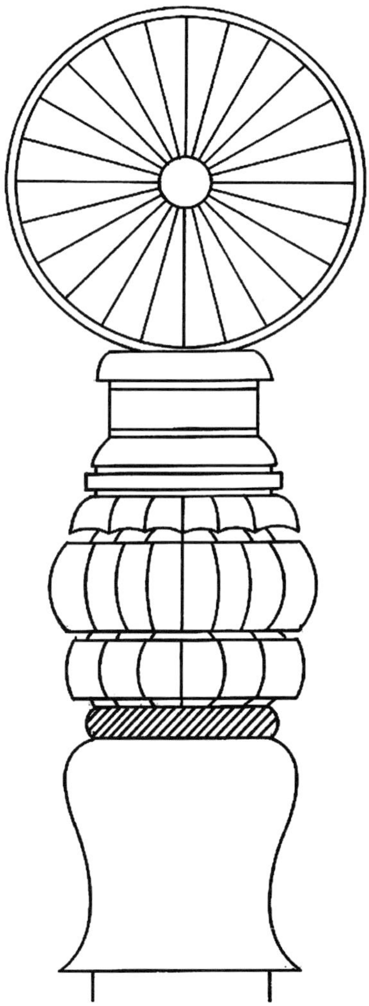

Fig. 2.7: *Reconstruction of the Delhi Iron Pillar capital with the chakra image atop the capital.*

(a) (b)

Fig. 2.8: *(a) Vishnu of Cave 6 at Udayagiri and (b) high magnification view of the* chakra. *(Photograph courtesy: Ellen M. Raven).*

most forceful argument for the *chakra* image atop the Delhi iron pillar capital. The circular disc is also in tune with the cut that is seen on the top surface of the capital and this will be addressed later.

The astronomical aspect of the Iron Pillar's erection site needs to be addressed in detail. Based on the hierarchy of inscriptions at Udayagiri, it was concluded that the pillar was located in front of Cave 7 facing the passage (Dass and Balasubramaniam 2004: 54-71). The original erection site of the Delhi Iron Pillar at Udayagiri has recently been deduced based on epigraphic and archaeological evidence (Dass and Balasubramaniam 2004: 54-71). This location is in front of the passageway, ahead of Cave 7. This has been marked in **Figure 2.6a**. The shadow of an erect object (placed approximately at the location where the Iron Pillar must have been located) was closely monitored at Udayagiri during significant periods round the year, that is, solstices and equinoxes. The results of this study indicate that the Iron Pillar was erected in an astronomically intelligent manner. At one of the significant periods in the year, that is, the summer solstice, the early morning shadow of the Iron Pillar fell in the direction of the foot of Vishnu in the *Anantasayin Vishnu* panel. Moreover, it is only in the period before and after summer solstice that the early morning shadow of the Iron Pillar fell on the passageway in the direction of *Anantasayin Vishnu*. This is due to the special angle of the cut of the passageway with respect to the cardinal directions. There are several other interesting details connected with the movement of the sun and the direction of sunrays, as the function of time of the year, with respect to the *Varaha* and *Anantasayin* panels. This can be obtained from the reference (Balasubramaniam and Dass 2004 86:1134-1142) provided in the bibliography.

Therefore, the Iron Pillar was not only a symbol of Indian metallurgical heritage, but also a symbol of the astronomical knowledge that existed in India during the time of the Guptas. The engineering, architectural and story-telling genius of the creators of the Udayagiri site is revealed by the allegorical representations of both Vishnu *pada* and Vishnu's cosmic sleep, by intelligently blending astronomical and architectural knowledge. The creation and development of the Udayagiri site appears to have been clearly guided by a highly developed astronomical knowledge, which existed during the time of Chandragupta II Vikramaditya. Therefore, the Udayagiri site, in general, and the Iron Pillar location, in particular, provides firm evidence for the astronomical knowledge that existed in India around 400 CE. The flowering of astronomical knowledge under prominent astronomers like Aryabhata, Varahamihira and Brahmagupta during the Gupta period has been well-established.

The positioning of the Iron Pillar would have additionally served to highlight the astronomical intelligence, knowledge and advancements prevalent during Chandragupta II Vikramaditya's time. Considering the astronomical significance of the Udayagiri site, it is interesting to note that there exists, on the northern edge of the northern hilltop, a relatively large flat platform commanding a majestic view of almost the entire skyline. Several astronomical marks have been identified at this platform, thereby suggesting that this must have been the site of an ancient astronomical observatory. Its location has also been indicated in **Figure 2.6a**.

Movement to Delhi

The Iron Pillar was brought to its current location at the Quwwat-ul-Islam mosque from its original location in Udayagiri by Iltutmish. It was installed in the mosque courtyard. Iltutmish was the first Muslim invader to loot and plunder Malwa. A contemporary historian Minhaj-us-Siraj has documented the details of Iltutmish's expedition to Malwa. His accounts must be considered fairly accurate because he served in the court of Iltutmish. His historical documentary is titled *Tabkat-i-Nasiri* and it contains the history of Early Slave Dynasty up to the period of Nasiruddin Mahmud (1246-65 CE).

The details of Iltutmish's expedition to and from Malwa in 1233 CE are interesting in that it has been mentioned "the effigy of Vikramjit.....together with other effigies, which were formed of molten brass.... were carried away to Dhilli, the capital". The possibility of the Iron Pillar being one of the brass effigies carried away to Delhi exists because several earlier observers of the pillar have stated that it was made of brass. For instance, a writer, about hundred years from Jehangir's time refers to the pillar as "an obelisk of brass of great antiquity". Several European visitors have also mentioned that the pillar was made of brass. Quoting from these sources and from the colour of the Iron Pillar, even Cunningham originally stated that the pillar was a brass pillar. It was only after a detailed chemical analysis of the material of construction of the pillar (sent by Cunningham), which was carried out by Dr Percy Brown of the Roorkee University in 1876 CE, that it was established that the pillar was constructed of pure iron.

A European tourist writing in a travel document called *Tour in the Upper Provinces* referred to it as "the wonderful brazen pillar". Emma Roberts in her travelogue titled *Views in India* mentioned it as "a pillar of mixed metal", while W.H. Sleeman referred it in his *Rambles and Recollections of an Indian Official* as a small pillar of bronze or a metal that resembles bronze. Cunningham himself initially thought that the pillar was made of a "mixed metal" similar to bronze and had a sample from the pillar analysed before concluding it was made of iron. It will be shown later that the brass-like appearance of the pillar, when viewed from certain directions, is due to the protective passive film which forms on the surface and also protects the pillar against atmospheric corrosion.

In the process of reassembling the Iron Pillar (after it was brought to Delhi from Udayagiri), part of the pillar, which was initially buried underground at Udayagiri (nee Vishnupadagiri), has been placed above the ground level. This is apparent based on the presence of round-shaped hammered cavities in the base of the pillar (provided for better gripping of the pillar to the ground) and deep corrosion pits. We shall see later that the bottom region of the pillar was deliberately made rough, by the original engineers of the Iron Pillar, in order to grip the pillar firmly to the foundation. The pillar has been, ever since 1233 CE, lying in this location.

Engineering Design

Let us explore some engineering aspects of the pillar. We have just described how Iltutmish relocated the pillar to its current location sometime in 1233 CE. We first realise that the current burial level of the pillar was not the original burial level of the pillar when it was located at Udayagiri. The rough portion of the pillar was originally buried in the courtyard of the temple and later left exposed outside when the Iron Pillar was displaced from its original position. Notice the hammer-marked cavities which are visible on the surface of the pillar in the rough region just below the smooth surface-finish region (**Figure 2.9**). We shall see later that this rough surface was the original condition in which the pillar was manufactured. It was left rough in order to aid gripping of the pillar to the buried underground region at Udayagiri. Careful archaeological excavations at Udayagiri at the location proposed in **Figure 2.6** will provide valuable information on how the pillar actually gripped the ground originally.

Fig. 2.9: *Bottom region of the Delhi Iron Pillar. The rough portion was originally buried in the ground.*

The possible philosophical reason for the pillar's rough surface region to be left exposed when it was placed in the mosque, could be hypothesised. It may have been left exposed outside to reveal the "imperfection" in Hindu art, as exemplified by the Iron Pillar.

There is a stone platform currently seen surrounding the pillar base. However, this was not present before 1861 CE. In the Annual Report of the Archaeological Survey of India (Volume IV) for the years 1871-72, Beglar reported the extensive studies he conducted at the Qutub Complex. His original report, available as a reprint from ASI, should be consulted for all the exciting details of his excavations (Beglar 1874: 28-30). Most importantly, he excavated the buried underground regions of the pillar in order to find out how deep the pillar was actually below the ground level. Before this, there was speculation that the pillar went all the way up to 60 ft below the ground level! Beglar's excavations revealed that the pillar's buried depth below the ground was only 2'8". Upon reassembling the pillar after the excavations, Beglar constructed the stone platform around the base of the Iron Pillar. The stability of the Iron Pillar must have become suspect after he excavated the buried underground region around the pillar.

Early sketches (Nath 1984) and published photographs (Cole 1872; Ritter von Schwarz 1901: 209-211, 277-283) of the pillar, before the construction of the stone platform, attest to the absence of the stone platform before Beglar's excavations. One example is the free hand sketch of the pillar by an artist named Mirza Shah Rukh Beg, commissioned for publication in Syed Ahmed Khan's Urdu work *Athar'al-Sanadid* in 1846 (**Figure 2.10**). Most of the monuments in the Qutub Complex were photographed extensively by almost all the leading British photographers who visited India in the period immediately after the invention of photography. Famous photographers who have photographed the Delhi Iron Pillar include Bourne, Bealto, Impey, Tytler, etc. All these old photographs of the Delhi Iron Pillar have been reproduced in the author's exclusive book on the Iron Pillar (Balasubramaniam 2002a). One good example is the photograph that appeared in Herbert Henry Cole's book *The Architecture of Ancient Delhi, Especially the Buildings around the Kutb Minar*, which was published in London in 1872. This is reproduced in **Figure 2.11**.

A critical analysis of the dimensions of the main body of the pillar provides conclusive evidence for the original burial level of the pillar and also an appreciation of the pillar's symmetrical design (Balasubramaniam 1997b: 1057-1067). If the start of the smooth surface section is taken as the original burial level, the relative dimensions of the pillar

Fig. 2.10: *Free hand sketch of the pillar by an artist named Mirza Shah Rukh Beg for publication in Syed Ahmed Khan's Urdu work* Athar'al-Sanadid *in 1846. In this illustration, a beardedperson is seen clasping the pillar (without the stone platform) at the top of the rough section.*

are as provided in **Figure 2.12a**. Considering the basic unit as U, the rough surface occupies one-fourth (60U) and the smooth surface three-fourths (180U) of the pillar's main body length, excluding the decorative top. The burial of the pillar body to one-fourth of its height would have provided the necessary stability to the structure. The decorative bell capital (Balasubramaniam 1998a: 40-47) is again a symmetrical object and its relative dimensions are provided in **Figure 2.12b**. The *chakra* (disc) that was originally located atop the Iron Pillar would have been approximately 20U in length, thereby providing the total length of the decorative top as 60U. The length of the decorative capital (60U) would now be exactly one-fourth of the total pillar height exposed above the ground level (240U). Therefore, it is reasonable to state that the depth of burial

Fig. 2.11: *One of the oldest published photographs of the Delhi Iron Pillar that appeared in Herbert Henry Cole's book* The Architecture of Ancient Delhi, Especially the Buildings around the Kutb Minar, *which was published in London in 1872. Notice the absence of the stone platform around the base of the pillar.*

(a) *(b)*

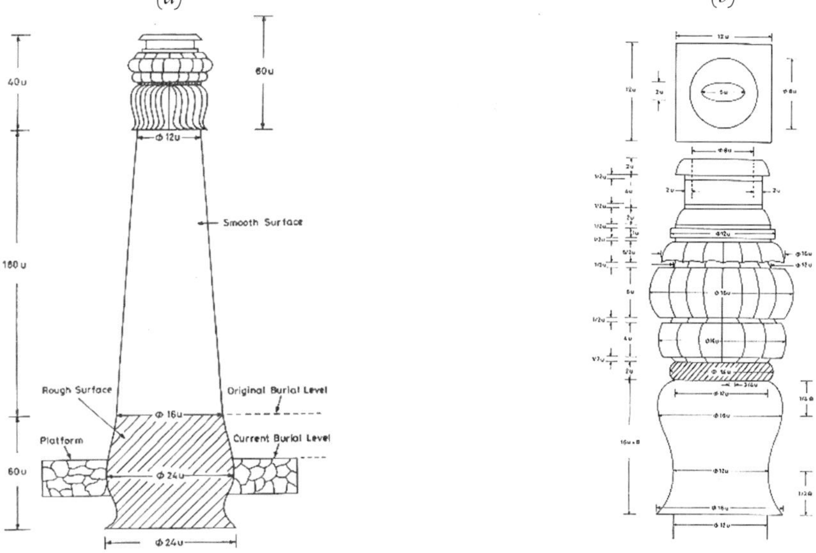

Fig. 2.12: *(a) An appreciation of the pillar's symmetrical design obtained in this schematic showing the relative dimensions of the pillar, and (b) the relative dimensions of the decorative bell capital indicate its symmetry.*

below ground level was equal to the height of the decorative capital, indicative of the engineering design of the pillar. What is the unit U, which excellently measures the Delhi Iron Pillar's proportions? The unit U is equal to 1 modern inch. The *angulam*, the ancient Indian unit of measurement, equals 0.75 of the modern one inch.

The buried underground region was excavated in 1961, on the centenary of the Archaeological Survey of India. The underground portion below the ground level is shown in **Figure. 2.13a**, before any conservation treatment. It was observed that the base of the pillar was flat. Eight small projections were seen at equal intervals. These projections appeared from the sheet of almost pure lead, placed at the bottom of the pillar. A heavy slab of stone was found placed horizontally on the original upper layer of the temple floor on which the lead sheet rested. Beglar's excavations revealed that the floor of the mosque "consisted of two layers of well-dressed stone close set, nine and ten inches thick respectively, resting on a basis of rubble stone of enormous dimensions and indefinite depth, the excavations having been carried down over fourteen feet without coming to the bottom of the layers of rubble stone. These two layers of dressed stone extend throughout the entire area of the mosque courtyard, and cloisters of inner enclosure. In the courtyard, however, these layers are overlaid by another layer of stones of irregular shape and size, and evidently belonging to various portions of some ruined structure; the consequence of this is that the level of the courtyard is higher than the level of the floor of the mosque and cloister."

Therefore, the beautifully constructed double flooring of the original temple resting on the massive foundation was left intact by the Muslims and they placed a superficial layer of broken material over the dressed Hindu stones in the courtyard when the mosque was built. The pillar is therefore supported by the upper layer of the old Hindu temple floor and surrounded by the superficial layer of broken stones laid down later.

No one has commented on the nature of arrangement of these iron rods because the pillar was not completely lifted up vertically for studying the base of the pillar. The observations were only made with the pillar resting on the ground and a part of the ground surrounding the pillar removed. It is, however, possible to reconstruct the placement of the iron rods in the bottom of the pillar based on available photographs (**Figures. 2.13a and 2.13b**). It appears that the two iron rods were placed parallel to each other and another two iron rods were placed above these such that they were perpendicular to the initial rods. This provided a grid-like structure. These iron rods were placed on a lead sheet. The Iron Pillar base was then fixed atop this iron grid structure, thereby providing the necessary support at the bottom.

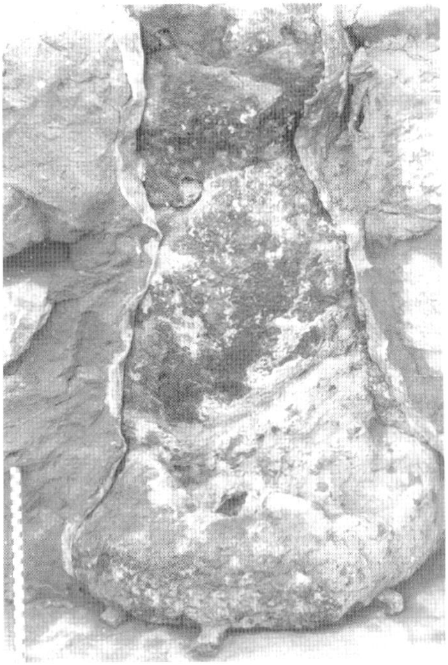

(a)

(b)

Fig. 2.13: *The underground portion of the pillar below the ground level (a) before conservationtreatment and (b) after provision of a new lead coating beforebeing buried again in 1961.*

Ghosh has analysed the composition of the lead sheet at this location and it is nearly pure lead with trace impurities of Au and Ag. It appears that the lead sheet must have been present when the pillar was located at Udayagiri because the people who had removed the pillar from its original position must have also ensured that the method of erection that was followed at the original erection site was strictly followed when it was re-erected in the Quwwat-ul-Islam mosque courtyard. Why was the lead plate provided at this location? The lead sheet would have acted like a cushion in case of seismic disturbances. However, the main purpose of the lead sheet appears to be to grip the pillar to the supporting stone underneath.

A coating of lead is currently evident on parts of the surface of the Iron Pillar that is in contact with the soil. This is also clearly seen in the photograph of the underground portion of the pillar (**Figure 2.13a**). A coating of material, white in colour in the photograph, is clearly distinguishable on the outer surface of the pillar. Beglar was responsible for the lead coating in the buried underground surface of the pillar when the pillar was re-erected. This uneven coating of lead (of about 3mm thickness) was found to be in an excellent state of preservation when the buried region of the pillar was excavated in 1961. However, the iron in the buried portion was found covered with rust layers ranging from a few mm to 15mm. Interestingly, numerous cavities and corrosion pits were also observed on the surface. The soil samples in the nearby vicinity were found loaded with soluble sulphates and chlorides. The iron in the buried regions is corroded more than the exposed surface due to the galvanic action with the lead layer, as lead is cathodic with respect to iron. The surface was cleaned and the cracks were consolidated during the recent studies. A new lead coating was provided on the pillar in the buried underground region (**Figure 2.13b**) and the pillar again buried under the ground.

Material

The underlying metal of the pillar would be discussed briefly in order to elucidate its characteristic features. Incidentally, these features are also characteristic of ancient Indian irons. We shall look at the composition and microstructural aspects of the Delhi pillar iron.

Composition

It was the chemical analysis conducted by Dr Percy Brown of Roorkee University in 1876 CE that established that the pillar was constructed of pure iron. This was the first analysis of the material of construction of the pillar. Hadfield (1912) published the first detailed chemical analysis of the Delhi pillar iron in 1912. He was a famous British metallurgist, who had a keen interest in ancient iron and steel-making practices of the Indian subcontinent. Several analyses of the pillar's iron composition are available since Hadfield first published his analysis.

The published chemical analyses (Hadfield 1912: 134-174; Ghosh 1963: 31-45; Lahiri *et al.* 1963: 46-5; Lal 1996: 22-58) of the pillar iron are presented in **Table 2.2** from which the variation in the iron's composition can be noted. A sample of the pillar iron was also subjected to microprobe analysis in order to determine the composition of the elements Mn, Cr, Cu and Ni in the near surface regions and it was found that the composition of Cu (0.05%), Ni (0.05%), Mn (0.07%) and Cr (Nil) was uniform through several millimetres into the sample from the surface (Bardgett and Stanners 1963: 24-30). This also clearly proved that there was no surface coating provided specifically for enhancing the corrosion resistance of the pillar. Excluding the analysis of Lal (1996) (**Table** 2), the average composition of the pillar iron is 0.15%C, 0.25%P, 0.005% S, 0.05%Si, 0.02% N, 0.05% Mn, 0.03% Cu, 0.05% Ni and balance Fe. The high P content of the pillar iron must be particularly noted.

Microstructures

In material engineering, the close correlation between structure and properties is well-known. Structure indicates arrangement of the material. When one views the arrangement of electrons, neutrons and protons, we term it atomic structure. The ordered (or disordered) arrangement of atoms is called atomic structure. On a microscopic scale, in the order of micrometers, the grain structure of engineering materials is understood. Finally, the macrostructure refers to observations made in the millimetre range. Structure affects the properties of engineering materials. We shall concentrate on the microstructure of the Delhi pillar iron, that is, the arrangement of the constituent phases and grain sizes.

TABLE 2.2

Published Composition Analyses of the Delhi Iron Pillar

	Hadfield (1912)	Ghosh (1963) Above	(1963) Under	Lahiri *et al* (1963)	Lal (1945)
C	0.08	0.23	0.03	0.26	0.90
Si	0.046	0.026	0.004	0.056	0.048
S	0.006	trace	0.008	0.003	0.007
P	0.114	0.280*	0.436-0.48	0.155	0.174
Mn	Nil	Nil	Nil	Nil	Nil
N	-	0.0065			
Fe	99.720	Diff			99.67
Others	0.246				0.011
Specific gravity	7.81	7.672-7.747			7.5

* 0.100 fixed and 0.180 in solid solution P

We shall discuss some important aspects of the underlying microstructure of the pillar iron. In fact, the microstructure of the pillar iron is highly heterogeneous and this is a characteristic that is observed in almost all ancient Indian irons. The Delhi pillar iron possesses a non-uniform microstructure. A published microstructure illustration of the Delhi pillar iron is presented in **Figure 2.14.** In the unetched condition, the specimens showed slag inclusions irregularly distributed in the microstructure. A recent *in situ* microstructural study also revealed similar features (Raj *et al.* 2005). In fact, the non-homogeneous nature is typical of ancient irons.

Some important aspects of the underlying microstructure of the Delhi pillar iron would be initially discussed as these have a bearing on its corrosion behaviour. The intimate relationship between structure and properties is well-established in materials

Fig. 2.14: *Microstructure of the Delhi iron pillar (Ghosh 1963).*

engineering. The Delhi pillar iron possesses a non-uniform grain structure (Ghosh 1963: 31-45; Bardgett and Stanners 1963: 3-10, 24-30) (**Figure 2.14**). In the unetched condition, the specimens showed slag inclusions irregularly distributed in the microstructure. The etched specimens revealed medium to coarse polyhedral grains of ferrite with slip bands in some grains near the surface. The surface regions were free from pearlite which seemed to increase towards the interior (Ghosh 1963: 31-45). Many slip bands were seen in the surface ferrite grains. Elongated slag particles and oxide particles were also seen in the deformed structure in the near surface regions. Lahiri *et al.* (1963) also conducted metallographic examination of the Delhi pillar iron and the irregular distribution of pearlite was also noted. The absence of a uniform distribution of pearlite is indicative of the segregation of P because in such areas of P segregation, C diffuses out and the material becomes poorer in C content. The interior portions were comparatively rich in C (Ghosh 1963: 31-45; Bardgett and Stanners 1963: 3-10, 24-30). Therefore, a wide variation in structure is exhibited by the Delhi pillar iron and this is a characteristic feature of ancient Indian iron. The non-uniform structure could be the reason for the difference in the chemical analyses of the Delhi pillar iron's composition as determined by several investigators (**Table 2.2**).

The Delhi pillar iron was characterised by a relatively high proportion of slag inclusions and the microstructure near the slag showed wide variations (including normalised and annealed structures) (Ghosh 1963: 31-45). Moreover, microstructures containing 0.2% to 0.3% C were present next to the slag particles, in addition to carbon-free grains. As a result of slag particles in the structure, the specific gravity of the Delhi pillar iron is lower than that for the purest form of Fe (**Table 2.2**). Note also that the specific gravity from different analyses is not uniform, which is indicative of the non-uniform distribution of the slag particles in the microstructure. The non-uniform nature of the slag particles in the Delhi pillar iron can be clearly seen in the microstructures provided by Ghosh (1963), and Bardget and Stanners (1963). The slag particles present in the Delhi Iron Pillar are generally microscopic in nature with a few of them in larger sizes.

Slag results in the microstructure due to the processing method employed to obtain iron, as discussed in detail in the first chapter Microstructural investigations on iron produced during the Gupta period showed that fayalite and iron oxides were present in the entrapped slag inclusions in iron (Puri *et al.* 1997: 1-10; Ramesh Kumar and Balasubramaniam 1998: 1169-1178; Dillmann and Balasubramaniam 2001a: 317-322).

Some of the iron oxides also contained carbon, presumably due to charcoal used in iron extraction (Dillmann and Balasubramaniam 2001a: 317-322). The presence of carbon in these unreduced oxides would render these oxides cathodic in nature with respect to the surrounding matrix.

The ancient Indian iron-making furnaces were relatively small structures, compared to modern blast furnaces (see **Figure 1.1**). The end product of the bloomery furnace was a lump of direct reduced iron, which contained P as the major alloying element. Therefore, the end product of the ancient Indian direct process of extracting iron can be termed as phosphoric irons. On the other hand, the end product of modern blast furnaces is pig iron, in which carbon is the major alloying element. In contrast to macrosegregation of P in pig iron, microsegregation of P is realised in ancient phosphoric irons.

The slag particles in the Delhi pillar iron, therefore, are in fine microscopic form distributed unevenly in the microstructure. High-resolution transmission electron microscopic microstructural investigations in other ancient Indian irons indicate that the grain boundaries near slag inclusions are the ones generally covered with slag inclusions. Had the slag enclosed the individual iron lumps that were forge welded (in order to produce the large dimension of the pillar), it would have resulted in poor solid-state fusion of the iron lumps (discussed in the next section). The pillar is a solid body with moderate mechanical strength (yield strength YS of 23.5 tonnes per sq. in., ultimate tensile strength UTS of 23.9 tonnes per sq. in. and 5% elongation).

The similarity of YS and UTS are indicative of the composite structure of the pillar iron. In fact, a cannon ball fired at the Delhi Iron Pillar in the eighteenth century (either by in 1739 CE or Ghulam Quadir in 1787 CE) failed to break the pillar also suggesting that slag does not coat the individual lumps that were forge welded. The marks of this cannon ball shot can be seen in the southern face of the pillar, half-way up the height of the pillar (**Figure 2.15**).

Manufacturing Methodology

The manufacturing methodology of the main body of the pillar will be addressed initially (Balasubramaniam 1999a: 42-65) and later the decorative bell capital's design (Balasubramaniam 1998a: 40-47) will be explained. This section also deals with the connection of the decorative bell capital to the main body. It should be noted that the starting material is, of course, iron lump and the method used to fuse the lumps together

Fig. 2.15: *The mark of a cannon ball shot can be seen in the southern face of the pillar halfway up the height of the pillar.*

was forge welding. The individual iron lumps obtained from the metal extraction process had to be joined in order to produce large objects. This was accomplished by forge welding. Forge welding is an operation in which iron lumps are joined together by forging them in the hot state such that fusion is obtained between them. This process initially involves heating of the lumps to a relatively high temperature in a bed of charcoal in order to make them soft and amenable for deformation. One iron lump is then placed on top of another and force is applied in order to weld them in the solid state. As the force is dynamic is nature, it is called forge welding.

The likely method by which the main body of the Delhi Iron Pillar could have been manufactured is briefly described to provide an overview of the process. This is based on the critical analysis of the various aspects of the manufacturing methodology such as the hammering method, heating method, forging method, use of inserts, use of dies and ease of handling (Balasubramaniam 1999a: 42-65). The heated iron lumps were placed on the side surface of the pillar and hammered on to the same by the use of hand-held hammers (**Figure 2.16**). The addition of metal would have been sideways with the pillar in the horizontal direction. The pillar's vertical and horizontal movements would have been aided by handling clamps provided on the surface of the pillar, the protruding portion of which must have been chiselled away during the surface finishing operations. Visual proof of the presence of these clamps is available at two locations on the pillar. The first location is the previously-polished surface where the presence of a rectangular insert is seen (**Figure 2.17**). The region where the insert is located was previously brightly polished due to visitors clasping their hands around the pillar. Recently, an iron cage has been constructed around the pillar. A close-up view of the same, when the region

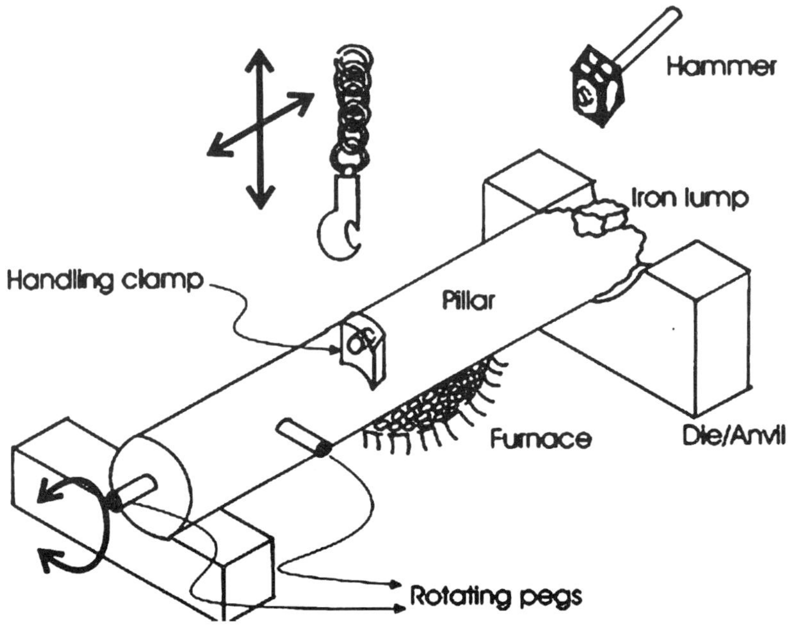

Fig. 2.16: *The side-way horizontal forge welding methodology of the Delhi Iron Pillar. The heated iron lumps were placed on the side surface of the pillar and hammered on to the same. The addition of metal would have been sideways with the pillar in the horizontal direction.*

Fig. 2.17: *Evidence of a rectangular insert (arrowed) in the previously brightly polished region of the pillar. A close-up view of the same, when the region appeared brightly polished, has been provided in Figure 8 in Balasubramaniam (1999a).*

appeared brightly polished, is provided in **Figure 8** in Balasubramaniam (1999a). This insert (originally containing the holding clamp) appears to have been inserted on to the surface of the pillar and this is indicated by the presence of cracks emanating from the insert periphery on to the surrounding lumps of iron. The second location where a handling clamp could have been present is situated at approximately about one- fourth of the height from the top of the main body of the pillar. There is a horizontal rectangular object currently missing from the surface at this location (**Figure 2.18**). Close observation of this region reveals that this rectangular slot is exactly of the same dimensions as that of the rectangular insert (that is, the remnant of the handling clamp) seen in the bright polished region. Moreover, it occurs exactly in line with the bottom insert (that is, it is aligned with respect to the bottom rectangular insert). The location of these inserts with respect to the pillar body dimensions should also be appreciated. The location of the top missing insert appears at a distance of approximately 150 cm from the top of the pillar main body (that is excluding the decorative capital). The rectangular insert seen in the bright polished region appears at a distance of 375 cm from the top of the pillar's main body and, therefore, 225 cm from the bottom of the pillar. The distance between these two inserts is 225 cm These dimensions should be compared to the overall dimensions of the pillar which has been analysed in detail earlier. The body would have been rotated with the aid of rotating pegs inserted in the holes provided on the surface

Fig. 2.18: *Missing clamp located at a vertical distance of about 6 ft above the insert seen in Fig. 2.17.*

for this purpose. These holding supports would have aided heating the surface to be forged and then bringing this heated surface on top of an anvil. The anvil would have served additionally as a die. The hot lump to be forged is placed on top of this side section and then forged with the aid of hand-held hammers. Once a certain length of the pillar was manufactured, the handling of the pillar becomes more tedious and therefore, to aid this process, handling clamps must have been provided on the surface of the pillar at regular intervals. The protruding portion of the insert must have been chiselled off leaving behind the remnant of the insert in the form of a rectangular block on the surface of the material. Finally, the surface of the pillar (that was supposed to be exposed) must have been smoothened by chiselling and burnishing the surface of the pillar and, thereby, providing it a smooth tapered cylindrical appearance. Finally, the Sanskrit inscriptions were die-struck on the surface of the pillar (Balasubramaniam and Prabhakar 2007). Cold dies must have been used for die striking the inscriptions. The decorative bell capital must have been finally fit on to the top portion of the Delhi Iron Pillar and then the whole pillar erected at Udayagiri.

The manufacturing methodology of the decorative bell capital will now be described. The decorative bell capital of the Delhi Iron Pillar has been described in great detail by Balasubramaniam (1998a). We shall summarise the main features of the capital. The decorative bell capital consists of seven distinct parts (**Figure 2.19**). The bottom-most part is the reeded bell structure which has been manufactured by utilising iron rods of uniform diameter (**Figure 2.20**). Atop this comes the slanted rod structure (**Figure 2.21**). Notice the presence of a black filling in between the joints. There are several evidences at the joints between these two members to indicate that lead solders were utilised for joining the pieces together (Balasubramaniam 1998b: 19-39; 1999b: 681-686). The next three members are rounded structures, with the top one being only half rounded (**Figure 2.22**) because when the pillar is viewed from the bottom, this part would appear curved when viewed in perspective from the bottom. A round disc comes above this and finally the box pedestal is placed on the top of the capital (**Figure 2.23**). The box capital contains holes that are empty at the four corners (Balasubramaniam 1998a: 40-47) and

Figure 2.19: *Decorative bell capital of the Delhi Iron Pillar: (a) bottom and (b) top.*

Fig. 2.20: *Details of the bottom region of the reeded-bell component of the decorative capital.*

Fig. 2.21: *Details of the slanted rod structure above the reeded bell structure. Notice the presence of a black filling in between the joints.*

Fig. 2.22: *Half-rounded component of the decorative bell capital.*

Fig. 2.23: *Top box pedestal of the capital.*

these could originally have been utilised for holding different animal figures, depending upon the season of the year (Dass and Balasubramaniam 2004: 54-71). The top of the pillar presently contains a hollow slot (**Figure 2.24**) in which the *chakra* image must have been originally fit. The fitting methodology of the various components is illustrated in **Figure 2.25**, where the individual components are shown shrunk fit around a hollow

(a)

(b)

Fig. 2.24: *The top of the pillar presently contains a hollow slot in which an image of* Chakra *must have been originally present. The presence of a circular cylinder of diameter 8", intersecting the surface, is evident. (a) vertical view and (b) oblique view.*

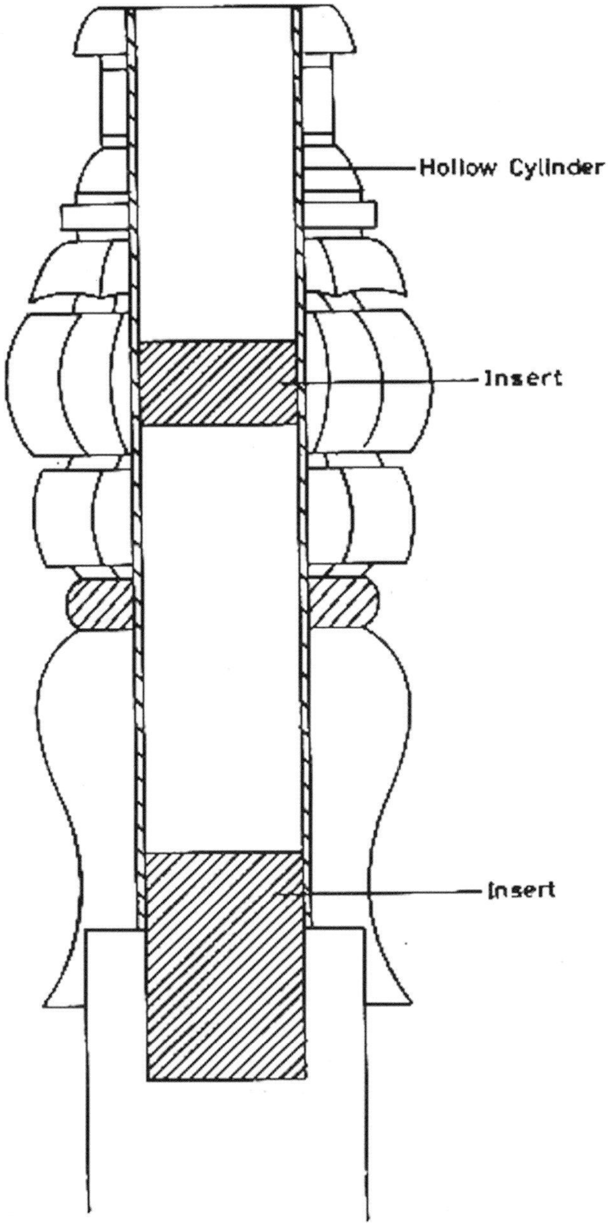

Fig. 2.25: *Shrink fitting methodology of the Delhi Iron Pillar decorative capital around a hollow cylinder. Notice that the decorative bell capital is attached to the pillar's main body by means of an insert.*

cylinder. Evidence of this kind of fitting method has been presented earlier (Balasubramaniam 1998a: 40-47). The cylinder would have also helped in the handling of the pillar and also for joining the capital with the main body by the aid of inserts. It is interesting to note the cross marking in **Figure 2.20**. Another such marking is seen in the half-rounded disc. These markings could be related to the alignment of the individual components, although they are not strictly aligned with each other in the overall context of the decorative bell capital.

Corrosion Resistance

The most fascinating aspect of the Delhi Iron Pillar is its remarkable corrosion resistance in the atmospheric environment. We know that the pillar is at least sixteen hundred years old based on the identification of *Chandra* of the Gupta-Brahmi inscription on the Iron Pillar with Chandragupta II Vikramaditya (375-414 CE). Let us explore and understand the reason for the Pillar's excellent atmospheric corrosion resistance.

Several theories have been proposed to explain the pillar's excellent corrosion resistance. They can be broadly classified into two categories: environmental and material theories (Balasubramaniam 1995: 123-145; 1997a: 23-35; 2000b: 2103-2129).

It is well-known in corrosion science and engineering that moisture must be present on the surface of objects in order to initiate and propagate corrosion. Moisture is the electrolyte that supplies and withdraws the ions involved in the electrochemical reactions leading to corrosion. Electrolyte, in the general sense, is one of the four components of the basic wet electrochemical cell. The other three components are the anode, the cathode and the electrical conductor between the anode and the cathode. The anode is the location where the corrosion anodic reactions occur. Similarly, the cathode is the location where the reduction reactions occur. It must be noted here that the anodic corrosion reactions will not occur without the supporting cathodic reactions. Finally, it is also necessary that there is electrical contact between the anode and the cathode (that is an electrical conductor must connect the anode and the cathode) in order to conduct electrons liberated by the anodic reaction to the cathodic regions, where the electrons are consumed. In the case of corrosion occurring on the surface of metals, the metal itself is the electrical conductor, while regions on the surface will support both anodic and cathodic reactions.

The proponents of the environment theory state that the mild climate of Delhi is responsible for the corrosion resistance of the Delhi Iron Pillar by quoting that the relative humidity in Delhi does not exceed sixty percent for significant periods of time in the year. This factor has been stated to be the main reason for the very mild corrosion of the pillar. It is well known that atmospheric rusting of iron is not significant for humidity levels less than 60%. When one analyses the atmospheric conditions in Delhi over a one year period (see **Figure 2.26**), it is observed that high humidity (that is, greater than 16% for significant periods of time) conditions exist during the monsoon season

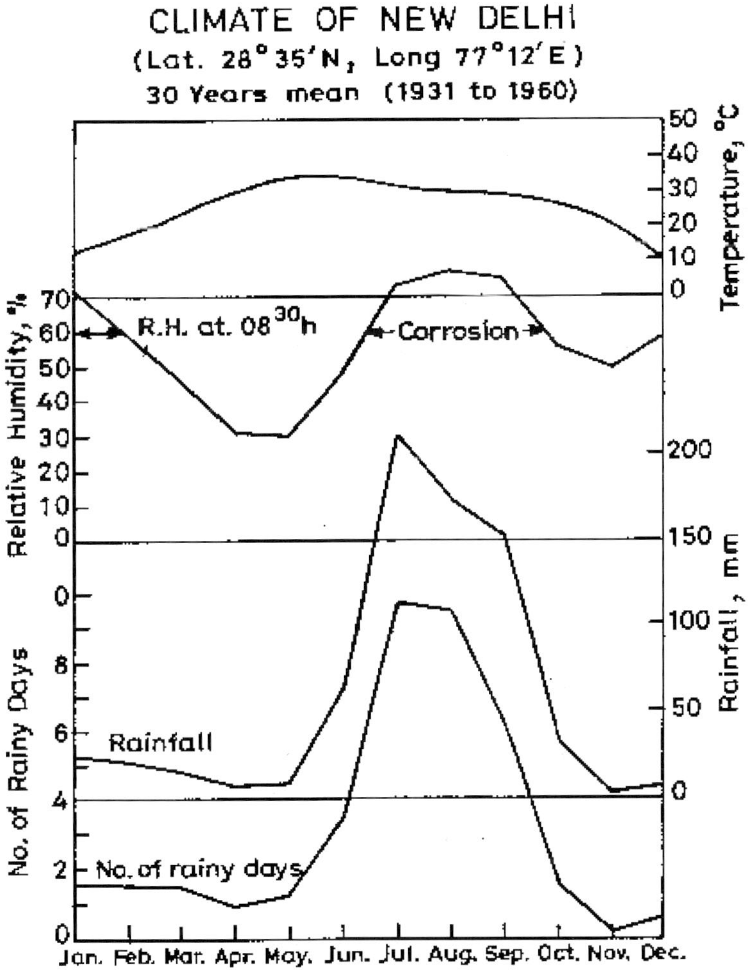

Fig. 2.26: *Atmospheric conditions at Delhi averaged over a period of fifty years (Wranglen 1970).*

(July to September) and in the peak winter season (January and February). Moreover, the pillar remains wet during the monsoon season for a significant period of time. Therefore, the atmosphere of Delhi is not "mild" as claimed by the foreign scholars.

On the other hand, several investigators have stressed the importance of the material of construction as the primary cause for its corrosion resistance. The ideas proposed in this regard are the relatively pure composition of the iron used, presence of phosphorus and absence of S/Mn in iron, its slag enveloped metal grain structure, passivity enhancement in the presence of slag particles and formation of a protective passive film. The absence of S and Mn implies the absence of corrosion-inducing manganese sulphide inclusions in iron. These MnS inclusions are cathodic in nature and are therefore responsible for corrosion and localised pitting attack in the case of modern mild steels.

Other theories to explain corrosion resistance are also to be found in the literature such as the mass metal effect, initial exposure to an alkaline and ammonical environment, residual stresses resulting from surface finishing (hammering) operation, freedom from sulphur contamination both in the metal and in the air, presence of layers of cinder (entrapped charcoal pieces coming from the iron extraction process) in the metal, thereby not allowing corrosion to proceed beyond the layer, (cinder theory), and surface coatings provided to the pillar after manufacture (treating the surface with steam and coating with slag) and during use (coating with clarified butter).

The large mass of the pillar is certainly a contributory factor because the pillar heats up relatively rapidly compared to its surroundings, and therefore the residence time of condensed moisture is reduced. It must be emphasised that the presence of condensed moisture layer on the surface is essential in order to cause corrosion. As mentioned above, moisture is the electrolyte, one of the four basic components of a wet corrosion cell.

That the material of construction may be an important factor in determining the corrosion resistance of ancient Indian iron is attested by the presence of ancient massive iron objects located in areas where the relative humidity is high all round the year. Good examples for this case are the iron beams in the Jagannath temple at Puri, the Sun temple at Konark and the iron pillar at Adi-Mookambika temple at the Kodachadri Hills. Puri, Konark and Kodachadri are situated on the coast. The distance from the location of these massive iron objects to the actual seacoast is less than 20km, thereby implying that these iron objects are constantly subjected to a saline environment due to their proximity to the seacoast. There are other examples of massive iron objects in several other parts of the Indian subcontinent that have successfully withstood atmospheric corrosion. These include the iron pillar at Dhar (Balasubramaniam and Ramesh Kumar 2003) and the numerous large forge-welded iron cannons scattered all over the Indian subcontinent. Two examples are the 22-tonne *Rajagopala* cannon at Thanjavur in Tamil Nadu (Balasubramaniam *et al.* 2005a: 269-294) and the 20-tonne *Dalmardan* cannon at Bishnupur in West Bengal (Balasubramaniam *et al.* 2005b: 295-320).

It is therefore obvious that ancient Indians, especially from the time of the Guptas (300-500 CE), produced a grade of iron that was capable of withstanding corrosion. This grade of iron contained a relatively higher P content. This is primarily due to the high P content of ancient iron meant for corrosion resistance applications. It is interesting to note that the ancient iron extracting metallurgists were very particular in choosing the ore that was fed into the bloomery furnace. The ore selected for extraction depended on the end-application of the iron that was extracted. In applications where corrosion resistance was required, it is reasonable to propose that the high P containing ores were selected to extract iron, which will be called, in modern terminology, as phosphoric iron. The ancient Indian metallurgists must have developed this knowledge by empirical means, through a highly keen sense of trial-and-error observation and analysis. We now know that phosphoric irons must have been produced in Ancient India by the use of high P containing iron ore, and aided by the absence of limestone in the bloomery furnace charge.

A freshly-cut surface of the pillar acquires the colour of the rest of the pillar within a short period of time (about three years). We know this is based on observations recorded on a significant cut made on the pillar surface when two specimens were removed for analysis in the year 1959 by scientists from NML, Jamshedpur, and TISCO, Jamshedpur, in collaboration with the ASI. This indicates that the protection offered to the pillar comes from within the material rather than due to surface coatings. This was also corroborated in a recent study by the author (Balasubramaniam 2002c: 1357-1365).

The excellent corrosion resistance of the Delhi Iron Pillar is due to the formation of a protective passive film on the surface (Balasubramaniam 2000b: 2103-2129). Passivity is defined as a condition of corrosion resistance due to the formation of surface film on the surface even under electrochemical conditions that favour corrosion. It is the formation of a protective passive film that protects the pillar from atmospheric corrosion. It should be borne in mind that alternate wetting and drying conditions are implied while considering atmospheric corrosion. This is a very important factor in the formation of the protective film at the metal-rust interface. In case ancient iron, containing second phase particles (slag and oxides), is exposed to a more severe environment, for instance complete immersion in acidic solution, rapid localised attack occurs at the second phase-matrix interfaces, and the material corrodes at a much faster rate than normal mild steel. Therefore, it is important to stress that the iron of the pillar exhibits excellent corrosion resistance only for atmospheric exposure, with its typical alternate wetting and drying conditions.

It is interesting at this juncture to note that the corrosion rates determined by constant immersion testing of the Delhi pillar iron samples in 0.001% NaCl and 0.003% SO_2 solutions were 6 mg/sq dm/day (mdd) and 54 mdd, respectively. Utilising these values, it can be easily seen that had the pillar been completely immersed in an aqueous solution, it would have severely corroded.

Rust Characterisation

In order to understand the nature of the protective passive film that offers such excellent corrosion resistance, rust samples from the top portion of the main body of the pillar were subjected to several advanced techniques (Balasubramaniam 1999c: 13-20; Ramesh Kumar and Balasubramaniam 1999a: 37-41; 1999b: 57-61; Balasubramaniam and Ramesh Kumar 2000: 2085-2181). As the rust samples were obtained from the region just below the decorative bell capital, this is the oldest undisturbed rust on the pillar because this area is inaccessible to the public.

The process of protective film formation on the Delhi Iron Pillar has been scientifically verified by conducting rust characterisation studies on the collected pillar rust. Rust samples were studied using X-ray diffraction, infrared spectroscopy, Raman spectroscopy and Mössbauer spectroscopy. It is beyond the scope of this book to delve into the principles behind all these techniques and therefore, all the results obtained using these techniques will not be presented. However, relevant examples would be provided below with explanations.

One may ask why several different structural characterisation techniques must be used and not just one. This is because different techniques provide different ideas about the material structure and therefore the characterisation techniques must be judiciously selected to obtain a complete picture of the rust. This is very much like the story of the blind men and the elephant. When the blind men were asked to describe an elephant, each of them touched a particular part of the elephant and concluded that the elephant must be like the part that they had touched. Of course, the overall picture of the elephant was entirely different from their individual perceptions. In a similar manner, by utilising just one technique, the complete nature of the rust cannot be precisely known and therefore it is important to analyse the rust using different structural characterisation techniques. In this manner, the unambiguous nature of rust can be obtained.

Two powerful techniques to understand the nature of rust are X-ray diffraction and infrared spectroscopy. Let us understand the useful information that can be obtained from these methods.

One of the most powerful techniques for structural characterisation of materials is X-ray diffraction. The basic principle behind all diffraction methods is the same. A monochromatic beam is focussed on the sample and the diffraction of waves is studied. The diffraction pattern thus obtained provides ideas about the nature of the compound(s) that comprise(s) the specimen. Different kinds of waves (of different wavelengths) can be used for probing materials and accordingly, we have different techniques. The scale of dimensions, which a particular wave probes, is of the same order as its wavelength. X-rays are one kind of electromagnetic waves that were discovered by Roentgen in 1896. The wavelengths of the X-rays are of the order of spacing between atoms in a crystalline material. The power of utilising X-rays to analyse material structures was revealed within a short period after Roentgen discovered X-rays. Since then, the X-ray diffraction technique has been widely used to understand material structures. We shall briefly explain what is meant by crystalline structure. Any material is composed of atoms or ions, which are bound by strong and weak forces. In the case of crystalline materials, the atoms or ions are arranged systematically at the atomic level and this periodic arrangement at the atomic level is known as its crystal structure. In the crystal structure of a unique chemical compound, the spacing between the atoms and ions (in different directions) that make up the structure is unique. Therefore, if this characteristic spacing can be determined, the material can be identified, using the known database of the planar spacing of a large number of compounds. The atoms or ions that make up the structure can also be viewed as an arrangement of planes of atoms or ions. The spacing between the planes in different directions would be different and characteristic for the particular compound. These planes act like a grid for the incoming monochromatic X-ray beam and diffract the X-ray beam in all directions. However, depending on the interplanar spacing, the X-ray intensity along some specific diffracted directions (that is, diffraction angles) is amplified (due to constructive interference of the diffracted X-ray beam). The intensity of the diffracted beam can be recorded as a function of the diffraction angle. The interplanar spacing can be easily calculated based on the angles where the diffracted beam exhibits maxima. Therefore, based on simple experimentation, it is possible to reconstruct the structure of the compound and, more importantly, identify the compound that provided the diffraction by comparison with standard published data.

Such an exercise was first undertaken with the Delhi Iron Pillar rust and the X-ray diffraction pattern obtained from the rust is shown in **Figure** 2.27. From the diffraction peaks occurring at specific angles and the known diffraction peaks from the compounds of iron, oxygen, hydrogen and phosphorus, all the peaks were identified as belonging to one phase, namely iron hydrogen phosphate hydrate. It must be understood that there are hundreds of compounds which are possible with different combinations of Fe, O, H and P, and the analysis of X-ray diffraction patterns is a rigorous procedure requiring experience and scientific skill. Only after a detailed comparison of the experimental data with the database of hundreds of compounds, the diffraction lines from the Delhi pillar rust were unambiguously assigned to the iron phosphate phase. What about the presence of the oxyhydroxides and oxides of iron that are normally expected in any rust? Were

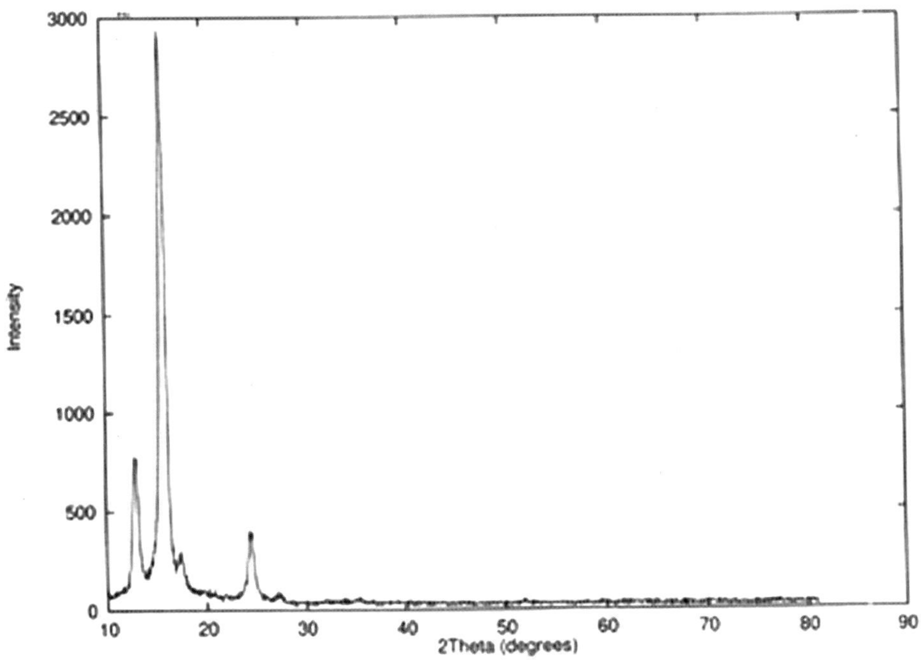

Fig. 2.27: *X-ray diffraction pattern of the Delhi Iron Pillar rust.*

they not present in the Delhi Iron Pillar rust? No iron oxide or oxyhydroxide was identified in the X-ray diffraction pattern. Based on this, one possible conclusion could be that they were not present in the rust. Of course, we should remind ourselves about the story of the blind men and the elephant because it is likely that the characterisation technique used, that is X-ray diffraction, did not provide the necessary "signatures" indicating the presence of iron oxides and oxyhydroxide. Is there then any problem with the X-ray diffraction method?

The main drawback with the X-ray diffraction method is that it cannot be used to identify non-crystalline or amorphous materials. Therefore, one probable reason why the X-ray diffraction technique did not indicate the presence of iron oxides and oxyhydroxides could be because they were present in a non-crystalline state in the rust. Non-crystalline state is synonymous with amorphous structure. As we had defined, in contrast to the ordered arrangement of atoms or ions in a crystalline material, the atoms or ions that make up the non-crystalline material are arranged in a totally random manner. Therefore, there is no periodic interplanar spacing present, like in the case of a crystalline material, with the end result that distinct X-ray diffraction peaks will not be obtained from a non-crystalline material. Therefore, the major disadvantage of the X-ray diffraction technique is its inability to identify the presence of non-crystalline phases.

Therefore we have to utilise other structural characterisation techniques, which can reveal and identify amorphous phases. One such technique, which is especially useful in the case of iron rusts, is infrared spectroscopy. This method is used for determining the molecular vibration (due to bending and stretching of the bonds) between the ions that constitute the compound, in our case, principally iron and oxygen. As the molecular vibration in all known iron oxides and oxyhydroxides are well-understood and available in literature, comparison of the infrared spectra from the Delhi pillar rust with standard data can reveal the precise nature of the iron oxides and oxyhydroxides. In this technique, the incident infrared radiation is absorbed or transmitted, depending on the nature of vibration of the atoms or ions that make up the structure. A complimentary technique is Raman spectroscopy where the incident waves used are of visible light.Remember that Sir C.V. Raman was awarded the Nobel Prize in physics for his discovery of the effect, which goes by his name as the Raman Effect. This effect was discovered by Professor Raman based on research work done in India. He was the first Indian scientist to receive the Nobel Prize in science. In fact, Raman spectroscopy is based on the Raman Effect. We shall not discuss this method here.

As the characteristic nature of vibrations in several phases is well- known, the presence of a particular phase can be identified using certain specific peaks in the Fouriet transform infrared (FTIR) transmission spectrum. Such a spectrum obtained from the Delhi Iron Pillar rust is provided in **Figure 2.28**. Comparing this spectrum with known peaks of the iron oxide and oxyhydroxide phases, the identities of the phases present in the rust were revealed. In this case, the radiation does not differentiate between crystalline or non-crystalline states of matter because the vibrational frequencies are similar in crystalline and non-crystalline forms. The phases identified in the Delhi Iron Pillar by infrared spectroscopy were lepidocrocite, goethite, magnetite, d-FeOOH and phosphate. The spectrum also indicates that the rust is hydrated, that is, contains moisture.

In summary, the significant result of the XRD analysis of the Delhi pillar rust was the identification of iron hydrogen phosphate hydrate in the crystalline form. The FTIR spectroscopic study of the Iron Pillar rust clearly established that, in addition to iron hydrogen phosphate hydrate, the scale also consisted a-FeOOH (goethite), g-FeOOH

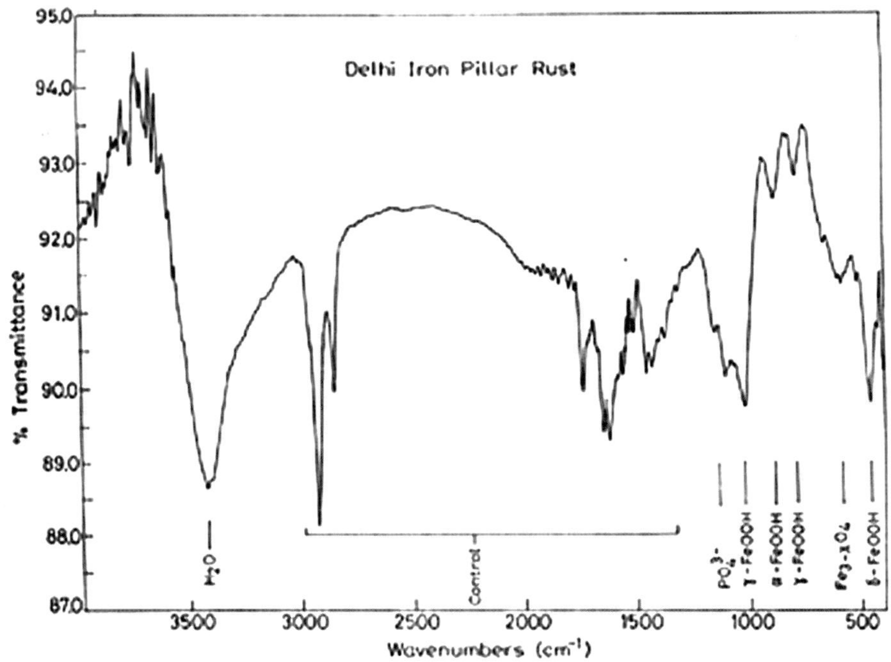

Fig. 2.28: *The infrared spectrum of the Delhi Iron Pillar rust infrared.*

(lepidocrocite), magnetite and phosphates. The hydrated nature of these products was also indicated. It was also seen in the XRD pattern that there was a very small amount of iron oxide/oxyhydroxides present in the crystalline form. The identification of the oxide/oxyhydroxides of iron by FTIR clearly established that they are present in the amorphous form. The FTIR study also provided that phosphate ions were present in the rust, confirming the results of XRD. In addition to these two techniques, Mössbauer spectroscopy was also performed using the Delhi pillar rust. The Mössbauer spectroscopic study of the Delhi Iron Pillar rust samples proved conclusively that oxyhydroxides and magnetite were present in amorphous form, in a finely divided nanocrystalline state (**Figure 2.29**). Moreover, iron in the phosphate was present in the +3 oxidation state. In summary, while XRD analysis proved the existence of crystalline iron hydrogen phosphate hydrate, FTIR and Mössbauer spectroscopy proved the presence of magnetite and several oxyhydroxides in an amorphous form. The scientific aspects of how these identified phases (phosphate and iron oxyhydroxides) form during rusting exert a beneficial influence will not be explained here in detail because it is beyond the scope of the present work.

The above discussion has been provided to inform the readers that there is no magic or supernatural phenomenon involved in the pillar's corrosion resistance. The protective

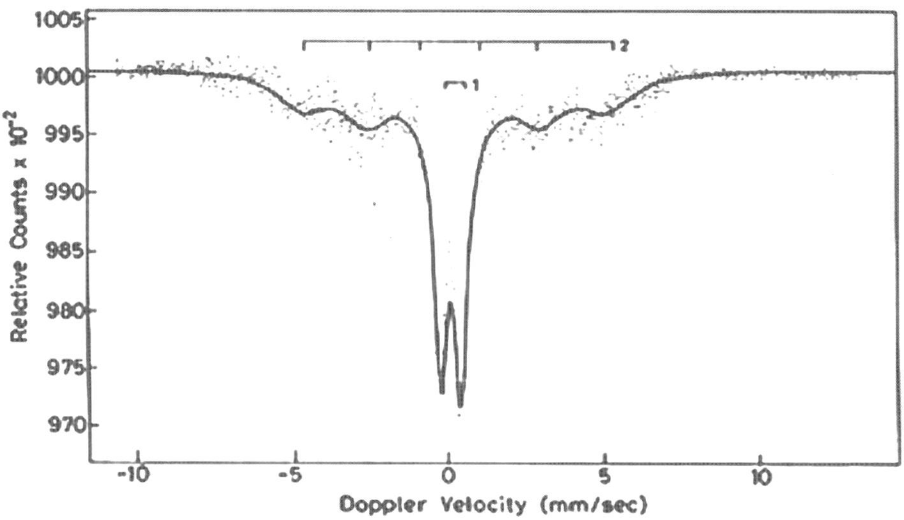

Fig. 2.29: *The Mössbauer spectrum of the Delhi Iron Pillar rust.*

passive film mechanism of the Iron Pillar's excellent atmospheric corrosion resistance is confirmed based on scientifically sound principles. Therefore, when people comment on supernatural origins for the pillar's corrosion resistance, it is totally wrong. We are now well-aware of the science behind the pillar's corrosion resistance. In fact, all observed natural phenomena have a sound scientific basis. Let us now understand the process of protective passive film formation on the pillar iron.

Protective Passive Film Mechanism

The process of protective film formation on the exposed surface of the Delhi Iron Pillar is now well-understood, based on the detailed characterisation of rust. It must be remembered that alternate wetting and drying conditions are implicit in the following discussion on atmospheric corrosion.

Initially, the corrosion of the iron matrix is relatively fast due to the presence of second phase particles in the microstructure. The usual corrosion products that are observed in the case of mild steels (exposed to the atmosphere without any chloride ions) are precipitated on the surface. It is well-known that the corrosion products that form on iron on atmospheric exposure are a-FeOOH (goethite), g-FeOOH (lepidocrocite), $Fe_{3-x}O_4$ (magnetite) and X-ray amorphous matter. These are the constituents of rust that you notice on any surface of iron. Their relative amounts and physical nature (like adherence and compactness) depend on a host of factors. In case of exposure to marine environments (that is, where chloride ions are present), the formation of b-FeOOH (akaganeite) is also favoured. In the case of the Delhi Pillar Iron, the formation of lepidocrocite and goethite was confirmed by XRD analysis of a half-year-old rust from the Delhi Iron Pillar surface (Lahiri *et al.* 1963).

The rust that forms on normal mild steels (that is, carbon containing iron) is non-protective because it is readily cracked and this allows for easy ingress of moisture and oxygen to the metal surface (that is, to the metal-scale interface). This results in further corrosion of the metal underneath. The rust structure on normal mild steels is schematically depicted in **Figure 2.30a**. The non-protective nature of rust on normal mild steels leads to further rusting because these rusts do not hinder the diffusion of moisture and oxygen to the metal surface.

The rusting of phosphoric irons, a good example of which is the Delhi Iron Pillar, is quite different from mild steels (that is, carbon containing iron). Of course, in the case of ancient irons, the entrapped slag inclusions will have an effect on the corrosion

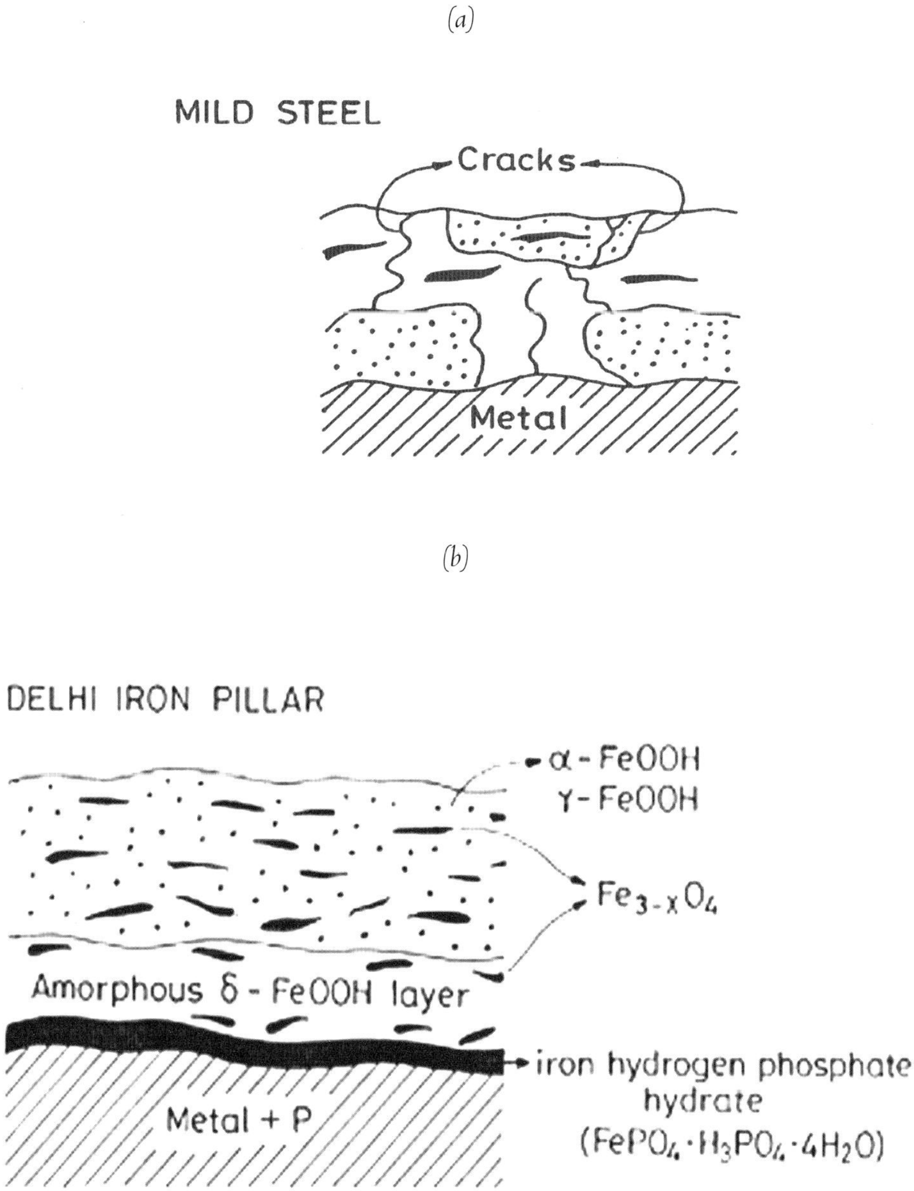

Fig. 2.30: *Rust structure on (a) carbon-containing iron (mild steel) showing its non-protective structure, and (b) phosphorus-containing iron (phosphoric iron) showing its protective nature.*

rates. They tend to enhance the corrosion of the matrix in the initial stages of exposure to the environment. This is beneficial because the initial enhanced corrosion of the iron matrix leads to the enrichment of P concentration at the metal-rust interface. However, it is also important to note, as discussed earlier, that the concentration of P is relatively high near the surface regions of the Delhi pillar iron than in the bulk. This is due to the depletion of carbon and enrichment of P due to surface heating operations during the pillar's manufacture.

Coming back to the corrosion of phosphoric irons, we note that there are several processes that lead to enhanced corrosion resistance, all due primarily to the high P content at the metal-scale interface. These processes will be described now. In the presence of P at the interface between the metal and rust, the formation of a compact layer of amorphous oxyhydroxide layer next to the metal-rust interface is favoured. This has been experimentally confirmed in the case of P-containing weathering steels. Weathering steel is the name given to steel that is specifically designed to provide good atmospheric corrosion resistance. This amorphous phase has been named as *misawite* (of corresponding chemical formula d-FeOOH) by the author, in view of the Japanese scientist Misawa's significant contributions in establishing the importance of this phase in the atmospheric corrosion resistance of weathering steels. In scientific terms, recent research has shown that this phase may be also identified as nano-crystalline goethite (that is, a-FeOOH phase). The formation of *misawite* layer confers the initial corrosion resistance to the Iron Pillar. It must be noted that this phase forms in a discontinuous manner in the case of normal mild steels while it forms as a compact layer next to the metal-rust interface in the case of P containing weathering steels and in phosphoric irons. The compact *misawite* layer formation at the metal-rust interface is aided by the presence of P due to catalytic action. The superior atmospheric corrosion resistance of P-containing weathering steels has been attributed to this compact amorphous *misawite* layer next to the metal surface. This lowers the diffusion of oxygen and moisture to the metal surface. This layer is also enriched with the element(s) added to provide weathering resistance (that is, P, Cu, Cr and Si in very small amounts of about 0.5%). Some investigators identify the amorphous layer with amorphous or nano-crystalline goethite. As we have stated earlier, we recollect that crystalline goethite (a-FeOOH) and lepidocrocite (g-FeOOH) could be identified by the X-ray diffraction technique, while it is generally not possible to identify the amorphous *misawite* phase by this characterisation technique.

It is important to note that the oxyhydroxides and magnetite present in the long-term rust of phosphoric iron may be nanocyrstalline/amorphous in nature. Amorphous is the term that applies to any material that is not crystalline, that is, does not possess a long range period ordered arrangement of atoms or ions that make up the material. Nanocrystalline implies that the grain sizes are of the order of 10^{-9} metres. As it is known that the initial oxide and oxyhydroxides that form on the iron are crystalline in nature, the long-term conversion of the crystalline forms of these oxyhydroxides to the nanocrystalline and amorphous form is indicated. The crystalline oxide/oxyhydroxides of iron are converted to the amorphous state due to the process of alternate wetting and drying, as has been shown in P-containing weathering steels. There is a benefit to corrosion resistance due to this because the defects in the rust, like pores and fine cracks, can be filled up efficiently by the nanorust particles, thereby further enhancing the resistance to diffusion of oxygen and moisture.

The mechanism of protective passive film formation on phosphoric irons does not end here. The corrosion resistance is further enhanced by further modifications in the rust of the Iron Pillar. The enrichment of P in the inner amorphous layer continues with prolonged exposure. This has been experimentally verified in P-containing weathering steels. This enrichment leads to the precipitation of the insoluble phosphates. The phosphate phase is precipitated at the metal scale interface and its precipitation further lowers the corrosion rate of the pillar iron.One can further imagine the above process repeating itself over a long period of time (like in the case of the Iron Pillar) resulting in a phosphate layer right at the metal-scale interface. This would greatly enhance the atmospheric corrosion resistance and the growth of the rust would practically stop with the formation of this phosphate film at the metal-scale interface. The protective passive film mechanism is schematically depicted in **Fig. 2.30b** where the long term rust on phosphoric iron has been shown in a cross-section.

The process of formation of iron phosphates and the beneficial effects on corrosion resistance are well-known. In fact, there exists vast scientific literature on phosphating of steels. Phosphating refers to surface treatment with phosphoric acid, which leads to corrosion resistance by the formation of a protective passive film on the surface. Phosphating is a very important modern industrial surface treatment procedure.

There are some additional subtle points involved in the mechanism of protective passive film formation on the Delhi Iron Pillar. First, let us understand phosphate formation in some more detail by understanding an important commercial operation known as phosphating. Phosphating of iron is a commercially important coating method that involves the formation of relatively insoluble, electrically non-conducting thin films of metallic phosphates on the surface. It is known that the formation of a protective layer on Fe surface involves the following four steps. In the first step, electrochemical attack of iron by orthophosphoric acid occurs over a wide range of concentration and temperature. In the case of pillar iron, the formation of orthophosphoric acid next to the metal surface has to be first understood. The enrichment of P at this location was earlier established due to the initial corrosion of matrix. Enrichment of P in the Delhi pillar rust has been experimentally determined by Ghosh who mentioned that the P content in the pillar rust was 0.35% whereas the P content in the pillar iron was 0.18%. The enrichment of P in the rust and the presence of condensed moisture would initially result in the formation of phosphoric acid at the metal-rust interface. Free energy considerations also favour its formation. The moisture that is required for phosphoric acid formation is realised in the alternate wetting and drying cycles, which also concentrates the acid thus formed. In contact with phosphoric acid, the dissolution potential of iron becomes less noble and it causes the dissolution of Fe to phosphate. The specific reactions involved are not mentioned here but it is easy to understand that a variety of phosphates can form. The phosphates that form initially are amorphous in nature. However, the dissolution and re-precipitation of phosphate (due to alternate wetting and drying) leads to a change in the pH of the rust. In this process, the amorphous phosphates are converted to the crystalline state, which results in a large decrease on the porosity of the phosphate layer. This further enhances the corrosion resistance by providing an excellent barrier to the diffusion of oxygen and moisture to the metal surface.

In summary, the excellent atmospheric corrosion resistance of the pillar is due to the protective passive film that forms on the surface of the Delhi Iron Pillar, in particular, and phosphoric irons, in general. Three processes of protectiveness have been identified. These are the formation of a compact amorphous layer next to the metal-rust interface, the precipitation of amorphous phosphates (either locally or as a thin layer at the metal-rust interface) and conversion of the amorphous phosphates to crystalline phosphates. Therefore, the cross-section of the rust on phosphoric irons is ideally expected to consist of at least two layers. The outer layer will contain the usual corrosion products of iron (that is, iron oxyhydroxides). The inner layer will consist of the compact amorphous/nanocrystalline phases, enriched in P (**Figure 2.30b**). This kind of multilayered rust has been confirmed in the Delhi Iron Pillar rust microstructure. The protective passive film that forms at the metal-rust interface is therefore responsible for the superior atmospheric corrosion resistance of the Delhi Iron Pillar, in particular, and phosphoric irons, in general.

In fact, Moni Ghosh of TISCO, Jamshedpur, who was one of the investigators of the pillar iron during the 1959-61 studies, anticipated this mechanism in his excellent study of the pillar iron. He stated that "P accumulates in a new phase at the base of the main oxide layer in the oxide form in combination with iron" and "so long as the new phase at the base of the main oxide film was not formed, the metal behaviour was similar to that of exposure surface of ordinary irons". Ghosh performed some simple experiments with the pillar iron piece to assess the influence of P on rusting. The sample was polished and allowed to rust. When a thin and unequally distributed film of rust was formed, it was photographed and slightly polished to remove the rust from the surface. This surface was treated with Stead's solution (which will colour different regions depending upon P concentration) to observe the distribution of P on the surface. In was found that P was generally low in the areas where rust appeared more intensely.

It must be noted here that the first scientist to attribute the Delhi Iron Pillar's corrosion resistance to the high P content in the iron was Neogi. In his classic book *Iron in Ancient India*, published in 1914, he compared the composition of several corrosion resistant ancient Indian irons and proposed that the common factor noticed in them, namely a high P content and low Mn and S contents, must be responsible for their corrosion resistance.

Alternate wetting and drying conditions play an important role in the case of atmospheric corrosion of the pillar because they accelerate the precipitation of phosphate phases and the amorphisation/conversion of the pillar rust to a nano-crytalline state. Interestingly, the amorphisation of rust is also aided by the presence of phosphate ions in the rust. We also note that the large mass of the pillar (the Iron Pillar's weight is estimated to be approximately six tonnes) plays a contributory role in aiding alternate wetting and drying. The large mass of the pillar implies a large heat capacity for the iron and therefore, the pillar will heat up faster or cool down faster than its surroundings. This provides the right conditions of alternate wetting and drying of the Iron Pillar surface. The intensity of wetting and subsequent drying would be much more in the case of the pillar iron because of the large mass of the pillar. The effect of atmosphere on the wetting and drying cycles experiences by the Pillar has been recently modelled by the author (Halder *et al.* 2004: 559-566).

In summary, the superior atmospheric corrosion resistance of the Iron Pillar is due to a protective passive film formation. The conclusion drawn is unambiguous as it has a strong experimental support from actual Delhi Iron Pillar rust characterisation.

Protective Passive Film Properties

Let us look at some characteristic properties of the protective passive film that forms on the Delhi Iron Pillar. We have seen the chemical nature of the protective passive film in the above section.

The passive film is relatively thin, which is indirectly revealed by the highly reflective surface of the pillar (**Figure 2.31**). Moreover, the phosphate phases in the protective passive film appear as yellow flecks, if the pillar is viewed from certain angles. Similarly, at certain times in the day when the sunlight reflects at some particular angle to the pillar surface, the whole surface takes on a golden hue (**Figure 2.32**). This is again due to the nature of the protective passive film. This may have been one of the reasons why some early observers of the Iron Pillar commented that it was constructed of bronze.

The protective passive film on the surface is not of uniform thickness throughout the entire length of the pillar. The pillar surface in the bottom regions was in contact with people before the construction of a circular iron grill cage in 1997 (**Figure 2.33**). This circular cage has been replaced by a square cage in 2005 (**Figure 2.34**). Therefore, the passive film is expected to be thinner in the lower regions of the pillar. The differences in passive film thickness will not be revealed by any technique used for determining coating thickness. However, the differences in passive film thickness can be readily observed in the electrochemical free corrosion potentials measured at different locations on the pillar (Balasubramaniam 2003b: 378-382). Noble potential will be observed at locations where the protective passive film is relatively thick (that is, in the top regions of the pillar) while active potentials at locations where the protective passive film is relatively thin. This has been, in fact, experimentally determined (Raj *et al.* 2005: 1948-1956). We must, of course, keep in mind that in both these cases, we are talking of nanometer-thick protective passive film and the terms "thick" and "thin" have been used in a relative manner.

The amount of P in the underlying metal (that is, iron) is the deciding factor in the formation of the protective passive film. Of course the subsequent enrichment of P at the metal-scale interface will also increase the amount of P, which results in the protective film formation. In view of this, the underlying microstructure does not really play a major

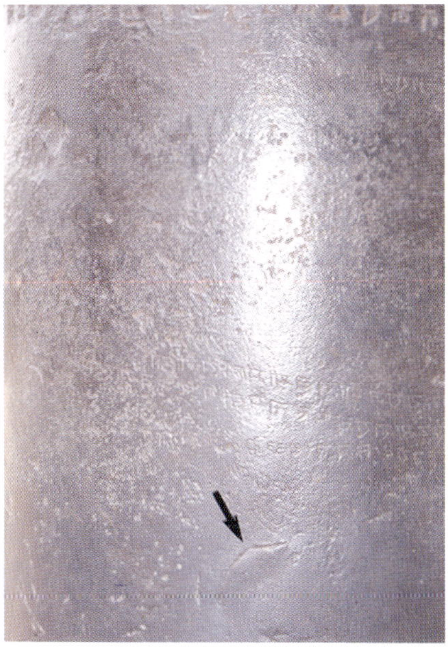

Fig. 2.31: *Highly reflective surface indicating that the protective passive film is relatively thin.*

Fig. 2.32: *The pillar appears golden-coloured when viewed at an angle, due to the dispersed phosphates in the atmospheric rust.*

Fig. 2.33: *A circular iron grill cage was constructed around the Delhi Iron Pillar in 1997.*

Fig. 2.34: *The circular grill cage around the Delhi Iron Pillar was replaced by a square grill cage in 2005.*

role in determining the general long-term nature of the protective passive film (Balasubramaniam 2003a: 534-541). This can be illustrated with an example. We had noted the non-uniform microstructure of the sample of iron that was sectioned from the rough bottom region of the pillar in **Figure 2.14**. However, when this same cut was viewed in 1993, that is, nearly thirty years after the cut had been made, it was difficult to distinguish its surface from the rest of the pillar. The nature of surface on the cut, as observed in 1993, is shown in **Figure 2.35**. The uniform nature of the protective passive film on the entire previously cut surface must be noticed in this plate. Therefore, it is also important to realise that the underlying microstructure does not play a major role in determining the nature of a long-term protective passive film on the surface of phosphoric irons and the chemical composition (that is, P content) is the deciding factor.

A kinetic model for the growth of the rust (protective and non-protective) on the Delhi Iron Pillar has been proposed (Balasubramaniam 2002c: 1357-1365), based on the known nature and structure of the rust on Delhi Iron Pillar and other corrosion resistant ancient Indian irons (Ramesh Kumar and Balasubramaniam 1998: 57-61; Balasubramaniam

Fig. 2.35: *There is no effect of underlying microstructure because the protective passive film covers the surface uniformly on the cut made in the surface in 1959. The microstructure of the metal from this location has been provided in Figure 2.14, from where it can be noticed that the microstructure is highly heterogeneous.*

and Ramesh Kumar 2003: 2451-2465; Dillmann *et al.* 2002: 2231-2242). The initial fast rate of corrosion is aided by the entrapped slag inclusions, and this leads to the enrichment of P at the metal-scale interface. The presence of P at the metal-scale interface promotes protective film formation processes (catalytic formation of d-FeOOH and phosphates). Once the protective passive film forms on the surface at the metal-scale interface, the corrosion rate reduces drastically (**Figure 2.36**). Growth rates have been roughly estimated for these two regions based on the available Delhi Iron Pillar rust thickness measurements (Balasubramaniam 2002c: 1357-1365).

We finally end this section on the Delhi Iron Pillar by again emphasising that all the benefits of phosphoric irons are realised only when relatively mild atmospheric exposure conditions are involved, with its characteristic alternate wetting and drying conditions. The phosphoric irons will fare as good or as bad as carbon steels if exposed in complete immersion conditions. Therefore, relevance of the studies conducted on the Delhi Iron Pillar to modern technology is that phosphoric irons are the materials of choice in

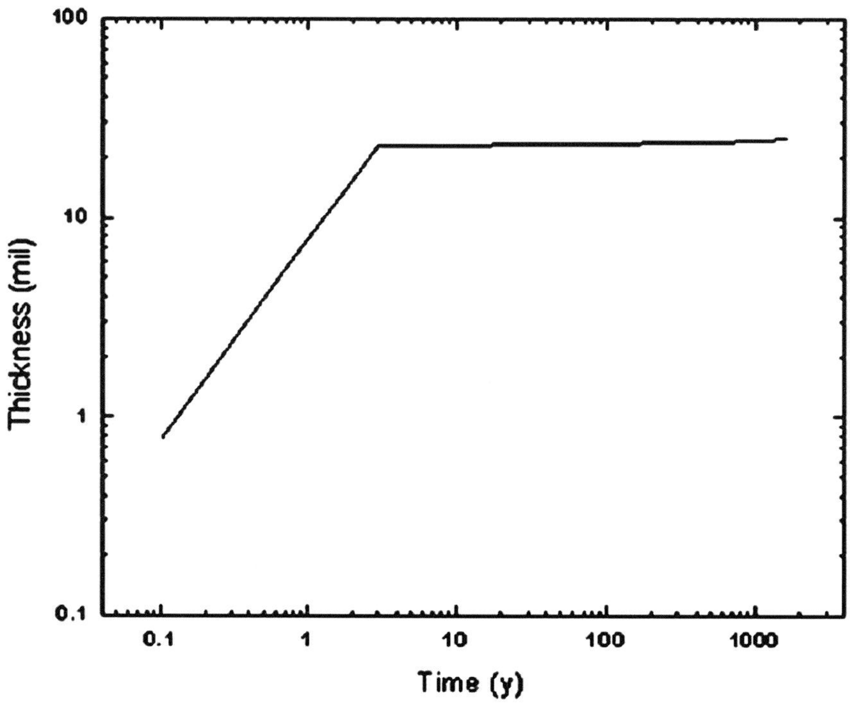

Fig. 2.36: *Proposed kinetics of the protective passive film growth on the Delhi Iron Pillar.*

practical modern applications,where atmospheric exposure conditions are involved. Recent research at IIT Kanpur has revealed the excellent corrosion resistance of phosphoric irons in concrete environments, thereby making then candidate concrete reinforcement materials. The manufacturing and heat treatment schemes to realise ductile phosphoric irons on a large scale have also been worked out. We note that if phosphoric irons can be applied in modern applications, it will go a long way in conserving and preventing the corrosion of steel. We must remember that a major portion of the steel produced is lost every year due to corrosion. This loss must be really huge, both in terms of material volume and its cost because the world production of iron and steel in the early 2000s was approximately nine hundred million tonnes.

The future is bright for phosphoric irons as the studies on the Delhi Iron Pillar have revealed. This is not surprising because, as an old adage informs, "the best of the new is often the long forgotten past".

DHAR IRON PILLAR

The attention of scientists and archaeometallurgists has not been drawn to the Dhar iron pillar, although this pillar is of larger dimensions than the Delhi Iron Pillar. Vincent Smith (1898) remarked that "while we marvel at the skill shown by the ancient artificers in forging a great mass of the Delhi pillar, we must give a still greater measure of admiration to the forgotten craftsmen who dealt so successfully in producing the still more ponderous iron mass of the Dhar pillar monument with its total length of 42 feet (13m)". It is currently lying in three broken pieces in front of the Lat Masjid at Dhar (**Figure 2.37**). The history of the pillar is first addressed followed by a description of the structural features of the pillar and its manufacturing technology. The original erection method of this pillar is also discussed. Finally, a detailed metallurgical analysis (composition, microstructure and corrosion behaviour) of the Dhar pillar iron is presented.

History

Dhar is situated near Indore in Madhya Pradesh and in medieval times, it was the capital of Malwa, when it was called Dhâra. The city was founded as the capital of King Bhoja (1010-1053 CE) (Choudhary 1963: 96-115). Dhar suffered the usual vicissitudes of cities in ancient and medieval India, and its security depended on the power of its rulers to resist aggression. During the Mohammedan period, it became known as Piran Dhar due

Fig. 2.37: *The three pieces of the Dhar iron pillar. The longest piece is of square cross-section, while the second changes from a square to octagonal section and the third piece is octagonal throughout.*

to the many Mohammadan saints associated with this place (Imperial 1908: 294-295). Dhar first came into Muslim hands around 1300 CE when Alauddin Khilji subdued Malwa up to Dhar. Muhammad bin Tughlak halted at Dhar in 1344 CE and found the whole place desolate due to famine. In 1399 CE, Dilawar Khan was made the governor of Dhar who soon became practically independent, with his son and successor Hoshang Shah being the first Muslim king of Malwa. Dhar became second in importance to Mandu, which Hoshang Shah made his capital (Imperial 1908: 294-295). Under Akbar, Dhar became the chief town of the *mahâl* in the Mandu *sarkâr* of the *sûbah* of Malwa.

The history of the Dhar pillar is shrouded in mystery. Smith (1898) supposes that the Dhar pillar, like the Delhi Pillar, was also erected during the Gupta period. There is no inscription on the pillar providing information about its donor and purpose. Prakash (1989) mistakenly mentions that there is an inscription on the square part of the pillar, which showed that some southern king Tilungavidya erected a pillar of victory at

Ujayapuri. However, there is no such inscription on the pillar and Cousens (1902) quoted this inscription (*Epigraphica Indica* Vol. VII, p. 121) to show that the pillar could have been erected as a *jayastambh* (victory pillar). Cousens (1902) hypothesised that Raja Arjunavarma Deva constructed the pillar in 1210 CE with the molten implements of war left in the battlefield by his enemies during his attack on Gujarat, as a mark of victory. Local tradition holds that Raja Bhoja, who was the king of Malwa between 1010 and 1053 CE, constructed the pillar. He was a great patron of poets and scholars, and advanced multifarious activities to promote learning. He is credited with more than two dozen scholarly works on a wide variety of subjects (Choudhary 1963: 96-115). The achievements of the iron industry in Malwa during Raja Bhoja's reign have been well-documented (Sohoni 1990: 104-109). Bhoja was well-versed in iron metallurgy as he, in his *Yuktikalpataru*, discusses the manufacture of iron weapons and refers to earlier texts on iron metallurgy like *Louhârnava, Louhadspa* and *Louhapradîpa* (Biswas 1996). Moreover, there was a spurt in construction activities during his reign. Bhoja was a Shaivaite (that is, worshipper of Shiva, one of the trinities of the Hindu pantheon) and this fact was expressed in the structural design of the Dhar Iron Pillar, which will be discussed later.

Cousens (1902) hypothesised that the pillar was originally set up before the principal temple of Mandu. Mandu is a mighty fortress located close to Dhar. According to him, the pillar was probably intact before Mandu's capture by the Muslims. There are no archaeological or literary evidences to support Mandu's claim for the original location of the pillar. A strong case, however, can be made for Dhar as the original location of the pillar because it was the capital city of Malwa founded by Raja Bhoja. The pillar must have been originally topped with a *trishul* (trident) capital and must have been originally placed in front of a Shiva temple. The probable name of the Shiva temple must have been *Latesvara,* based on the general name of *Latesvara Mandala* given to this location within the Malwa region. The use of the word *lat* (pillar) appearing in the name of Lat Masjid further reveals that the original temple name could have been *Latesvara,* in front of which the pillar must have been originally erected. This temple would have formed the very site at which the present Lat Masjid stands, and the masonry basement where the stone boulders are seen must have been the original erection site of the Dhar iron pillar.

After being thrown down by the Muslims, its shaft was broken into at least two pieces, which lay about for a hundred years. One smaller piece (most probably without the currently missing fourth piece of the pillar) was planted at Dilawar Khan's mosque in Mandu (in a position similar to that of the Delhi Iron Pillar in the Quwwat-ul-Islam mosque). The greater length was erected before the mosque built by Dilawar Khan at Dhar in 1405 CE. He gave the name Lat Masjid to the mosque erected by him after the *lat* (pillar) in front of it. The masjid was erected out of the remains of Hindu and Jain temples in 1405 CE. The Hindu and Jain columns in the mosque are handsomely carved, while the *mihrabs* and *mimbar* are fine specimens of Muslim workmanship (Führer 1893: 21).

The larger piece remained in front of the Lat Masjid before Bahadur Shah of Gujarat, in 1531 CE, captured the area and wiped out the dynasty at Mandu. The Mughal emperor Jahangir notes that Bahadur Shah wished to carry the pillar to Gujarat. In attempting to do so, the pillar fell down and broke into two pieces of 22' and 13' (~6-4 m). Jahangir writes the following in his autobiography (Beveridge 1968: 406-408) "Outside this fort (of Dhar) there is a Jami Masjid and a square pillar lies in front of the Masjid with some portions embedded in the ground. When Bahadur Shah conquered Malwa, he was anxious to take the pillar with him to Gujarat. In the act of digging out, it fell down and was broken into two pieces (one piece 22' long and the other 13'). I (Jahangir) have seen it lying on the ground carelessly and so ordered the bigger piece to be carried to Agra, which I hope to be used as a lamp-post in the courtyard of my father's (Akbar's) tomb". It is clear that Jahangir's instructions were not carried out as the pillar piece is still at Dhar.

In 1598 CE, Akbar stopped at Dhar for seven days, while directing the invasion of Deccan. This fact is recorded on the Dhar iron pillar by an inscription of Akbar in Persian. By the manner in which the inscription has been inscribed, it can be concluded that the pillar was lying down rather than upright when the inscription was inscribed (Cousens 1902: 205-212). Cousens also remarked about names and letters in Devanagari character on other parts of the largest piece of the pillar. They were engraved with the pillar's proper side up. Among these inscriptions are several names of visitors of the goldsmith caste, each name having "*soni*" for "*sonar*" attached to it, and Cousens read the last as "Jasu Soni" for "Yasvant Sonar". The date immediately after the names was very indistinct. These names are between 6'11" (3.3m) and 7'6" (3.6m) from the proper lower end of the largest pillar piece. All the Devanagari letters and names are at about the same level, and none occurs on the upper parts of the largest pillar piece or on the other two pieces, which clearly indicates that these characters were engraved before the first fall of the pillar. Cousens (1902) noticed several small symbols and a Persian word or two, but they were all scratched in rather than engraved.

The largest piece (that is, the one that Jahangir measured as 22' and which had broken off from the erected pillar in front of the Lat Masjid) remained in the same position from the time of its fall in 1531 CE, when Bahadur Shah tried to remove the pillar, till the time it was removed by the Archaeological Survey of India (ASI) around 1980 CE and placed horizontally on a platform adjoining the mosque (**Figure 2.37**). The reports by Führer (1893) and Cousens (1902) show that it was lying in the same sloping position against the masonry terrace in front of the mosque (**Figure 2.38**) as Jahangir had described. Interestingly, kids in the nearby areas were using this piece as a slide (before the ASI set it up on the platform) and therefore, the top surface of the largest piece appears smoothly polished.

Fig. 2.38: *Photograph taken in the early 1900s showing the longest piece of the Dhar iron pillar lying in a sloping position against the masonry terrace in front of the Lat Masjid. This piece remained in this position from 1531 CE till about 1980 CE. (Photograph courtesy: Archaeological Survey of India).*

As regards the second piece that was broken during the time of Bahadur Shah, Führer (1893) mistakenly reports that it was standing outside the Jami Masjid in Mandu. Both Campbell (1895) and Smith (1898) have presented Führer's incorrect observations. (The iron pillar standing outside the Jami Masjid in Mandu, even today, is the iron flagstaff known as Allaudin's *Sang* (spear), and this pillar will be described later in this chapter). The second piece was lying within Dhar. Cousens, in February 1903, saw the same at the Anand High School, where a museum had been established sometime in 1902. This museum was shifted to another location within Dhar, sometime between 1922 and 1942. The second pillar piece was not shifted to the museum at the new location but was placed horizontally on the ground, without any support, near the masonry basement where the longest piece lay. This piece was removed from this position by the ASI, around 1980 CE, and placed horizontally on concrete supports on a platform near the mosque (**Figure 2.37**).

One of the original broken pieces that was erected in the Dilawar Khan mosque in Mandu was also moved from this location during the British period, as stated by Cousens (1902). He quotes the following interesting account of the sighting of the third piece at Mandu by a Bombay subaltern, published in 1844: "there is a large piece of iron several tons in weight – a remnant of the blacksmith's stock-in-trade, which he forgot to convert into gold." Cousens (1902) mentions that the account refers to the smallest piece of the *lat* that was subsequently brought down to Dhar. Führer (1893) mentions that the smallest piece was in the garden of the Maharaja's Guest House at Dhar in 1893 (which was later called the Agency House and currently a heritage hotel), while Cousens reports that in February 1902, this was fixed in a masonry basement in the public gardens known as Lal Bagh, quite close to the Anand High School. Cousens had this pillar piece removed from the masonry basement in order to determine its accurate dimensions. It was then placed in the museum at Anand High School and, similar to the second piece, was shifted to its current location. Therefore, this piece has also been shifted from one location to another in Dhar, after being bought down from Mandu.

The three pieces of the Dhar iron pillar are currently lying horizontally on concrete supports on a platform beside the Lat Masjid (**Figure 2.37**).

Dimensions

Führer (1893) first reported that the largest piece was 24' long and 10" on each side, while the second piece was 12' long and the third, 6' long. He mistakenly quotes the third piece as a square cross-section of 10" width. Smith (1898) quotes Furhrer's measurements *verbatim*. Cousens (1902) reported that the total length of the three pieces was 43'4", with an average cross-section 10.25". The longest portion was measured as 24'3" of the square section; the second 11'7" (of which 8'6" was square and 3'1" was of the octagonal section); and the third piece, 7'6" in length, and, with the exception of a circular collar at the end, about 8' deep, was of octagonal section throughout. He also reported that the proper lower end of the largest piece was slightly bulbous (see **Figure 2.37**), being about 11" wide at 2' from the end, while the rest of the cross-section measured 10.25" to 10.50". Prakash (1989) and Roessler (1995) also measured pillar parts. Roessler mentions that the first and the biggest part of the pillar had a length of 24'2", with a nearly square section of 10'7" × 11'1". The second piece was 11'8" long with a rectangular section of 10' 7" × 10'2" over a length of 9'2", which changed into an octagonal cross-section and finally ended with a cone shape of 5.5" length and 9.5" diameter. The third part of the pillar was 7'6" long and is octagonal, beginning with a cone shape of 8.3" length and 9.5" diameter (Roessler 1995: 143-154). The combined height of the pillar has been estimated to be 43'4", and this is nearly double the height of the Delhi Iron Pillar. Roessler estimated the weight of the three parts, utilising the measured dimensions and the specific weight of iron (7.81 g/cm^3) as 4.50 tonnes for the largest piece, 1.86 tonnes for the second and 0.94 tonnes for the third piece, thereby providing a total weight of 7.3 tonnes. Therefore, the combined weight of the Dhar iron pillar is at least a tonne more than the Delhi Iron Pillar.

As regards the original joined condition of the pillar, the matching fractured surface of the top of the largest piece and the bottom of the second piece (**Figure 2.39**) proves that both these parts of the pillar were originally joined together when manufactured by the forge welding process. However, the conical top of the second piece (**Figure 2.40a**) and the conical bottom of the third piece (**Figure 2.40b**) do not seem to be joined by forge welding. Roessler (1995), based on the original idea of Cousens (1902) of a collar connecting the two pieces, showed that the third part of the pillar was joined with the second part of the pillar by a forged ring (**Figure 2.41**). Roessler proposed that the ring could have been of the same dimensions as the octagonal portion. Cousens (1902) stated that he has "personally taken fresh measurements of the two smaller sections, as a doubt was expressed as to their both having been parts of the same pillar. The smallest piece, with the collar or neck at one end, measures 2' 9.5" round its octagonal shaft, while the other measures 3'2" round the octagonal end. The first gives 10 1/4" diameter

Fig. 2.39: *The matching fractured surfaces of the top of the largest piece and the bottom of the second piece.*

(a) *(b)*

Fig. 2.40: *(a) Conical top of the second piece, and (b) conical bottom of the third piece.*

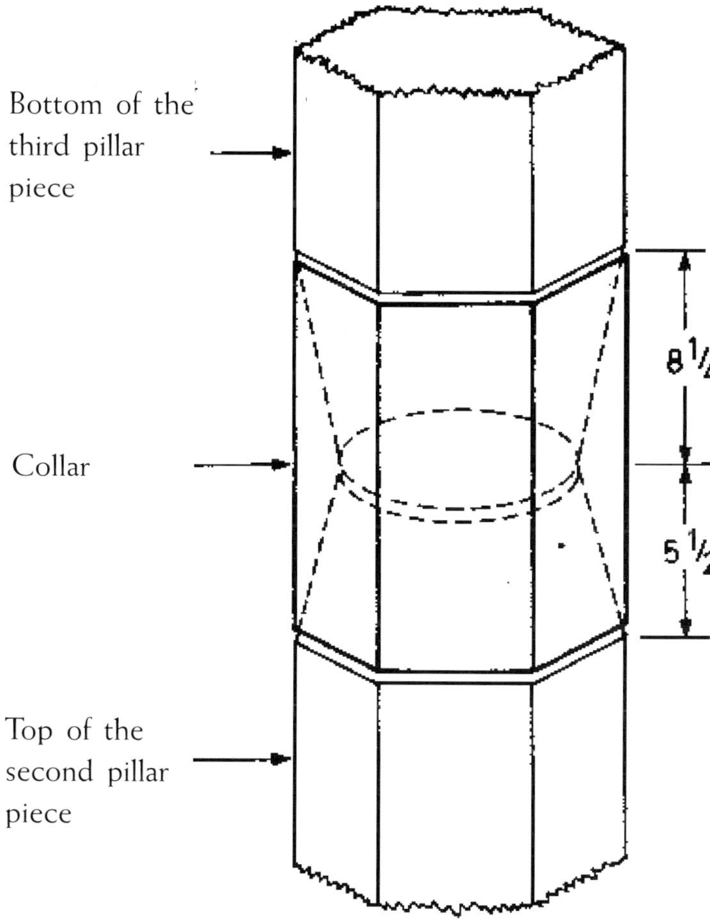

Fig. 2.41: *Proposed joining methodology of the second and third pillar pieces using a collar.*

from one face to an opposite face, through the pillar, and the breadth of the square shaft of the largest section at the Lat Masjid is 10 3/8" at its upper end, while the breadth of the square part of the middle section is 10 1/8". The width then of the smaller section is practically the same as the square part in the other two sections. But the perimeter of octagonal end of the middle piece gives a diameter of 11 3/8", which shows how unequal the diameter is in different parts. It seems quite clear, however, that the shortest piece does not immediately join on to the middle piece as there would be a sudden lessening from 11 3/8" diameter to 10 1/4", and I think we must conclude that there is a missing piece which fitted between these". He further goes on to state that the conical ends of the second and third pieces must have been intended to hold a collar.

The fractured top of the third section (**Figure 2.42**) indicates a missing fourth piece of the pillar. The relatively higher percentage of slag inclusions on this fractured surface should be noted. This must be the reason for the fracture at this location, when the erect pillar was first thrown down. Based on the fact that the proportion of the octagonal part of the whole pillar to the square portion required greater length in the former, Cousens (1902) proposed that the total length of the original pillar was probably a little short of 50'. On the other hand, Roessler deduced that there must be a missing fourth piece (about 3'3" in length) based on the relative position of the drill holes in the third piece. The size and complete cross-section of the missing part is not known with the available information. However, it has been speculated that it could be octagonal or octagonal-round (Roessler 1995: 143-154). This discussion on the missing fourth piece reveals that the Dhar iron pillar must have been higher than 43'4".

Fig. 2.42: *Fractured top surface of the third piece indicates that a missing fourth piece was present atop the third piece.*

Cousens (1902) first hypothesised that the pillar was surmounted by either a *garuda* or a *trishul*. Führer (1893) notes that the "third piece, a square of 10 inches, with a bell-capital, 6 feet high, is standing in the garden of the Maharajah's guest-house at Dhar". Cousens enquired about this in a letter to Mr Lele, State Superintendent of Education, stationed at Dhar. Mr Lele replied that he, as soon as he received the letter, he "drove to the Agency House and made a search for the bell-capital near the Havaldar's house. Nothing like it was found there, or anywhere else. But on further enquiries I found, near the *baghban's* house, a flat octagonal slab of ordinary black-stone, which old people say rested upon the *lat* while it was standing in the Agency garden. It formed the seat of a stone figure of Napoleon Bonaparte on horseback by which the *lat* was surmounted. When Dr Führer visited Dhar–this slab with its support might have looked to him bell-shaped". Roessler (1995) observed a bell-shaped structure (**Figure 2.43**) at the Dhar Fort Museum and proposed it to be the capital of the Dhar iron pillar. The author was also present during Roessler's trip to the Dhar Fort Museum. In the author's opinion, the bell-shaped structure appears to be the end-part of a forge welded cannon. There are

Fig. 2.43: *Bell-shaped structure currently lying at the Dhar Fort Museum. Roessler proposed that this was the original decorative bell capital of the Dhar iron pillar.*

numerous forge welded iron cannons in the Dhar fort, and the bell-shaped structure must have originated from one of these cannons. In summary, although it is proved that there is a missing fourth piece, the nature of this piece and the pillar's capital are not known.

As regards the possible original height and the capital of the pillar, insights will be obtained by a dimensional analysis of the Dhar pillar. Recourse will also be taken to Hindu iconography in order to glean ideas about the original condition of the pillar. As the pillar was set up by Raja Bhoja, it is clear that it must have formed a pillar in a Shiva temple. As a staunch Shaivaite, Raja Bhoja (Choudhary 1963: 96-115) constructed several temples dedicated to Shiva. Firm support for the pillar being associated with a Shiva temple is obtained from the observed cross-sections of the Dhar pillar. In Hindu iconography (Banerjea 1956: 93), Shiva is depicted as *Shivalingam*, symbolically represented by an erect phallus. The *Shivalingam* consists of three distinct parts. The lower part of the *Shivalingam* is square in cross-section, indicating the *Brahma Khand* (the Portion of Brahma – God of Creation). This changes to an octagonal cross- section, which is indicative of *Vishnu Khand* (the Portion of Vishnu – God of Existence). Finally, the cross-section becomes circular in the upper regions, which is indicative of *Rudra Khand* (the Portion of Shiva – God of Destruction). Therefore, it is concluded, based on the above discussion, that the final cross-section of the pillar in the missing fourth piece must have been circular, based on the iconographic description of the *Shivalingam* and the resemblance of the pillar to the *Shivalingam* in symbolic terms. This brings us automatically to the conclusion that the pillar must have originally surmounted by a *trishul* or trident, which is the symbol (standard) of Shiva.

As regards the relative dimensions of the various cross-sections, dimensional analysis indicates that the square cross-section extends to a total distance of 33' and the octagonal cross-section currently seen is about 11'. Therefore, the octagonal cross-section must have formed a certain proportion of the original square cross-section and it is reasonable to assume that this was one third of the square cross-section height, which is symbolic of the trinity concept in Hindu pantheon iconography. The circular section must have been again one-third of the length of the cross-section below it (that is, the octagonal section) and therefore, based on the analysis above, its height must have been about 3'. This dimension fits well with the estimates of Cousens (1902) and Roessler (1995) who stated that the missing fourth piece should have been about 3' in length. Finally, the relative dimension of the pillar capital should appear at a fixed proportion to the pillar body, and it is again reasonable to assume that this must have been one-third of the height of the cross-section just below it and therefore, it is deduced that the *trishul* capital should have been 1' in height. With the above-deduced dimensions, the total height of the original pillar must have been 48'. The dimensional analysis described above has been reproduced in the schematic depiction of the possible original condition of the Dhar pillar (**Figure** 2.44).

It is tempting to propose that the iron pillar currently standing in Mandu (in front of the Jami Masjid) could have been the missing fourth piece of the pillar. First, the pillar is of circular section which is indicative of the final cross-section of the Dhar iron pillar. Second, this pillar is associated with Alauddin Khilji as it is presently called *Alauddin's*

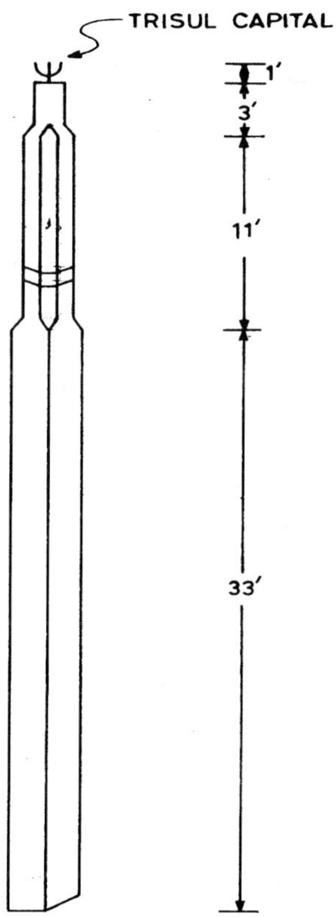

Fig. 2.44: *Schematic representation of the original condition of the Dhar pillar, showing the relative dimensions of various sections of the pillar. The circular cross-section of the final top regions of the pillar and its* trishul *capital have been deduced based on Hindu iconographic philosophy.*

Sang (spear). As noted earlier, Alauddin Khilji was the first Muslim ruler to plunder interior Malwa and therefore, the first fall of the Dhar iron pillar must have occurred during his raids. It is possible that Khilji could have modelled the fractured circular part of the pillar in the form of the pillar currently seen in front of the Jami Masjid at Mandu. It is also interesting to note a large joint towards the top of the Mandu iron pillar. This could be the location from where the *trishul* capital of the pillar could have been reshaped to form the presently-seen circular section.

Erection of the Pillar

Cousens (1902) first mentioned the presence of a number of small holes (see **Figure 2.45**) at irregular intervals on all its four sides, varying in depth from 1 ¾" to 3", and in diameter about 1 ¼". They run up each of the four sides of the square shaft and the corresponding faces of the octagon. The unequal distribution of the holes discounts the possibility of the pillar having been a *dipadana* (lamp-post) and Cousens (1902) assumed that these pits were used for the purpose of inserting some instrument like crowbars

Fig. 2.45: *Two holes are present in the front (arrowed) and back faces of the third piece and they are partly covered by the concrete support beams.*

while the pillar was being forged and welded. With the aid of these crowbars, it was suggested that the workmen could easily manipulate the heavy column and forge weld the semi-molten metal, lump by lump, on to the white hot stump of the shaft. Cousens did not mention the material and the length of the crowbar, while Roessler (1995) proposed that it was made out of steel. Prakash (1989) has also noted these small holes and related them to the manufacturing methodology. His views will be discussed while addressing the manufacturing methodology of the pillar. Roessler (1995) mentions that all the pieces contained holes of 1.2" to 1.6" in diameter and 1.6" to 3" in depth, which were distributed at irregular distances on all four sides of the first and the second pillar. Two holes in the front (arrowed in **Figure 2.45**) and back of the third piece are partly closed by the concrete support beams. The arrowed hole in **Figure 2.45**, at a distance of 1.6" from the upper surface of the third pillar piece, is partially closed because a broken peg/crowbar is seen at this location. Cousens (1902) and Roessler (1995) have noticed this half-closed hole. Compositional analysis of the broken peg/crowbar from this location would provide insights into the material of construction of the peg/crowbar.

Roessler has provided a plausible explanation for the existence of these holes. He states that the pillar would have been impossible to fix in the stone stand (to be discussed below) due to the heavy weight of the pillar and its tremendous height. Roessler proposed that the holes, apart from being used for handling the pillar during the manufacturing process, were inserted with small pegs in order to fix cables or wires at different heights of the pillar in order to hold the pillar in the upright position. The reconstruction of the pillar in the upright position, as suggested by Roessler (1995), is provided in **Figure 2.46**. The proposed reconstruction was based on the estimation of the bending moment resulting from the weight of the pillar multiplied by the centre of gravity (nearly half the height of the pillar). Based on the existence of an ancient iron anchor near Jahaz Mahal at Mandu, Roessler (1995) further proposed that the cables were held in position by means of iron anchors (**Figure 2.46**). However, this may not be likely as the ancient iron anchor at Mandu (**Figure 2.47**) was used for anchoring the boats that sailed in the lake adjoining the Jahaz Mahal at Mandu.

The lower region of the Dhar iron pillar was not buried underground when it was originally erected, unlike the Delhi Iron Pillar. Cousens (1902) first reported the method by which the pillar was erected originally. Opposite to the Lat Masjid, there are three pieces of stone on a masonry basement (**Figure 2.48a**). Cousens, in 1902, observed that iron rings were used to bind together the three rock boulders together.

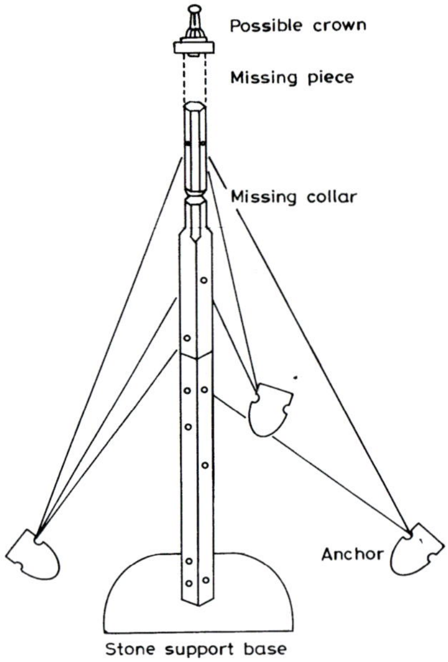

Fig. 2.46: *Proposed reconstruction of the Dhar iron pillar according to Roessler (1995).*

Fig. 2.47: *Iron anchor originally discovered from the lake adjoining Jahaz Mahal in Mandu. Its height is 30.7" and width at the top 22" and at the bottom 11.8". Its thickness is 6.3" at the bottom and 7" at the top.*

He states, "upon the masonry basement stand the three great rock boulders, which were bound together by iron bands and had a socket in the top, 20 inches deep (**Figure 2.48b**), where thc foot of the pillar was gripped. The iron bands securing these passed round them horizontally, and their pressure was spread over the bounders by vertical flat iron bars inserted at intervals under the bands in slots cut for the purpose. In fact the whole was faggotted around the end of the pillar". The slots for inserting the vertical flat iron bars can be noticed on the stone blocks (**Figure 2.48a** and **b**). The iron bands and the flat iron bars are currently missing. The bottom surface of the Dhar iron pillar possesses a circular hole, 2.3" in diameter and 3.8" in depth (see **Figure 2.49a**), to hold an insert for gripping the bottom of the pillar with the stone boulders. Additionally, the circular holes seen in the bottom region of the pillar (**Figure 2.49b**) must have been used for securing the pillar with the stone basement with the aid of inserts and ropes. Interestingly, the stone boulders themselves have circular holes provided at the bottom for gripping them to the platform.

(a)

(b)

Fig. 2.48: *(a) Three stone boulders currently on the masonry basement opposite the Lat Masjid, and (b) The author is standing on the 20" deep socket in between the stone boulders, in which the bottom of the pillar was originally gripped.*

(a) (b)

Fig. 2.49: *(a) and (b) Hollow slots in the bottom region of the Dhar iron pillar. These hollow slots were used for gripping the pillar to the basement by means of inserts and ropes.*

Manufacturing Methodology

The iron pillar has been forge welded by the horizontal forge welding technique, as outlined for the construction of the main body of the Delhi Iron Pillar in the above section. The surface is not as well forged as the Delhi Iron Pillar. Roessler (1995), however, admired the forge welding methodology by noticing that "at the bottom of the longest part there is a perimeter of 3'8", in the middle 3'7" and on the top 3'5", which means the square is reduced by only 0.4" each side from the top to the bottom of the 24'2" height pillar. It shows the exactness of the forging".

Prakash (1989) provides an interesting alternative account of how the pillar may have been manufactured. He notes that the four surfaces of the first section and the square part of the second section are covered with flat plates 2" to 6" thick and 2' to 2'4" long. He further states that the holes have been punched about 2" to 4" before the end of each of these plates, and in the process deforming them and piercing into the main body (**Figure 2.50**). He concludes that the pillar has been fabricated by joining 2'4" to 2'9" long pieces of square cross-section and the plates have been fixed and forge welded as butt welded re-enforcement on the joints. He also suggested the horizontal forge welding technique for fabrication of the other pieces of the pillar, while ruling out the possibility that the cross-section was changed by chiselling out the excess material to give the desired shape. As noted earlier, while discussing the manufacturing methodology of the

Delhi Iron Pillar in Chapter 2, the possible presence of a thick circular pin in the fractured end of the first piece can be noted (see **Figure 2.51**). He attributed the fracture of the pillar to improper forge welding technique due to insufficient pressure and to the presence of a higher amount of slag inclusion in the Dhar pillar iron. He proposed that

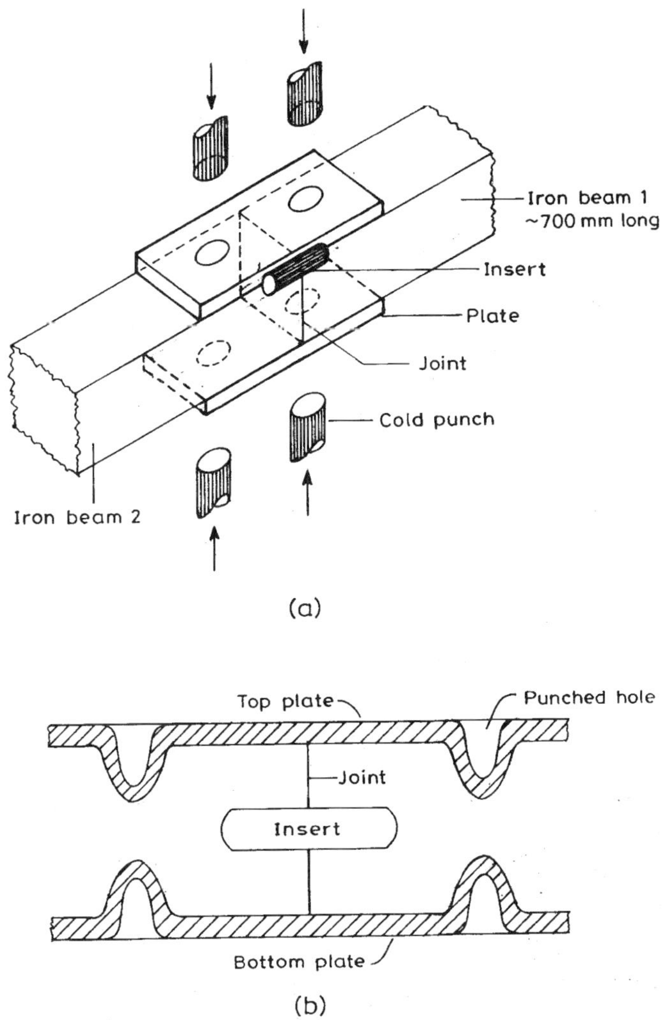

Fig. 2.50: *The method of joining the iron blocks and butt welding of the plate on the pillar surface, as proposed by Prakash (1989): (a) isometric view and (b) cross-section.*

Fig. 2.51: *Fractured cross-section of one of the Dhar iron pillar pieces indicating the possible presence of a circular insert in the centre (marked with an arrow).*

the iron required for the construction of this pillar was smelted near Ujjain and first forge welded into square blocks of 2'4" to 2'9", and then transported to Mandu or some nearby area for final fabrication. These hot forged square sections were supposed to possess a circular tapered hole in the centre of the square cross-section, with the holes (of 1.6" to 2.4" diameter) being punched in to these blocks in red hot condition. In the second stage of manufacture, Prakash envisaged that these 2'4" to 2'9" long sections were joined together in the hot condition by fixing a common iron pin and forge welding two adjoining faces (**Figure 2.50**). He further speculates that for handling the hot sponge, highly skilled craftsmen must have used forging hammers weighing 20 to 40 kg, based on his observation of such heavy swing forge hammers in operation in the cottage industries for producing heavy forgings. The possibility of drop forging methodology was also mooted by Prakash (1989). In this way, Prakash proposed that several 2'4" to 2'9" long sections were joined together to fabricate a long pillar or shaft which was further forged in the horizontal position to give it a proper shape. As noted earlier, Prakash proposed that the joints were further strengthened by butt welding of the iron plates, by first forge-welding these plates on the joint and later securing them in position (as well as weld them with the main body) by hammering a cold punch through the hot stock under heavy pressure (**Figure 2.50**). This, according to Prakash (1989), was the reason for the holes noticed on the pillar. He also accepts that these holes must have further facilitated the handling of the iron shaft, as originally suggested by Cousens (1902). Ultrasound measurements by the author and Roessler, conducted in December 1996, using a hand-held ultrasound equipment did not provide conclusive evidence for the presence of the surface plates. The largest pillar piece does show large weld joints spaced at about 2'4" to 2'9" (**Figure 2.37**). Moreover, the plate-like structure of the faces can be noticed in the bottom cross- section of the second piece and top cross-section of the first piece. Therefore, the manufacturing method proposed by Prakash (1989) needs to be looked into carefully in future studies of the pillar. However, there is no doubt that the Dhar iron pillar has been manufactured by the horizontal forge welding technique.

Finally, it is important to join the three parts of the Dhar pillar, for which sophisticated welding techniques are currently available. The Dhar pillar in the completed state would be the largest ancient forge welded iron pillar in the world.

Corrosion Resistance

There is only one published composition of the Dhar pillar iron. According to Tylecote (1979), with a quotation of Hadfield (1912) and Graves (1912), the chemical composition of Dhar pillar iron is 0.02% C and 0.28% P. A small piece of the Dhar iron pillar was obtained from the lower face of the second largest pillar piece, with the permission of the ASI, and characterised (Balasubramaniam and Ramesh Kumar 2003: 2451-2465). As the Dhar iron pillar is a product of forge welding, there was one location where the small piece of metal, in the form of a thin sheet about 0.1" thick, was protruding out of the surface. A chisel was used to gently ease out this flat piece of metal without damaging the surface of the pillar. This piece of Dhar pillar iron was used in all further studies reported here. Local compositions were determined using an electron probe microanalyser (EPMA). The composition varied from one location to another, depending on the microstructure. The composition from one region (containing pearlite) was (in weight percent) 0.683% C, 0.693% P, 0.013% Mn and no sulphur, while from another location (containing both ferrite and pearlite), the composition was 0.276% C, 0.851% P and 0.075% Ag. Interestingly, the Ag content was insignificant in all the locations analysed. Cousens (1902) commented that the local people believed that the pillar was made of *pancharasa* or *astadhâtu*, an alloy of five or eight metals. He speculated that some bright appearing regions on the surface were silver, imperfectly mixed with iron from the silver mounted weapons. A detailed compositional analysis of the pillar is required to determine whether Ag is present in significant amounts or not. The entrapped slags were also analysed and it was found that they were essentially fayaletic. A typical composition obtained was 55.8% Fe, 27.8% Si, 0.1%Mn and 16.3% P. The relatively higher amount of P in the Dhar pillar iron must be noted.

Microstructural analysis indicated that there were some regions devoid of carbon; while at other locations there was a significant amount of carbon as revealed by the presence of a higher volume fraction of pearlite. The entrapped slag inclusions were generally surrounded by a higher volume fraction of pearlite (**Figure 1.4**). This aspect has been discussed in detail in Chapter 1.

Potentiodynamic polarisation experiments were conducted with the Dhar pillar iron, Eran iron and mild steel specimens in a borate buffered solution of pH 8.5. All the specimens exhibited stable passivity in the solution (**Figure 2.52**). The Dhar pillar iron exhibited the lowest passive current density, thereby indicating its superior corrosion

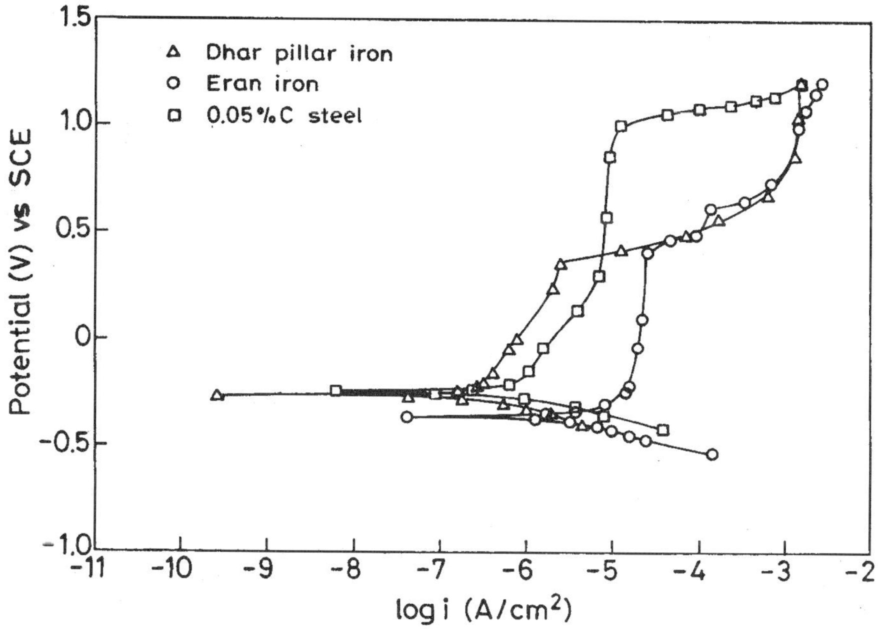

Fig. 2.52: *Experimental potentiodynamic polarisation diagrams for the Dhar pillar iron, Eran iron and 0.05% C steel in borate buffered solution of pH 7.6.*

resistance. The pitting potential of the Dhar pillar iron was more active compared to that of mild steel and similar to that of Eran iron. This indicates the deleterious effect of the slag inclusions on passivity breakdown in both the ancient Indian irons (Puri *et al.* 1997: 1-10). The interfaces between the iron matrix and slag inclusions provide ideal initiation sites for pitting corrosion and hence the passive ranges in both the Dhar pillar iron and Eran iron are lower compared to mild steel (**Figure 2.52**).

In order to understand the atmospheric rusting process, samples of rust from the Dhar pillar iron piece were characterised by X-ray diffraction (XRD), Fourier transform infrared spectroscopy (FTIR) and Mössbauer spectroscopy (Balasubramaniam and Ramesh Kumar 2003: 2451-2465). The results of the characterisation of the atmospheric rust of the Dhar iron pillar indicate the existence of crystalline ferric oxides and phosphate phases, and amorphous hydroxide phases..

Cross-sectional microscopy of the iron sample indicates that the atmospheric rust consisted of two layers, an optically dull inner thin layer and an optically bright thick outer layer (**Figure 2.53**). The layered structure of the protective rust in the case of weathering steels is well- established (Misawa *et al.* 1971: 35-48, 1974: 279-289; Yamashita *et al.* 1994: 283-299). Regarding the optical nature of the layers on weathering steels, it has been pointed out that the inner optically isotropic layer of the surface rust is composed of X-ray amorphous spinel type iron oxide which can protect the steel matrix (Okada 1968: 705-7709; Okada *et al.* 1969: 355-365). Therefore, based on the above studies, it is reasonable to state that the inner optically dull layer seen in the Dhar iron pillar rust microstructure is amorphous in nature while the outer layer is crystalline in nature. The innermost thin layer seen next to the metal surface must be the amorphous d-FeOOH layer and this may be enriched with phosphorus or may contain crystalline phosphates, as has been found in corrosion-resistant ancient Indian iron (Dillmann *et al.* 2002: 2231-2242). The outer layer must consist of the usual corrosion products expected on atmospheric corrosion of iron (that is, magnetite, hematite, goethite and lepidocrocite) and can also be enriched in phosphorus or may contain phosphates. As the Dhar pillar iron contains a significant amount of phosphorus, the formation of phosphates is expected. The golden reddish brown colour of the surface of the pillar pieces also indicates that phosphates must be present in the atmospheric rust. The present analysis was performed on one of the pillar pieces at a specific location and it

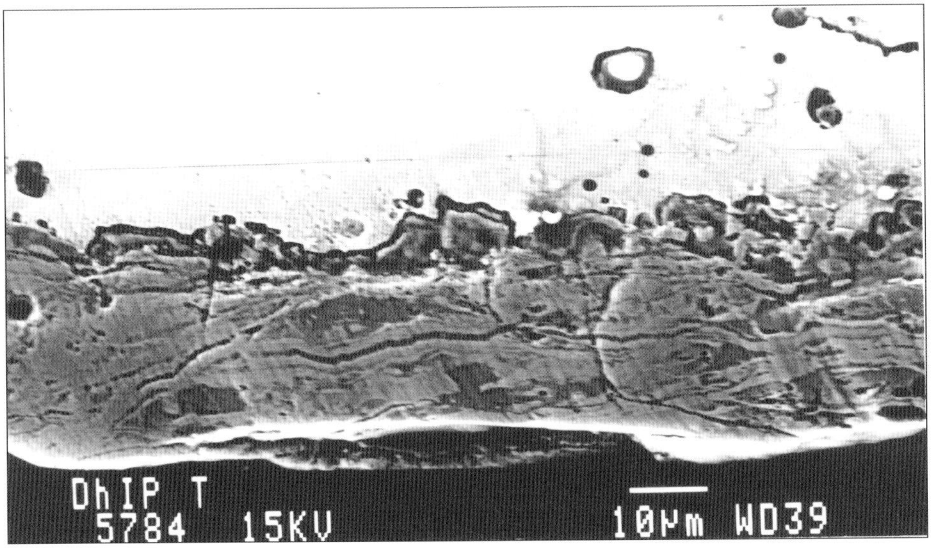

Fig. 2.53: *Cross-section of the atmospheric rust of the Dhar pillar iron showing an optically dull thin inner layer and an optically bright thick outer layer.*

is likely that the relative amount of phosphate in the rust at this location could have been low. Therefore, a detailed study of the rust from several locations of the three pillar pieces must be undertaken to elucidate the nature of the protective passive film and its mechanism of formation. This is all the more important in the case of the Dhar pillar iron because, as noted earlier, the three pillar pieces have been handled and shifted around several times during their history.

IRON BEAMS IN THE ORISSA TEMPLES

There is evidence of the use of large iron beams in the temples of Orissa. The Bengal-Bihar-Orissa region had the benefit of accessibility to good quality iron ores and king Bhoja, in the eleventh century CE text *Yuktikalpataru,* mentions several places in this region where iron metallurgy was prevalent (Biswas 1996). Iron clamps and beams were extensively used to join the long projecting cornices and roof stones of the big temple at Bhubaneswar, built in 640 CE. An illustration of the same is provided in Brown (1976). Extensive use of large iron beams has been recorded at the Jagannath temple at Puri (built in the twelfth century CE) – both in the main temple and the *Gunduchibari* garden temple (Neogi 1914: 32-40) (**Figure 2.54**). As many as two hundred and thirty nine iron beams up to 17' in length and up to 6" × 4" or 5" × 6" section have been counted in this garden temple (Graves 1912: 187-212). The complete list of these beams, along with their dimensions, has been reported in Graves (1912). Based on the enumeration of these iron beams in the *Gunduchibari* temple, it has been postulated that iron beams have similarly been used extensively in the temples at Bhubaneshwar, dating to the period between the sixth and the thirteenth century CE (Neogi 1914: 32-40).

The iron beams at the now-ruined Surya temple at Konarak are of even larger dimensions. The main temple was built in the latter half of the ninth century while the *Natamandir* was constructed in 1241 CE (Neogi 1914: 32-40). The first report of nine iron beams (nearly 1' square and 18' to 21' long) at Konarak was provided by Stirling (1824). Fergusson visited the site in 1838 and recorded that the lengths of the iron beams were longer (23') with a slightly smaller cross-section of 8 inches by 9 inches (Neogi 1914: 32-40). The Konarak temple was in complete ruins and everal portions of the temple were buried in drift sea-sand before excavations commenced in 1901. It was during these excavations that beautiful sculptures and more iron beams were discovered. In 1912, Graves counted as many as twenty nine iron beams at the Konarak temple. The

Fig. 2.54: *Iron beams used in the construction of the Jagannath temple at Puri.*

largest iron beam was 35' long and 7" to 7.5" in square cross section and weighed about 2.5 tones. There was another beam 23.5' in length and 11" by 10.5" in cross-section, which was part of a much larger beam, with the other end missing (Graves 1912: 187-212). Graves further notes that 'some of the pieces are only 5' or 6' in length and, could they be matched, it would probably result in not fewer than twenty complete beams'. The iron beam found in the superstructure (**Figure 2.55**) was placed in the courtyard of the complex (**Figure 2.56**).

The forging of the beams was not perfect, as in the case of the Delhi Iron Pillar, as the weld lines were perfectly visible in several beams. The comments of Graves (1912) regarding the nature of forge welded iron lumps have been mentioned earlier in this chapter, while discussing the possible presence of iron inserts in the main body of the Delhi Iron Pillar. Ghosh (1963) proposed that the iron beams were forge welded using square rods of small sections, based on a study of the fractured surfaces of the beams. When a small piece of 8" square cross-section was hammered, instead of breaking off crosswise, the piece broke longitudinally and appeared to be laminated, being composed of two square pieces joined together (Ghosh 1963: 31-45). Jena and his associates have found traces of lead between two pieces forged together, and it seems that a large lead

Fig. 2.55: *Iron beam used in the superstructure of the Sun temple at Konarak*

Fig. 2.56: *Iron beams placed on a platform in the Sun temple complex at Konarak*

bath might have been used for uniform heating of a bundle of wrought iron bars to the required temperature, before forging them together (Prakash and Tripathi 1986: 568-579). The yield point of Konarak iron was 14 tonnes per sq inch, which was much less than the maximum stress of 23 tonnes per sq inch (Ghosh 1963: 31-45). These two values are not close, unlike the Delhi pillar iron (Ghosh 1963: 31-45), and it has been postulated that the Delhi pillar iron is less porous and subjected to better forge welding and heavier mechanical working (Biswas 1996).

Chemical analysis of the iron from one of the beams by Neogi (1914) confirmed that it was wrought iron of composition 99.64% Fe, 0.15% P, traces of C, traces of S and no manganese. Its specific gravity was 7.8. Neogi (1914) noted that the nature of this iron was almost similar to the iron of the Delhi pillar, with manganese being absent and phosphorous being high. Chemical analysis of Konarak iron samples by Ghosh (1963) and Friend and Thorneycroft (1924) provided lower P values, when compared to the analysis of Neogi (1914). Ghosh (1963) performed compositional analysis on three samples and the results were almost similar. For example, sample KT/3 assayed 0.27% C, 0.04% Mn, 0.015% S, 0.018% P and 0.096% Si, 0.16% Cu and 0.0025% Cr. The analysis by Friend and Thorneycroft (1924) provided 0.11% C, 0.024% S, 0.015% P and 0.100% Si. Friend and Thorneycroft (1924) also found the presence of carburised phase in a Konarak beam iron and decarburisation was noticed, which was supposed to have taken place during welding.

The rust scales from the Konarak beams have been analysed by Ghosh (1963). The magnetic portion of the rust was 98% whereas for the Delhi pillar iron, it was 80% (above the ground) and 99% (below the ground). X-ray diffraction analysis showed that the magnetic portion of the rust in the Konarak iron was mainly composed of magnetic goethite and a small proportion of lepidocrocite.

Hudson (1953) stated that the Konarak sample, having composition similar to the Delhi pillar iron, corroded much more due to the moist and salt-laden air of the Orissa coast. However, Ghosh (1963) pointed out that there were several modern iron beams lying in the yard of the Konarak temple that had corroded much more than the ancient iron beams. Ghosh maintained that the composition of the Konarak iron did play a role in its corrosion resistance. Based on his chemical analysis of the Konarak iron, the superior corrosion resistance of the Delhi Iron Pillar was attributed by Ghosh to the higher P content in the Delhi pillar iron when compared to the Konarak iron. However, when the chemical analysis of Neogi (1914) is also included, it is noticed that the P content was also significant in the Konarak iron, and therefore the presence of P must be an important consideration for its corrosion resistance, as has been outlined earlier for the Delhi pillar iron.

Further studies have not been conducted on the iron beams of the temples at Orissa. It is important to conduct a detailed study of these iron beams and record their present condition. There have been so many of these beams recorded by Graves (1912) that each of these iron pieces must be understood. It is quite likely that they are lying in a neglected state. Conservation activities need to be undertaken, based on a scientific study of these beams. This is important as these beams hold valuable clues to the method of manufacture of large iron objects in ancient India.

IRON PILLAR AT KODACHADRI HILL

The iron pillar at the Mookambika temple at Kodachadri hill has been addressed in one study (Anantharaman 1999: 1428-1430). The salient features of this study will be summarised below. The iron pillar is popularly known as the *dwajasthamba* (flag staff) of the Adi-Mookambika temple at Kodachadri hill (**Figure 2.57**). Kodachadri is about 40km from Kollur, a town located about 120km north of Mangalore in the southern Canara district of Karnataka. Local tradition mentions that the flagstaff is actually the top portion of the *trishul* (trident) with which the "Mother Goddess nailed down the demon into the bowels of the earth!" (Anantharaman 1999: 1428-1430). During recent renovations of the temple, the iron pillar has been stabilised with a concrete platform. The pillar rises to a height of about 33' above the ground and it possesses a rectangular cross-section of 3.4" by 2.3". The surface is not smooth like the Delhi Iron Pillar, but is rough with a slightly reddish colour. This is reminiscent of the reddish hue of the protective passive film of the Delhi Iron Pillar. During the rainy season, the Iron Pillar acts like a lightning arrester and evidences for local melting, flow of metal and solidification are found at the pillar top. Anantharaman (1999) estimated the weight of the pillar to be about 500kg by assuming the pillar to possess a total length of 45'. Anantharaman (1999) obtained a small iron piece from the pillar and subjected it to microstructural and X-ray diffraction (XRD) analyses. XRD analysis indicated that the specimen was almost pure iron. The XRD pattern presented in Anantharaman (1999) showed the peaks between the deviation angles (that is, 2q) of 20 and 80 degrees. The pattern revealed the strong 110 and 220 plane reflections from iron. It has not been mentioned whether the XRD pattern was

Fig. 2.57: *The iron pillar at the Adi-Mookambika temple at Kodachadri hill.*

obtained from the surface or from a polished section. If the XRD pattern was from the surface, it can be concluded that no significant peak from any iron oxyhydroxide is found in the pattern. The presence of phosphate cannot be confirmed by the pattern provided because the major reflections from iron phosphates generally appear at lower 2q values (JCPDS 1996).

The microstructure of the iron was almost ferritic, with a small percentage of pearlite. Small globular second phase inclusions were identified as silicates containing some Ca and P. The larger irregular- shaped inclusions were identified as iron oxides with traces of Si, Ca and P. These large inclusions possessed a microhardness of 165 VHN (Vickers Hardness Number). The microhardness was about 140 VHN for the iron grains and about 155 in the pearlite-cum-matrix areas. The volume fraction of the inclusions was estimated by image analysis to be 2.0%. The pearlite volume fraction could not be accurately determined and, assuming it to be about 1.0%, the carbon content of the pillar iron was estimated as less than 0.05% (Anantharaman 1999: 1428-1430). Based on the microstructural analysis, Anantharaman (1999) concluded that the iron was not a product of modern iron-making processes. The excellent corrosion resistance of the pillar must be due to the material of the pillar and not due to environmental factors because the Adi-Mookambika temple at Kodachadri hill, at 1450 m above sea level, receives an annual rainfall of about 500cm to 750 cm, and it rains for about eight months in a year. Moreover, the Arabian sea is only 50 km away from the pillar. The reddish colour of the protective rust of the pillar indicates a process of protective rust formation similar to that outlined for the Delhi Iron Pillar. The P content of the iron of this pillar has not been determined and it would not be surprising if it is in the range of the Delhi pillar iron. Detailed compositional analysis of the Kodachadri pillar iron and characterisation of its rust are required to provide precise answers to its excellent corrosion resistance.

3

CANNONS

CANNONS CONSTITUTE AN IMPORTANT PART OF ARTILLERY WHICH DECIDES THE FATE of nations and empires. The forge-welded cannons truly represent the high skill of the Indian blacksmiths in the art of working with iron. We shall first look into the developments in cannon technology in the Indian subcontinent, specifically related to forge-welded iron cannons. The incendiary devices used before the advent of cannons have also been briefly introduced. The design and construction of forge-welded iron cannons and composite (wrought iron+bronze) cannons have been explained. Some interesting Indian innovations in cannon technology are briefly reviewed. Some of the marvellous forge welded cannons, located in different parts of the subcontinent, will be presented.

The invention of cannons and their use in warfare added a totally different dimension to battles. The fate of nations was decided by the use of cannons. It was an effective arm of both the army and the navy, and still is. When it was used in the army, it added destructive power to the artillery. Its use in ships decided the final outcome of many a navy battle. The use of cannons in the navy posed its own unique requirements and alterations in cannon technology (Guilmartin 1974), but the basic operation of the cannon, the mighty fighting machine, remained the same.

The origin of cannon technology is not clear, as there are claims to this technology by the Europeans, Chinese and Arabs. The development of cannon was the outcome of the invention of saltpetre in China sometime in the tenth century, and the realisation of its propellant properties. India also lays claim on the discovery of salt-petre because of its reference in several ancient texts (Balasubramaniam 2007). Gunpowder contained a suitably combined mixture of saltpetre, charcoal and sulphur. The story of early gunpowder is available in literature (Guilmartin 1974; Partington 1999; Ágoston 2005). Some historical and technical aspects of saltpetre (Balasubramaniam and Jaikishan 2005: 663-672) and gunpowder (Biswas 2005: 539-572) production in the Indian subcontinent have been reviewed recently.

The first illustration of cannon in Europe is dated to 1326, wherein a gunner is shown firing an arrow-like projectile from a vase-shaped cannon using a red-hot iron. A handheld cannon of similar design, dated to about early 1300, has been recovered from the sea near Sweden, and is currently placed at the National Historical Museum in Stockholm. There are several references to the use of cannons in battles in Europe during the fourteenth and fifteenth centuries. The Ottoman Turks further advanced cannon technology in this period. They devastatingly used it in the siege and capture of Constantinople in 1453 (Ágoston 2005). It is clear that the Ottoman innovations reached the Indian shores through two routes, through land from the north-west and through the sea to the Deccan (that is, peninsular India). Cannon technology also appears to have independently reached India from China, by sea route to Kerala and by land route to Assam (Khan 2004c: 41-58). Before understanding the development of cannon technology in the Indian subcontinent, it is important to review the early incendiary devices that were used before the advent of cannons.

EARLY DEVICES

Prior to the advent of gunpowder and cannon technology, several incendiary throwing devices were used in the Indian subcontinent, during both field and water battles, as well as in sieges of fortifications. That the Indian subcontinent was witness to numerous battles and wars provided the necessary potential and zeal for inventing different types of war machines. In the early medieval period, we hear about the use of war devices called *naft-andaz* (naphtha throwers), *atish-bazi* (fire-playing devices), *hukkaba-e-atish bazi* (vessels filled with fire), *manjanik/maghribi/arrada* (elaborate tension machines for throwing fire arrows), *charkh* (magnified cross-bow catapult worked by tension by means of pulleys and ropes) and *ban* (iron cylinder containing gunpowder attached to a long bamboo or reed, which steadied its flight or, in simple word, rocket) (Jaggi 1989: 135-136). One of the primary ingredients was naphtha, an invention from Asia Minor that travelled to Europe through Greece, whence it was called "*Greek fire*" (Partington 1999).

The history of gunpowder usage in India originated with the use of the rocket-like object called *ban*. There is an excellent discussion on the use of *ban* and its history in Khan's book on the history of armed warfare in the Indian subcontinent (Khan 2004a: 17-91). The *ban* was the forerunner to rocket technology. The destructive use of rockets by Tipu Sultan in his battles with the English, towards the close of the eighteenth century, paved the way for the introduction of rockets in warfare by the European powers. One of the English officers (Congreve), who was present in the campaigns against Tipu Sultan, borrowed the idea of rockets and introduced them in Europe, whence it was known as Congreve rockets (Narasimha 1999: 123-125; Roy 2005: 635-656).

A comprehensive history of cannons in the Indian subcontinent has been presented by Balasubramaniam (2007). We shall not go into such great details. The developments in cannon technology in the Indian subcontinent through the medieval period will be first critically addressed from a technical viewpoint.

BEGINNINGS OF CANNON TECHNOLOGY

The use of gunpowder to project a missile was introduced in the Indian subcontinent in the fifteenth century. Scholars well-versed in Persian have carefully pondered over numerous texts of the early medieval period and have arrived at definite conclusions regarding the question of introduction of artillery in India.

It is clear that gunpowder was certainly used to project a missile, in the Indian subcontinent, sometime by the middle of the fifteenth century. In the manuscript *Maasir-i-Mahmud Shahi* (which was completed in 1467-68), there are several references to the use of cannon fire. The first mention is in 1442-43, wherein two cannons were supplied by Rana Kumbha (the Sisodia ruler of Mewar) to an ally, the chief of Gagraun, for defending against the Sultan of Malwa. The second mention is the use of cannons by Mahmud Khilji against the fort of Mandalgarh in 1456. The use of missile throwing device is described as follows, "By the impact of the balls of the *r'ad (gola-i r'ad)* and stones of the *manjaniq (sang-i-manjaniq)* the rampart of the fort was demolished". There is a clear distinction between the stone-throwing *manjaniq* and ball-throwing cannon. Therefore, it is clear that one of the earliest names for the cannon was *kaman-i-r'ad*, which translates as "lightning bow". The meaning of *r'ad* alone is "lightning". There is mention of another weapon called *kashakanjir*, which threw balls "by the extensive force of combustible substances *(daruha-i-atishin)*" (Khan 2004a: 17-91)

It is also certain that the Bahamanis used artillery to very forceful effect in 1470 against Belgaum Fort. This has been described by Mahmud Gawan in his *Riyazu'l Insha* (compiled before 1481). He was a Persian in the employment of the Bahamanis and he must have passed on his expertise in the use of artillery to the Bahamanis. Interestingly, Mahmud Gawan calls cannon as *r'ad.* He describes its effectiveness as follows: "The flood of blood-shedding arrowheads and the lustre of the sword and roaring *r'ad,* having the effect of a thunderbolt, were showered (on the Belgaum Fort) in such a manner that the battlements, niches, windows and porticos of that lofty fort were razed to the ground." (Khan 2004a: 17-91).

Some other early references to the use of artillery in the later part of the fifteenth century are as follows. The *Tarikh-i-Ferishta* mentions that, in CE 1368, Muhammad Shah Bahamani I captured three hundred gun carriages in a battle with the Hindu king of Vijayanagar. There is a record that Mahmud Shah II of Gujarat, in 1482, sent out a fleet consisting of gunners and musketeers against the pirates of Bulsar. Moreover, Mahmud Shah II used cannons to break the walls of Champanir and fired shells at the palace of the Raja in 1484. Immediately after the Portuguese set foot in India in 1498, they noted that a vessel from Gujarat fired several guns at them in CE 1500. Even more notable is the Portuguese report of the fleet of the Zamorin of Kerala carrying three hundred and eighty guns in 1503.

It is relevant to note that the kingdoms in the south, both Muslim and Hindu, were advanced in artillery compared to the Delhi rulers of this period because of their contact with the outside world, especially Turkey and China through the sea route. The South Indian kingdoms sometimes imported their gunners (*topchi*) and artillery from Turkey and the Arab countries, with which they had developed good relations.

A big impetus to cannon technology was provided from the beginning of the sixteenth century with the introduction of new skills and concepts from Europe and Ottoman sources. Khan (Khan 2004b: 91-127) attributes this to two reasons, namely the arrival of the Portuguese at Calicut in 1498 and Babur's occupation of Delhi and Agra in 1526. The latter event appears more significant because Babur's destructive use of artillery in field warfare (in the First Battle of Panipat) provided the thrust to the adoption of artillery in the subcontinent.

Wrought Iron Cannons

Khan contends that one of the most important skills borrowed from Europe in the beginning of the sixteenth century was the making of cannons out of wrought iron.

Shipwreck finds have confirmed that the Europeans were using a type of forge-welded iron cannon in their ships in the sixteenth century, which were known as "port pieces" (Smith 1993: 1-10). An example of a European port piece is shown in **Figure 3.1**. Therefore, the design of early Indian forge-welded cannons may have been based on this European model. That the Europeans designed forge-welded cannons even prior to the sixteenth century is proved by the early forge-welded bombards like *Mons Meg* in Edinburgh, England, and *Dulle Griet* in Ghent, Belgium, (Ritter 1938: 113-129; Smith and Brown 1989). These important forge-welded cannons are seen in **Figure 3.2**. However, the forge-welded cannons fell into disuse in Europe, with the last one reported to have been made around 1520. One of the causes for this was the ease of casting bronze cannons when compared to the difficulty in manufacturing forge-welded cannons. Another probable cause must have been the perfect bore that could be obtained with the case of the cast cannons in contrast to the rougher surface created in the case of forge-welded cannons by the use of staves. Therefore, the engineering was more involved in the case of forge-welded cannons as compared to bronze cannons. Another possible reason could be the advent of cast iron technology in Europe by the sixteenth century. This drastically affected cannon production.

Cast iron cannons were not viewed with favour initially because they tended to fail without notice. The bronze cannons were more reliable because they were tougher and bulged at the breech (i.e. rear portion of the gun barrel before failing, thereby providing sufficient warning to the gunners. One of the first major applications of cast iron was for producing cannon balls.

Fig. 3.1: *Typical example of European "port-piece" cannon. This is on display in Segovia in Spain.bThe bed on which the cannon rests in a modern construction (Photograph courtesy: R.D. Smith)*

(a)

(b)

Fig. 3.2: *The massive European cannons named (a)* Mons Meg *at Edinburgh, England, and (b)* Dulle Griet *in Ghent, Belgium. (Photograph (a) courtesy: R.D. Smith).*

It is very interesting at this point to compare the forge-welded cannons of the Indian sub-continent with the forge-welded cannons (bombards) of Europe. Unlike the European examples of *Mons Meg* and *Dulle Griet* (Ritter 1938: 113-129; Smith and Brown

1989), the Indian cannons do not reveal a smaller diameter powder chamber and a larger diameter stone chamber. There are two exceptions to this, namely the *Bachhawali* cannon (**Figure 3.3a**), now located at the Hazaraduari palace complex at Murshidabad in the state of West Bengal and a cannon atop Gavilgarh fort in Maharastra (**Figure 3.3b**). The

(a)

(b)

Fig. 3.3: *(a) The* Bachhawali *cannon of Murshidabad and (b) forge welded cannon on top of Gavilgarh fort.*

date of manufacture of the *Bachhawali* cannon is not known because the brass plates that were fixed to the cannon, which provided this information, are missing (Chattopadhyay 2005: 465-486; Chatterji 2001). Like the case of many archaeological objects placed in the public domain in current day India, the brass plates have been vandalised. The location where the larger diameter chamber meets the smaller diameter chamber is interesting.

Lack of precise dates is a problem with forge-welded cannons because we obtain precise dates (or inscriptions) only in few forge-welded iron cannons. According to Khan (Khan 2004c: 41-58), the earliest dated forge-welded cannons are two wrought-iron guns lying in the public gardens at Khandwa (Madhya Pradesh). They bear inscriptions of dates 1585 and 1589. Forge-welded cannons preceding these dates are available, based on the dating of bastions on which the cannons are located. For example, the *Lambacharri* cannon on the Haidar Burj at Bijapur has been dated to 1582 (Cousens 1916: 29-33; Deloche 2005a: 573-596).

Incidentally, inscriptions are more readily available on bronze cannons. Therefore, this may suggest that bronze cannons were more prized than forge-welded iron cannons, probably due to the greater cost of raw material and manufacturing of bronze cannons. It could also be due to the relative ease of carving out inscriptions on the softer bronze surface.

Some of the earliest dated wrought iron cannons belong to Sher Shah Suri's time (Khan 2004c: 41-58; Banerji 1911: 44). They are dated to 1542-3, based on a Persian inscription on one of them, stating that it was made by one Saiyid Ahmad Rumi (Abdul Karim 1992: 387-8). They are of roughly the same design and length as his light cast-bronze cannons, classified as *zarb-zans*, of the period. The *zarb-zan* was a smaller cannon, about 4 to 5 feet in length with a muzzle diameter of 1 to 2 inches, which was much more mobile than large cannons (called *kazan*). One light cannon of Sher Shah, now located at Indore, is seen in **Figure 3.4** (Dishalkar 1944: 40; Bhatt 2005: 52-55). Although this cannon is made of copper alloy, it illuminates the reader as to how the *zarb-zans* looked like.

Cast Bronze Cannons

Around the beginning of the sixteenth century, the technique of casting bronze cannons also improved with knowledge inputs from external sources. The Turks were particularly skilled at casting massive bronze cannons (Ágoston 2005). The Turks were referred to

Fig. 3.4: *One of Sher Shah Suri's light cannons located at the Indore Museum.*

as *Rumis*. The Mughal emperor Babur successfully adopted several war tactics of the *Rumis* (*Babur Nama* 1979: 469, 536, 547). Some notable *Rumis* in the service of Babur were Ustad Ali Quli and Mustafa Rumi. Ustad Ali Quli was an expert gun-founder and his casting a large cannon is graphically recorded in *Babur Nama* (1979). The leading cannon founders were given the title *"Rumi Khan"* (Irvine 1962: 152). The Turks were experts in casting massive bronze cannons and they rendered their service to the North Indian as well as Deccani kings. One wonderful example of a massive cannon cast by a *Rumi* is the *Malik-i-Maidan* (King of Battlefield) cannon (see photograph of this cannon in **Figure 3.5a**) located on the Sherji Burj in Bijapur. This all-bronze cannon was cast by a Turkish engineer (Mohamed bin Hasan Rumi) for a Deccani king Nizam Shah in 1548-9 (Cousens 1916: 29-33; Forbes 1840: 84-85). Incidentally, this is one of the largest bronze cannons in India. Its length is 426 cm, muzzle diameter is 149 cm and the bore diameter is 71.2 cm. Its estimated weight is 55 tonnes. The wonderful design on the muzzle face, showing a lion devouring an elephant, is worth noting (**Figure 3.5a**). Another massive bronze cannon fabricated by the same engineer in located at Ausa fort (see **Figure 3.5b**).

It must be emphasised that the import of cannon technology in no way diminishes the engineering ingenuity of the Indians because the cannon technology was further

(a)

(b)

Fig. 3.5: *(a) The* Malik-i-Maidan *bronze cannon located on the Sherji Burj of Bijapur and (b) a bronze cannon from Ausa fort.*

developed based on local need and talent. These developments will be understood in the following section, with specific reference to the casting and forge-welding techniques.

DEVELOPMENTS IN CANNON CASTING

The destructive power of cast bronze cannons was clearly established in the Indian subcontinent by Babur, although cannons were introduced earlier. The developments in cast bronze cannon technology in the early sixteenth century appear to have been drastic as the distance travelled by mortar increased from about 1200 metres in 1527 (time of Babur) to about 5500 metres in 1540 (time of Humayun) (Khan 2004b: 91-127). There were several innovations affected by Sher Shah Suri, who deposed Humayun and ruled India for a short period. It is clear that he paid considerable attention to the use of gunpowder and was more interested in smaller arms than large massive cannons. Some of his earliest small sized cannons are known (Datta 1968,1969,1972). A typical light cannon of Sher Shah Suri is seen in **Figure 3.4**. These smaller cannons were put to effective use, both for waging offensive field battles and for defending fortifications.

Artillery progressed further under Akbar's (1556-1605) rule. It attained greater efficiency, and several innovations were affected. Cannons are depicted in several miniature paintings in *Akbarnama*. One painting showing cannons used in the siege of Ranthambore is seen in **Figure 3.6**. There is mention of one Fathullah Shirazi, one of the jewels of Akbar's court, who joined the court in CE 1583. Innovations carried out by Fathullah Shirazi included a machine for cleansing gun barrels, a portable cannon and a multi-barrel cannon (Alvi and Rahman 1968: 4-13). Jahangir inherited efficient artillery from Akbar, and there were not many improvements implemented by him.

The use of large sized artillery again gained prominence during Aurangzeb's reign. This was necessitated by his numerous war campaigns in the Deccan. He laid several long sieges on Deccani forts, such as those at Bijapur, Golconda and Senji. It is debatable whether the forts were captured due to his artillery or by deceit. More often, the impregnable forts were captured by clever trickery and outright betrayal, and not by damaging the bastions and fortifications with cannon fire power (Deloche 2005a: 573-596).

With the waning of the Mughal power, other states rose into prominence in the Indian subcontinent, aided by the efficient use of cannons. Notable among them were the Marathas and the Sikhs (Cooper and Wagle 1995: 58-78; Carleton 2002: 3-7; Carleton and Buck 2004: 57-66). Artillery played an important role in the rise of these powers

Fig. 3.6: *Miniatura painting from* Akbarnama *showing heavy mortars used in the siege of Ranthambore.*

Some excellent Maratha and Sikh cannons are preserved at the Royal Artillery Historical Trust Museum in Woolwich, England (HMSO 1963).

Most of the cannons captured after the Anglo-Maratha and Anglo-Sikh wars were destroyed. However, the British retained a few pieces as war trophies. Some were transported and gifted to the ruling monarch back in England, while others were donated to prominent personalities associated with these military campaigns. The excellent engineering and construction of these cannons must be appreciated. Some examples of cannons from Maratha, Mysore and Sikh kingdoms at the Museum of Artillery in the Woolwich Rotunda have been published recently (Carleton and Buck 2004: 57-66; Balasubramaniam 2007).

Types

Based on design features and size, cast bronze cannons were classified into different categories. In Europe, in the sixteenth century, almost all cannons fell into one of the three categories according to design: the culverins, the cannons, and the *pedreros*. Such classifications also existed in the Indian subcontinent (Khan 2004b: 91-127). Therefore, we hear about the use of *kazans, zarb zans* and *firingis* during the time of Babur. Based on the painting of the Battle of Panipat, prepared at Akbar's court in 1600 (Randhawa 1983: 121), Khan concluded that Babur's *zarb-zans* were lighter versions of his *kazans*, with modifications noticed in the handling arrangements. In both these types, trunnions were missing. The *zarb-zans* were placed on carriages with two wheels and drawn by four pairs of bullocks. The larger cannons appear to have been drawn by eight pairs of bullocks. While the *zarb zans* discharged balls about 41 lbs in weight, the larger ones appear to have discharged lead balls almost 10 times this weight (Jaggi 1989: 135-136). The *firingi* appears to be what was referred to in the Deccan as *jinjals*. In fact this word was used even as late as 1821 to indicate a swivel cannon ('Abd al-Rahim 1921: 187). Khan also suggests that *firingi* may be related to the Chinese *fo-lang-chi Chhung* (similar to European breech-loading naval gun called culverine) (Needham 1986: 367-373).

The effectiveness of lighter cannons was also realised and different types were invented in the Indian subcontinent (Jaggi 1989: 135-136). We shall briefly address some of these because they were unique Indian innovations. The *firingi* appears to have been modified into these lighter cannon pieces. These lighter pieces were called by different names based on how it was rendered mobile. Smaller and lighter cannons that were carried by men were known as *mardum-kash* (men-drawn) and also as *narnal*. Small cannons mounted on camels were called as *shaturnal* or *pahar kalan*, while those mounted on elephants were referred to as *gajnals* and *hathnals*. These cannons were unique Indian innovations. Examples of these cannon types have been discussed by Balasubramaniam (2007). Other types of light cannons mentioned are *zamburk*, *shahin*, *dhamaka*, *ramjanki*, and *rahkula* (Jaggi 1989: 135-136). Bajwa states that they were usually built of cast brass with iron cylinders, and were between three and six pounders (Bajwa 1964: 6).

Cannons were also classified based on their specific use and purpose, because cannons were designed keeping specific functions in mind. Cannons known as *burji-shikans* (Breakers-of-Tower) were too heavy to move from one place to another and were generally lodged on bastions of forts. Cannons mounted on carriage and drawn by elephants were known as *fil-kash*. Ox-driven cannons were referred to as *gau-kash*. These cannons were of various sizes and weights.

Bronze Casting Technology

The early impetus to develop bronze cast cannons was provided by the Turks, who served the Indian chiefs as master gun founders. The Turks were famous for casting massive bronze cannons (Ágoston 2005). The requirement for a large quantity of molten metal for casting large bronze cannons was partly solved in the Islamic world of the fifteenth and sixteenth centuries by casting the powder-chamber and the stone-chamber of heavy mortars separately. This certainly seems to have been the case with the early bronze cannons of India, especially during Babur's time.

Babur described the casting of a mortar (*kazan* according to Babur) by his chief gun-founder, Ustad Ali Quli Khan, at Agra in 1526 (*Babur Nama* 1979: 469, 536, 547):

> October 22: Ustad Ali Quli had been ordered to cast a large mortar for use against Biana (Bayana) and other forts which had not yet submitted. When all the furnaces and materials were ready, he sent a person to me, and, on Monday the 15th of the month [corresponding to 22nd October] we went to see the mortar cast. Round the mortar mould, he had eight furnaces made in which were the molten materials. From below each furnace, a channel went direct to the mould. When he opened the furnace holes on our arrival, the molten metal poured like water through all these channels into the mould. After a while and before the mould was full, the flow stopped from one furnace after another. Ustad Ali Quli must have made some miscalculation either as to the furnaces or the materials.

> In his great distress, he was for throwing himself into the mould of molten metal but we comforted him, put a rope of honour on him, and so brought him out of his shame. The mould was left a day or two to cool; when it was opened, Ustad Ali Quli with great delight sent to say, the stone chamber (*tash-awi*) is without defect; to cast the powder compartment (*daru-khana*) is easy. He got the stone chamber out and told off a body of men to accoutre it, while he busied himself with the casting of the powder compartment.

Babur Nama's description of casting the mortar lacks technical details. However, we learn that the casting of cannons was a spectacular sight worthy of personal visit of the supreme monarch. In the European context, we hear about casting of cannons being public events when common people specifically came to the foundries to view the actual casting process. It must have been an exciting experience for the general public to view casting of large cannons, due to large quantities of hot metal flowing through the runners from the furnaces and then filling the cannon moulds.

In this regard, it is interesting to note the technology used in the casting of the great Turkish cannon used against Constantinople in 1453. This account is as follows (Clark 1873: 363):

> [The founders] take a quantity of very fat clay, the purest and lightest possible, which they make plastic by kneading it for several days. The mass is knit together and prevented from breaking by the addition of linen, hemp and other fibres. The whole is worked into a tough and compact mass. Then they make a long cylinder to serve as the core of the mould. Another [hollow, cylinder] to receive the first is made, but larger in order to leave a void space between the two; it is the space intended to receive the bronze pouring into it from the furnace to take the form of a cannon. The exterior [of the mould] is made of the same kind of clay, but entirely surrounded and reinforced by iron, timber, earth and stones built up around it to prevent the immense weight of bronze from fracturing it and spoiling the cannon. They then erected two furnaces, one on either side and close to [the mould]. These lowers were made very strong and fortified internally with brick and a very fat well-worked clay, and on the outside built with large cut-stones and cement. And they cast into the furnaces, a mass of copper and tin [weighing] about 1500 talents [37 tons]. On it they threw, charcoal and wood,

arranging that the metal was covered below, above and on all sides. Round about were the bellows, working without intermission for three days and nights until the whole of bronze, melted and liquefied, became like water. Then the outlets being tapped, the bronze flowed through earthen pipes into the mould until it was filled and the interior cylinder covered so that the metal lay 30 inches deep upon it.

It seems that Ali Quli Khan's method may be similar to that, but there are fine differences to be noted.

If one compares the accounts, the second account provides more technical details regarding the mould and core used in the casting of the hollow barrel. Another interesting detail that we learn from these accounts is that the stone chamber and powder chamber were cast separately and then joined together.

The developments in bronze cannon technology of India in the sixteenth century closely followed those in Europe. Two distinct casting methodologies evolved in the sixteenth century (Guilmartin 1974b). The first method was used for casting relatively large cannons (called *pedreros*) and practiced by Ottoman Turks and the Portuguese. In this method, the gun was cast around a core, which was first lowered into the casting pit. The main part of the mould was made hollow to fit over the core. The mould was then lowered over the core. The material was poured such that the bottom of the cannon filled up last (see **Figure 3.7a**). In the other practice, which was followed by nearly all the Indian powers till the beginning of the nineteenth century, the gun was cast around a core that was lowered into the main "sleeve" of the mould. The core was maintained in position and centred by means of an iron cross or web, located at the breech or at other locations (see **Figure 3.7b**). These are known as chaplets, and they held the core in place during the casting process. These were made of wrought iron. These iron rods were incorporated into the casting and these types of cannons are also called as "cast-on" type. The presence of these rods can be clearly distinguished on the surface by their different colouration. A typical example of a large cannon cast by this method is the Sikh cannon now located at Fort William in Kolkata (**Figure 3.8a**), while a typical example of a light cannon is the *Machi Tope* at Mehrangarh museum in Jodhpur (**Figure 3.8b**).

Several wonderful examples of the Mughal bronze cannon manufacturing technology prevalent during the time of Aurangzeb. (1658-1707) are available at Golkonda fort in Hyderabad. One massive cannon is the *Fath Raibhar* located on the Petla Burj (Balasubramaniam 2005d: 409-430).

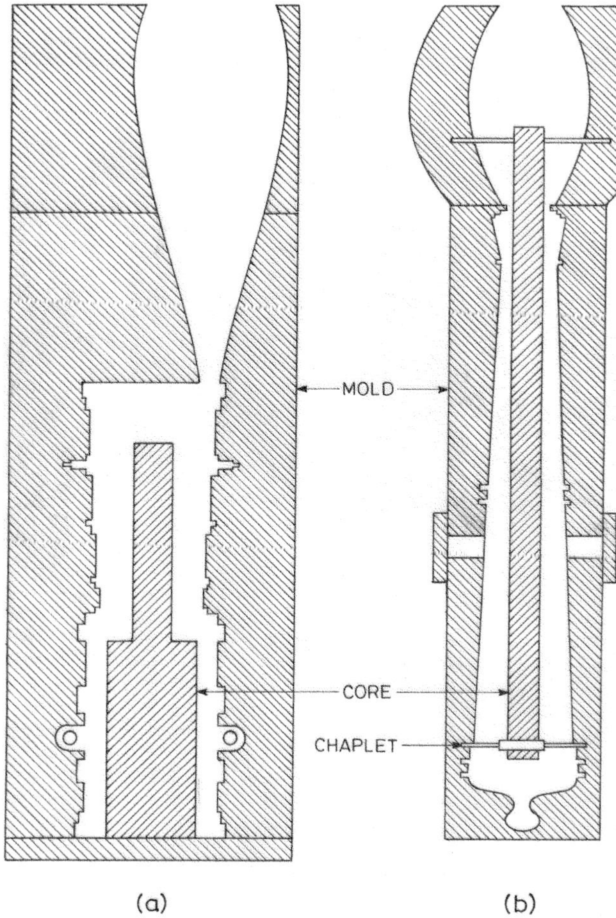

Fig. 3.7: *Comparison of two methodologies of casting cannons: (a) core placed in the centre of the mould and material poured over and (b) core placed in the sleeve of the mould and positioned using chaplets and material poured into the mould (adapted from Guilmartin 1974b).*

Later developments in Europe resulted in casting of a solid gun barrel, and later boring out of the central portion by drilling. This was known as the Maritz system of casting cannons. This was also adopted by the Indian powers by the eighteenth century. (Smith 1805; Poona 1800: 298). The method of casting of the entire cannon as a solid cylinder and later, using drilling machines to bore out the central portion, was a preferred option with the advancement of cannon technology. This was because the centre of the

(a)

(b)

Fig. 3.8: *(a) Large Sikh cannon captured by the British after the Anglo-Sikh war and now located at Fort William in Calcutta and (b)* Machi Tope *at Mehrangarh museum at Jodhpur.*

hole could be properly controlled, that is, there were no off-axes bores. Moreover, the surface also could be finished in a perfect manner. This also reduced the space/gap between the cannon ball and the barrel, resulting in better accuracy of the cannon ball and also in more velocity for the ball due to low windage.

It is certain that the latest techniques that were available in Europe were also available to the native Indian powers in the eighteenth and early nineteenth centuries. When the British defeated Tipu Sultan in 1799, they were astonished by the quality of his cannons. Nearly nine hundred and twenty seven cannons were captured after the fall of Srirangapatnam in 1799. Out of these, nearly four hundred brass cannons were manufactured in Tipu's foundries (one located at Bangalore and two in Srirangapatnam) (Carleton and Buck 2004: 57-66). Water powered boring machines were used in Tipu's arsenals and this provided the perfect finish to his guns (Carleton and Buck 2004: 57-66). Although some French technicians were employed by Tipu Sultan, as noted by Francis Buchanan, the foundries of Tipu Sultan were operated by Indian engineers (Carleton and Buck 2004: 57-66).

One important lacuna in Indian cannon research is the lack of specific information regarding the effectiveness of Indian cannon fire. The method of estimating the pressure developed in the powder chamber of the cannons, based on the amount of powder used and the size of the cannon bore, is known (Gillet *et. al.* 2004: 19-26; Ubranski 1985). Using similar procedures, it must be possible for scholars/engineers/scientists to calculate the firepower of Indian cannons, especially the ones that mention the weight of charge and the weight of the shot that was to be used in the cannon (Deloche 2005a: 573-596). This exercise needs to be performed by knowledgeable and interested scientists and engineers.

CATALOGUE OF FORGE-WELDED CANNONS

The forge-welded cannons can truly be said to belong to India. There are only a limited number of massive forge-welded cannons available in Europe, as per available literature (Ritter 1938: 113-129; Smith and Brown 1989; Smith 2005: 451-464). Therefore, this clearly indicates that making cannons by the forge-welding technique was not a popular European method. It appears that the invention of cast iron and its use in, first, cannon ball manufacture and later, casting cannons, was a major technological development. However, it took time for the cast iron cannons to find favour because the bronze cannons were tougher compared to the cast iron cannons. Unlike the bronze cannons that bulged before they failed, the cast iron cannons burst without any warning due to the inherent brittleness of cast iron. However, with developments in cast iron technology in Europe, improved cannons were manufactured. Cast iron cannons were critical elements in the establishment of European colonial power around the world in the pre-modern period.

In the Indian subcontinent, there was a great reluctance to adopt cast iron technology because of the proficiency of the Indian blacksmiths in the art of producing large iron objects by forge-welding. The brittle nature of cast iron did not enthuse the Indian blacksmiths, who were master forgers and could handle direct-reduced wrought iron more easily. A complementary reason is the lack of interest shown by the Indian rulers to find out more about cast iron technology from the Europeans, and adapt them to Indian conditions. By the time the Indian states realised the importance of cast iron in manufacturing cannons, and undertook steps to set up cast iron gun foundries in their kingdoms (like the Marathas, Sikhs and the Nizams of Hyderabad), the British colonial power in India was well entrenched. In order to understand the cast iron technology and its relevance to cannon technology, the developments in Europe have to be studied. This will not be attempted here.

Interestingly, the Chinese appear to have mastered casting of monumental iron objects quite early in history (Wagner 2000: 200-224), at least since the eighth century CE, as evidenced, for example, by the recently discovered magnificent 'iron oxen' and 'iron men' of Pujin. The massive Pujin castings were cast in 724 CE and served as anchor-weights for the Pujin Bridge, which crossed the Yellow River outside the ancient city of Puzhou in modern Yongji County, Shanxi (Paludan 1994: 61-68).

The forge-welding technique of manufacturing cannons will be specifically addressed in detail in this chapter. It must be again realised that compared to Europe, India is home to a large number of massive forge-welded cannons (Balasubramaniam 2005a: 259-268). These forge-welded masterpieces reflect the great glory of Indian blacksmithy skills during the late medieval period, like the Delhi Iron Pillar in the ancient period (Balasubramaniam 2002a), and the Dhar iron pillar (Balasubramaniam 2002b: 115-151) and iron beams in the temples of Orissa (Graves 1912: 187-202) in the early medieval period. We shall first catalogue some of the available specimens and then dwell on the salient technological features of Indian forge-welded cannons. It must again be emphacized that there is no other country in the world possessing such a large collection of massive forge welded iron cannons like in India.

The massive forge-welded iron cannons located in different parts of India are living testimony to the mastery of the Indian blacksmiths in the technology of extraction of iron and its forging into large shapes. While the history of these cannons is practically unknown, more conspicuous by its absence is the technical literature pertaining to their design, construction and use. When compared with forge-welded cannons available in the rest of the world, the Indian specimens possess certain unique design features. The relatively large number of existing Indian forge-welded iron cannons is also a important point to be noted.

There are scattered reports on many large cannons present in different parts of India (Ritter von Schwarz 1901: 209-211, 277-283; Neogi 1914: 32-40; Roessler 1997: 1; Kannan and Balasubramaniam 2000; Khan 2001: 321-336; Chatterji 2001; Kedareswari 2005). The prominent massive forge-welded cannons located in the Indian subcontinent will be presented. The wrought iron cannons found in different parts of India were manufactured by hooping iron rings over longitudinally placed iron staves. The medieval blacksmiths continued the rich tradition of manufacturing iron objects by the forge-welding technique, which was the method used to fabricate small and large iron objects like the Delhi (Balasubramaniam 2002a) and Dhar (Balasubramaniam 2002b: 115-151) iron pillars.

Panchanan Neogi (1914), in his landmark 1914 book *Iron in Ancient India*, provided the first catalogue of some of the wonderful forge-welded iron cannons of India. He followed the footsteps of P.C. Ray, who collected vast medical and medico-chemical Sanskrit literature, bearing the knowledge of ancient Indians on metals and their compounds in his well-known *History of Hindu Chemistry* (Ray 1909). Considering the time period in which the book was published, it must be appreciated that Neogi was the first person to recognise the importance and significance of these wonderful pieces of Indian engineering skill and to systematically catalogue them. His aim was to highlight the skill of the Indian blacksmiths and provide evidence for their skill in fabricating large iron objects. Neogi described some notable forge-welded cannons in Dhaka, Murshidabad, Bishnupur and Bijapur.

Some of the locations in India where massive forge-welded cannons are present are indicated in the map of the Indian subcontinent in **Figure 3.9**. Although forge-welded cannons appear to be concentrated in the Deccan, they are located all over the country.

Thanjavur

In view of its weight and size, the forge-welded iron cannon at Thanjavur must be regarded as among the most massive forge-welded iron cannons in the world

(Balasubramaniam *et. al.* 2005a: 259-268). The cannon was manufactured in Thanjavur during the reign of Raghunatha Nayak (1600-1645 CE). The Thanjavur cannon formed an important component of the fortification scheme (Balasubramaniam 1994: 312-337) and it was located at the eastern entrance of the ancient fortified city (**Figure 3.10a**). The cannon is referred to as *Rajagopala*, according to local tradition.

There are several descriptions by European travellers that fortified centres in South India possessed firearms. Nicolau Pimenta, a Jesuit visitor to the city of Senji around 1600, noted the presence of "much ordnance, powder and shot". Similar tales are recounted by visitors to less mighty forts. Gasparo Balbi, a resident of the Portugese

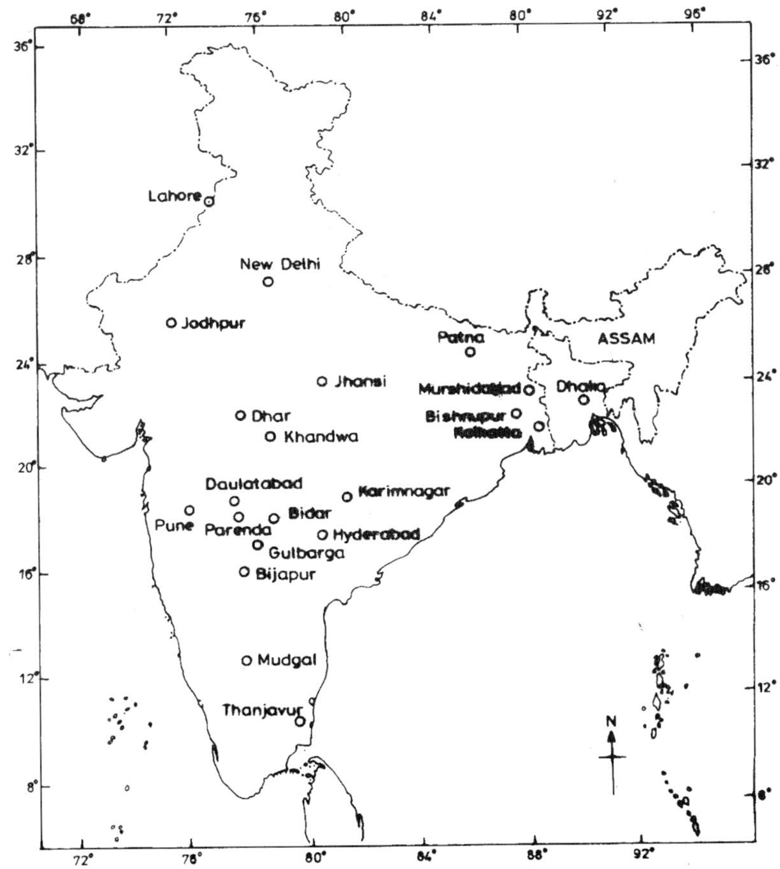

Fig. 3.9: *Map of the Indian subcontinent showing the location of places mentioned in this chapter.*

settlement of Sao Tome de Meliapor (Mylapur) in the early 1580s, describes a fortified centre (*palayam*) near Sao Tome and also about the *palegadu* (chief) who "when he goes out, is accompanied by many harquebusier on foot... with the carriage belts slung across their flanks". Jesuit description of Thanjavur from 1640 confirms that Thanjavur possessed "a prodigious quantity of pieces of artillery of every caliber" including one big cannon "in the mouth of which a man could conveniently hold himself couchant". It appears that the cannon being referred to is the *Rajagopala* cannon.

Dutch records also mention a considerable presence of firearms in the south. The Dutch possessed a fortress in Pulicat and factories down south along the Coromandal coast.

The Thanjavur iron cannon rests on three concrete supports (**Figure 3.10b**). The iron cannon is 751.5 cm in length from end to mouth, including the 31.5 cm projection at the end of the barrel (**Figure 3.10c**). The outside and inner diameters of the gun barrel are 93 and 63 cm, respectively. Assuming the hollow cylinder of the cannon barrel to extend to the complete end of the cylindrical barrel (length of 720 cm), the minimum weight of the cannon estimated from the known thickness of the barrel (that is, 15 cm) is 20.6 tonnes. Including the solid end portion, the minimum weight of the cannon adds to a staggering figure of over 22 tonnes. All holding clamp rings, but for two, are currently missing. Only two of the original eight rings still remain. Similar iron rings can be noted on several other large forge-welded cannons. The rear end of the cannon is made of successively smaller diameter rings (**Figure 3.10d**).

The handling rings seen on several forge-welded iron cannons were used to adjust the direction of cannon fire. Unlike the cannons with trunnions, these types of cannons were usually placed on massive wooden logs. For example, the photograph of the largest bronze cannon at Bijapur, by the name *Malik Maidan*, (see Figure 3.5a) shows it resting on large wooden logs.

Dhaka

The first example to be quoted is interesting because the massive cannon is presumably lost. Some details of the cannon are known from eyewitness accounts. Rennel (1783), in his *Memoir of a Map of Hindoostan* written in 1793, quoted a gigantic wrought-iron gun located at Dhaka in the eighteenth century. Rennel commented that "there are the remains of a very strong fortress in it; and within these few years there was near it a cannon of extra-ordinary weight and dimensions: but it has since fallen into the river,

(a)

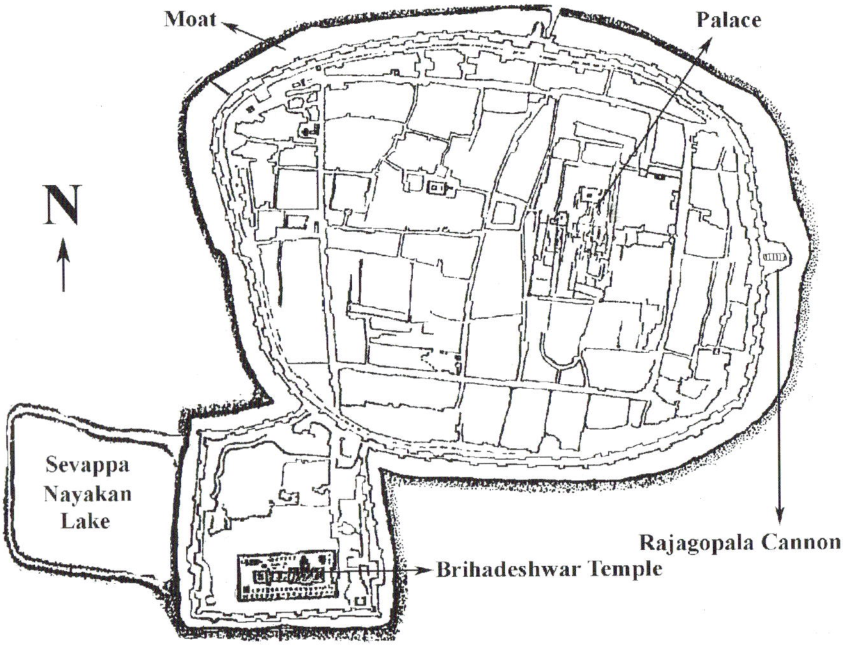
Moat
Palace
N
Sevappa
Nayakan
Lake
Rajagopala Cannon
Brihadeshwar Temple

(b)

(c)

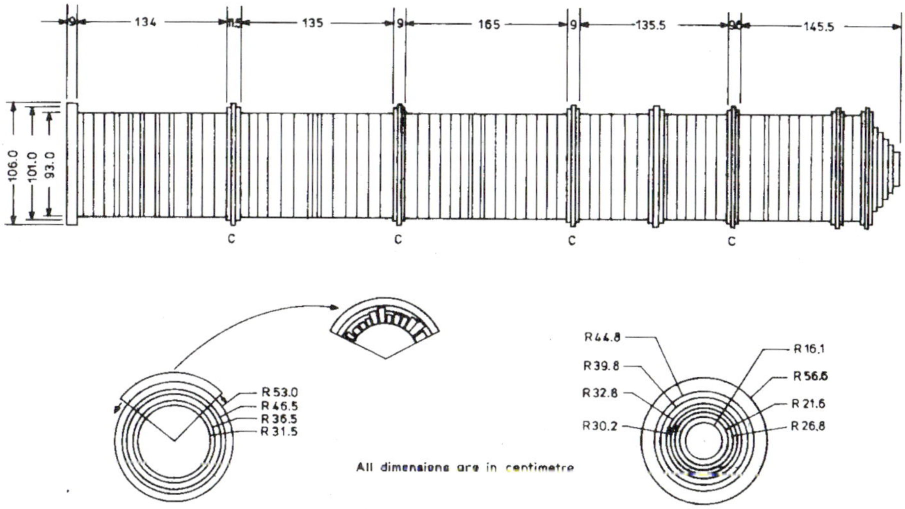

(d)

Fig. 3.10: *(a) Old map of Thanjavur Fort showing the location of the cannons (b) the historical forge-welded iron cannon at Thanjavur, (c) its engineering drawing and (d) rear side.*

together with the bank on which it rested". Luckily, Rennel took measurements of the gun very carefully. The length of the cannon was 22 feet 10½ inches, diameter at the breech 3 feet 3 inches, diameter of the muzzle 2 feet 2 inches and diameter of the bore 1 feet 3 inches. Rennel further quoted that this massive cannon "was made of hammered iron; it being an immense tube formed of 14 bars, with rings of 2 or 3 inches wide driven over them, and hammered down into a smooth surface, so that its appearance was equal to that of the best executed piece of brass ordnance, although its proportions were faulty. The gun contained 234,413 cubic inches of wrought iron and consequently weighed 64,814 pounds avoirdupois (about 30 tons), or about the weight of eleven 32-pounders. Weight of an iron shot from the gun, 465 pounds."

Rennel has noted that the cannon was sunk in the Ganga. The location of the cannon is presently not known. If proper investigations are conducted, it is quite possible to retrieve the cannon from the river. Quoting from local sources, Rennel stated that the name of the cannon was *Kaley Khan*. A cannon bearing the same name was mentioned by the Venetian traveller Manucci in the list of big cannons possessed by the Mughals in the seventeenth century (Manucci 1906).

A large forge-welded cannon is standing in Osman Garden in Dhaka (Chattopadhyay 2005: 464-486). It stands as a mute spectator to the happenings of history. A picture of the cannon is provided in **Figure 3.11**. The history of the cannon is not clear. The name of the cannon has been mentioned as *Kalu Jham Jham* and also as *Bibi Mariyam*. Its total length is 538 cm. Four rings were originally attached to the clamps.

Murshidabad

A large cannon at Murshidabad (**Figure 3.12a**) was first described by Neogi as follows: "The great iron gun at Murshidabad, called *Jahankosha* ("Conqueror of the World"), 17 feet 6 inches in length and with a circumference of 5 feet 3 inches, is of great historical importance owing to the existence of nine inscribed brass plates on it. From the inscription it is ascertained that this gun was constructed in 1047 Hijira, Jamadinssani (October 1637), during the reign of Emperor Shajahan (the then Subedar of Bengal being Islam Khan) at Jahangirnagar (Dacca) by chief mechanic Janardan under the supervision of Daroga Sher Mahammad and Inspector Harabullava Das."

Neogi noted that generally the cannons "were all manufactured by Hindu mechanics and metallurgists under the orders of the Mohammedan rulers. It appears that the Hindus were skilled workers in iron in all ages and their remarkable skill was utilised by the

Fig. 3.11: *Large forge-welded cannon in Dhaka located at Osman Udhan (Garden) (Photograph courtesy: Pranab Chattopadhyay).*

Mohammedan rulers in the manufacture of wrought-iron guns which must be really regarded as specimens of Hindu art". The cannon is now protected by the Archaeological Survey of India (ASI) and placed on a platform in the city (**Figure 3.12b**). The total length of the cannon is 530 cm and its bore diameter is 15 cm. The estimated weight of the cannon is about 8 tonnes. The excellent designs of the cannon are to be noted in the front (**Figure 3.12b**) and rear (**Figure 3.12c**).

Another massive forge-welded cannon at Murshidabad is the *Bachhawali* cannon (see **Figure 3.3a**). This is at present located at the garden of the Hazarduari Palace Museum (Chattopadhyay2005: 465-486). The total length of the *Bachhawali* cannon is 461 cm, with the length of the powder chamber being 110 cm. The external diameters of the stone chamber and powder chamber are 68 and 42 cm, respectively. The bore diameter is 46 cm. The stone chamber displays ten raised rings, with the first one from the muzzle exhibiting a unique design. Holding rings are provided at the rear end of the *Bachhawali* as well as at the location where the smaller diameter chamber joins the larger diameter chamber. Notice that at this location, rings are provided both on the smaller as well as larger diameter chambers. These rings are 27 cm in diameter and 2.4 cm in thickness. These rings are used specifically for handling the cannon and not necessarily for screwing-unscrewing the two different diameter sections of the cannon. The earlier misconception

Fig. 3.12: *(a) Iron cannon at Murshidabad as first reported by Neogi (1914). The name of this cannon is* Jahan Kosha, *(b) current location of this cannon, and (c) some details of the rear side of cannon.*

that such a mechanism may be operative in the European examples has been conclusively proven to be false, based on X-ray radiography studies of *Mons Meg* (Smith and Brown 1989).

Bishnupur

Neogi first mentioned the cannon at Bishnupur. The massive forge-welded cannon at Bishnupur is popularly known nowadays as *Dolmodol*, which is a corrupt version of its original name *Dal Mardan* ("Crusher of People"). The cannon dates back to about 1650 CE. The cannon lay in a half-buried condition for a long time. In 1918, the governor-general of Bengal, Lord Ronaldshay, on a visit to Bishnupur, ordered it to be dug out from the ground and it was then placed on a laterite stone platform (**Figure 3.13a**). The discolouration of the bottom regions of the cannon is due to the fact that is was buried in the ground earlier.

The iron cannon rests on two concrete supports. The total length of the cannon from the front to the extreme rear is 3.84 m. The weight of the cannon, estimated on the basis of the dimensions, is 7.9 tonnes. The complete dimensions of the iron cannon are provided in **Figure 3.13b**. There are two protruding solid cylindrical supports (that is, trunnions) provided halfway along the length of the cannon, which were used for manipulating the cannon's direction and also for aiding its movement and transportation. A total of one hundred eight nine iron rings have been used in constructing the tapered cylindrical barrel of the iron cannon. The rear of the cannon has been skilfully designed such that the number of rings has been successively reduced in order to finally reach the solid iron cylinder at the extreme end of the cannon. The construction of the rear end and the trunnions indicate the mastery of the blacksmith over his trade.

Jhansi

There are two massive forge-welded cannons located at the Jhansi Fort, which is associated with the heroic deeds of Rani Laxmibai during the First War of Indian Independence (1857). The *Kadak Bijli* is located immediately on the left, when one enters the Jhansi Fort, through its present entrance. The other cannon, located near the Ganesh Temple, is slightly in the interior of the fort and this is called *Bhavani Shankar*. Both these cannons are placed on raised concrete supports.

The *Bhavani Shankar* cannon (for a full view of the cannon and its engineering details, see **Figures 3.14a** and **3.14b**) was constructed during the Maratha period in 1725 CE.

(a)

(b)

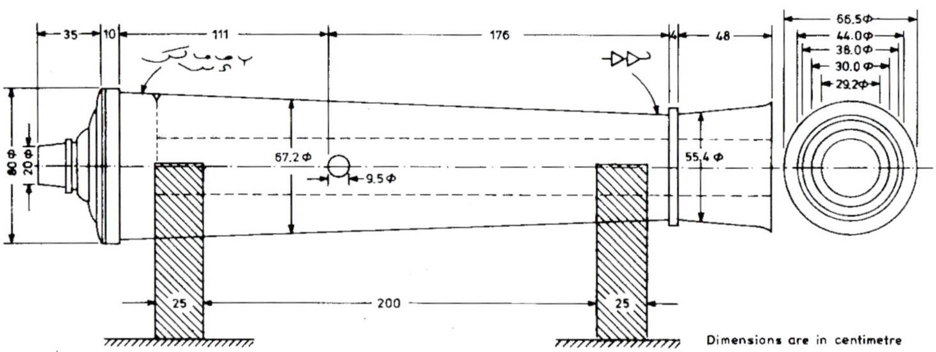

Fig. 3.13: *(a) The* Dal Mardan *cannon at Bishnupur. Notice the discolouration of the cannon in the lower portion, which is due to the half-buried condition of the cannon till 1918, and (b) its engineering drawing.*

(a)

(b)

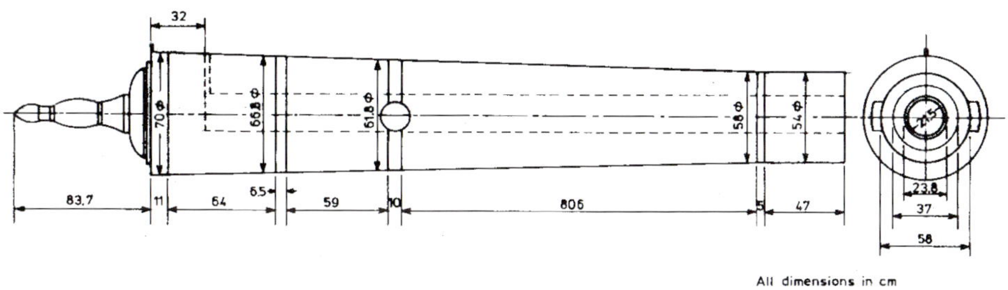

Fig. 3.14: *(a) The* Bhavani Shankar *cannon at Jhansi Fort, and (b) its engineering drawing.*

The total length of the cannon from the front to the extreme rear is 502 cm. The main barrel was manufactured by hooping two layers of iron rings over fifteen longitudinally placed iron staves. A minimum number of one hundred twenty five iron rings were used in the construction of the cannon. The interesting designs of lion and elephant in the front and rear portions of the cannon must be noted (see **Figures 3.14a**). The rear of the cannon is a marvellous construction, reminiscent of bronze cannons of similar design.

The *Kadak Bijli* cannon (see **Figure 3.15** for its overall design and engineering design) measures 5.5 m in length and weighs about 5 tonnes. The barrel of the cannon has been constructed by hooping two iron rings over eleven longitudinal iron staves. The iron rings were hooped over such that the second layer of rings closed the gaps between the rings of the first layer. Valuable information about the construction of forge-welded cannons is available in the damaged front (**Figure 3.16a**) and rear portion of the cannon (**Figures 3.16b** and **3.16c**). Notice that the iron staves progress all the way to the rear of the cannon and that they are thicker in the rear end of the barrel. The excellent engineering of the powder chamber and the design of connection of the iron staves with the rear must be noted (see **Figure 3.16d** and **3.16e**).

Assam

The independent rulers of Assam extensively utilised cannons in their wars. Chattopadhyay has described two forge-welded iron cannons of the Assamese king Jayadhvaja Simha (1648-1663), one lying at the Patna Museum (see **Figure 3.17**) and the other at the Asiatic Society, Kolkata (see **Figure 3.18**).

The cannon at the Patna Museum is 300 cm long, with a 28 cm muzzle diameter and 9 cm bore diameter. There are a total of seventy nine rings that are noticed on the top surface of the cannon. Four additional rings have been provided along the length of the barrel. A two line inscription in Assamese indicates that the master of the cannon was Jayadhvaja Simha and the date provided is Saka 1540 (that is, 1618 CE).

The cannon lying at the Asiatic Society, Kolkata, is 190 cm in length, diameter of the muzzle is 23 cm and bore diameter 6.5 cm. There are a total of fifty five rings visible on the surface. A two-line inscription on this cannon indicates that this also belonged to Jayadhvaja Simha, and the date provided is Saka 1548 (that is, 1626 CE). The legends on the cannons at Patna and Kolkata are almost identical but for the different dates.

Neogi (1914) referred to this gun as being "presented in 1891 by Captain Petley, being dug up at False Point, to the Asiatic Society of Bengal, in whose rooms it has been

(a)

(b)

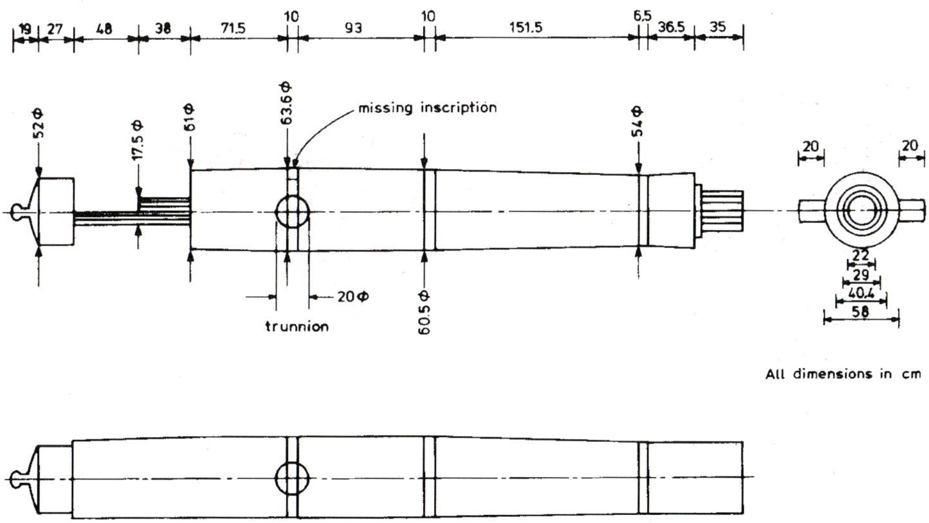

Fig. 3.15: *(a) The Kadak Bijli cannon at Jhansi Fort, and (b) its engineering drawing.*

(a)

(b)

(c)

(d)

(e)

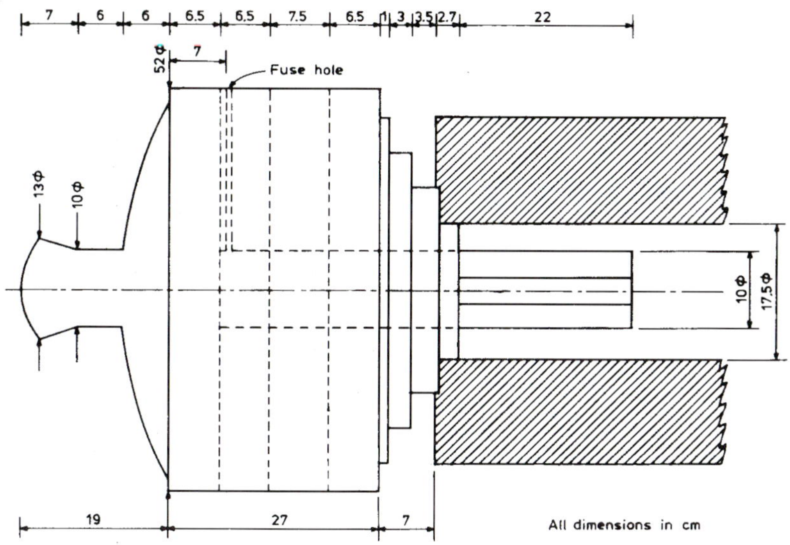

Fig. 3.16: *The damaged (a) front, (b) middle region viewed from the rear, (c) middle region viewed from the front of the* Kadak Bijli *cannon, providing insights on its method of manufacture, (d) rear region and (e) schematic of the rear portion.*

Fig. 3.17: *Forge-welded cannon of Jayadhvaja Simha now located at the Patna Museum. (Photograph courtesy: Pranab Chattopadhyay).*

Fig. 3.18: *Forge-welded cannon of Jayadhvaja Simha now located at the Asiatic Society at Kolkata.*

preserved". Wilson (1897) also read the date in the inscription as [1]548 Saka era and commented that "the gun was captured from Aurungzeb's General, Mir Jumla in 1662 by Svargadev Jayadhvaja Sinha, the then reigning Ahom Prince of Assam. From Assam it was carried away to Burma. It was taken by the English in the first Burmese war and on the completion of the light-house at False Point in 1838, seems to have been removed from the old fort at Cuttack and buried in the ground near the light-house to hold a flag staff". This gun was also manufactured in the same way as the Dhaka guns from wrought iron. Shastri (1890), who examined the gun, mentioned "the gun is made in the old-fashioned method of welding together a number of large iron rings, three inches thick, with an opening in the middle with a diameter of three inches".

Tripura

Cannons were also used in Tripura quite early in the history of cannon technology. Some aspects are discussed by Chattopadhyay (2005). According to this learned scholar, the earliest use of cannons has been mentioned around 1513-14 when the Sultan of Bengal, Hussein Shah used them against Dhanyamanika. The Sultan was defeated and a bronze cannon captured from him is still lying in the Ujjayant Palace in Agartala. Another cannon that was captured during the same time is still lying at Chowmohani in Agartala (see **Figure.** 3.19).

Fig. 3.19: *Forge-welded cannon at Agartala (Photograph courtesy. Pranab Chattopadhyay).*

Gulbarga

There are numerous cannons scattered all over the Deccani forts. Deloche mentions that in all the forts (such as Golconda, Bijapur, Bidar, Gulbarga, Parenda, etc.) that he studied, he found numerous cannons still present in their original condition and in their original location. In all the Deccani forts, the cannons are located on ramparts that make it difficult for people to negotiate and view these wonderful cannons. Moreover, the ramparts are not properly maintained, and it is difficult to move around with a thick outgrowth all around. Therefore, it is quite difficult to visit these forts first hand and record the technical details of the cannons located on the ramparts and within the forts.

Gulbarga was one of the important centres of Muslim power in medieval India. It served as the capital of the Bahamani kings of the fifteenth century. There are several forge-welded cannons located on the Gulbarga Fort rampart (Deloche 2005a: 573-596). The largest one (see **Figure 3.20**) was commented upon by Neogi (1914) as follows: "The long gun at Gulbarga seems to have been made in a similar way, but it is worthy of notice that there is double row of iron rings, ten on each side." This cannon is known locally as *Bara Gazi Tope* (12 yard cannon) and it is located on Shiraz Burj of the Gulbarga Fort.

Fig. 3.20: *Bara Gazi Tope located on Shiraz Burj of Gulbarga Fort. (Photograph courtesy: S. Kalyanaraman).*

The significance of this cannon is that it still rests on the pivot, and this provides valuable information about the actual operation of forge-welded cannons containing trunnions. The trunnions of the cannons were connected to a forked swivel, constructed usually of wrought iron. This swivel rested on an iron pivot, which was firmly fixed to the ground in an iron socket. The cannon could then be turned around to face different directions by swivelling over the iron pivot. A heavy segmental recoil wall was generally built at a very short distance from the back of the cannon (see **Figure 3.20**). This is a common feature noticed in Indian forts when cannons were placed on platforms atop bastions. The wall neutralised the recoil of the cannon when it was fired and thereby prevented stressing of the swivel and the pivot. Moreover, there must have been some equipment in front of the cannon for resting the cannon and also for aiding its movement for positioning purposes. This was usually a wooden arrangement moving on a grooved surface on the platform. In this way, the cannon's direction of fire and height could be adjusted.

Such is the working of the swivel of the massive cannon that the local children use this cannon as a see-saw! Therefore, this is locally known as *Jhula Tope* (see-saw cannon).

There are several other massive iron cannons located in Gulbarga. Let us take a look at a few of them. In one of the bastions of the rampart, we notice the *Char Gazi Tope*. This is also known as *Charmani Adil Shahi* (see **Figure 3.21**). A cannon located on the

Fig. 3.21: *Charmani Adil Shahi Tope located on one of the bastions of Gulbarga fort. (Photograph courtesy: S. Jaikishan).*

bastion inside the fort is called as *Haft Gazi Tope* and this is seen in **Figure 3.22**. Two cannons of similar design can be seen in two other bastions. While one cannon is lying flat in one of the bastions (see **Figure 3.23a**), the other is lying on the tower wall, half-buried in the stonework (see **Figure 3.23b**). Both these cannons are almost 12 feet in length.

Based on the size and design, these pieces must be considered as masterpieces of forge-welding technology.

Fig. 3.22: *Haft Gazi Tope located on one of the bastions of Gulbarga Fort. (Photograph courtesy: S. Jaikishan).*

Bijapur

The wonderful fort of Bijapur is home to some very fascinating forge-welded iron cannons (Cousens 1916: 29-33; Deloche 2002: 39-106).

The first cannon at Bijapur described by Neogi (1914) was the *Landa Kesab*. He writes, on the south wall of the city of Bijapur there is still to be seen the celebrated *Landa Kesab*

(a)

(b)

Fig. 3.23: *(a) and (b) Massive cannons located bastions of Gulbarga Fort. (Photograph (a) courtesy: S. Jaikishan and (b) courtesy: S.M. Khened).*

gun (**Figure 3.24**). It is also made of circular iron rings shrunk on longitudinal iron bars and then welded together. Aurangzeb is credited to have removed the original points on which it turned in order to make it practically useless. It is 21 feet 7 inches long, diameter at the breech is 4 feet 4 inches, calibre 1 foot 7 inches, length of bore 18 feet 7 inches and the estimated weight 47 tons". Notice a smaller mortar cannon beside the *Landa Kesab* cannon (see **Figure 3.24**) and assume it to be a mortar. Deloche has dated the *Landa Kesab* to 1646.

Fig. 3.24: *The* Landa Kesab *gun at Bijapur (photograph courtesy: Archaelogical Survey of India).*

The second cannon, described by Neogi, is the cannon on top of the Haider Burj (see **Figure 3.25**). He comments, "the long gun, named the *Farflier,* which is said to have been raised on the huge tower known as the Haider Burj at Bijapur by means of an inclined plane over a mile long, should be of interest in this connection. This gun, too, was constructed of iron bars of square section and laid longitudinally along the bore, over which rings were slipped, one at a time. As they cooled they shrank and bound the iron bars together. The gun near the breech was strengthened by the addition of a second layer. It is 30 feet 8 inches long and has a bore 1 foot in diameter". The name of this cannon is *Lambacharri.* Deloche provides a date of 1583 for this cannon. The interesting detail regarding its construction, at the location where the trunnions are located, must be noted Another wrought iron cannon on the same Haidar Burj of length 604 cm and bore diameter 20.3 cm can be seen in **Figure 3.26**.

Fig. 3.25: *The* Lambacharri *cannon on Haider Burj in Bijapur.*

Fig. 3.26: *Another massive forge welded cannon on Haidar Burj in Bijapur.*

There are some wonderful forge-welded cannons placed at the left and right entrance of the Archaeological Museum at Bijapur, near the Gol Gumbuz. Three forge-welded cannons each have been placed on either side of the entrance. One of the wonderful forge-welded cannons on the left side of the entrance is shown in **Figure 3.27**. Its outer diameter is 33 inches while the inner diameter is 15 inches. The complete length of the cannon is almost 18 feet. The muzzle has been reinforced with additional two sets of rings. Moreover, the delightful design of the necklace around the neck of the cannon must be noted. Another cannon of almost similar dimensions, but located at the other side of the entrance is seen in **Figure 3.28**. The length of the cannon is 16.5 feet, while the outside diameter is 25 inches, the inner bore diameter is 16 inches. Another cannon of similar length but having a smaller diameter of bore (of 8 inches) is seen in **Figure 3.29**. A smaller cannon placed beside (see **Figure 3.30**) shows a very interesting design of the muzzle.

Bidar

Bidar was another important centre in the Deccan in the middle ages (Yazdani 1947, 35-43, 85). One is lost in the maze of five Muslim kingdoms that erupted out of the Bahmani rule – Berar, Bidar, Ahmednagar, Bijapur, Golkonda. The Bahamani rulers operated from Gulbarga. On the fall of the Bahamani kingdom, five separate kingdoms came into prominence. Bidar was one of them. The small museum of the Archaeological Survey of India at Bidar Fort houses ancient weapons and hollow cannonballs filled with iron shrapnel. This is quite unique as the idea of shrapnel originated in the late eighteenth century by a Britisher named Shrapnel. However, the presence of these hollow iron cannon balls reveals that such ideas were known to Indians.

There are several wonderful massive bronze and iron cannons located in the Bidar Fort (see **Figure 3.31** for a map of Bidar Fort). The fort rampart consists of thrity-two bastions with seven gates. Yazdani has described some of these cannons in his book of 1947. Interestingly, he does not mention the material of construction of the major cannons that he had located in the fort. It is really fascinating to note that most of these massive cannons are indeed forge-welded wrought iron cannons. These include the *Ali Barid* on Mandu Gate (1542), *Fath Lashkar* on the north-west rampart (1580), *Tope-i-Haidari* on Lal Burj (1596), *Ali Barid* on Kala Burj (1569), *Tope-i-Mahmud Shahi* on Munda Burj (1591) and a long cannon on the western plateau. The dates of construction of these cannons are known from inscriptions on the cannons (Deloche 2005a: 573-596). These have been indicated within brackets.

Fig. 3.27: *One of the forge-welded cannons placed at the entrance of the Archaeological Museum at Bijapur, near the Gol Gumbuẓ.*

Fig. 3.28: *Another cannon of almost similar dimensions located on the other (right) side of the entrance.*

Fig. 3.29: *Another cannon of almost similar length but having a smaller diameter of bore (of 8 inches).*

Fig. 3.30: *A smaller cannon at the entrance of the Museum at Gol Gumbuz. shows a very interesting design of the muzzle.*

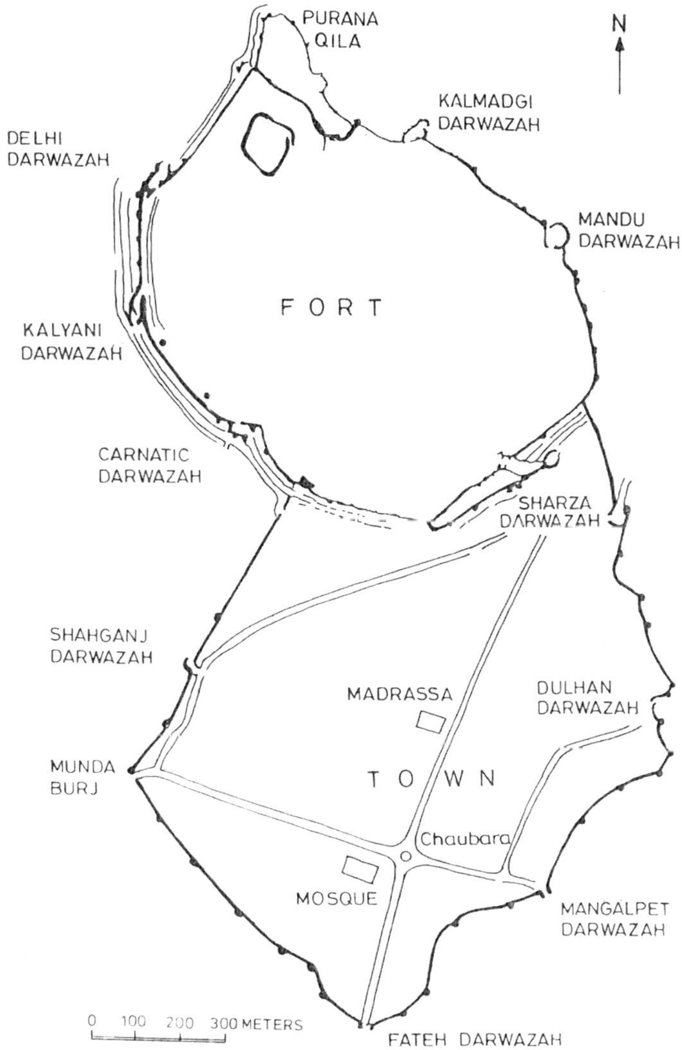

Fig. 3.31: *Plan of Bidar Fort.*

The long cannon is a wrought iron cannon (**Figure 3.32**). The ditch around which a wooden cart moved, in order to change the direction of fire, can be seen in this photograph. The cannon is 883 cm long, diameter at the muzzle is 53 cm and diameter of the bore is 15.2 cm.

Fig. 3.32: *The long forge-welded cannon at Bidar.*

The *Ali Barid* cannon located on the Mandu Gate is a massive cannon (**Figure 3.33a**). Its length is 450 cm, with an outer diameter of 106 cm and inner bore diameter of 48 cm. The cannon fired shots that weighed 136 kg, and the gunpowder for such a shot weighed 27.2 kg. Two sets of trunnions and two sets of handling rings are noticed on the cannon. The design and construction of the trunnion deserve attention (see **Figure 3.33b**). The handling ring is relatively large, with the outer diameter of the ring being 23 cm. Interestingly, this cannon is called locally as *Gaddha* (donkey) cannon.

The *Ali Barid* cannon on the Kala Burj bastion is shown in **Figure 3.34a**. This cannon is 350 cm long, with a muzzle diameter of 87 cm and an inner bore diameter of 48 cm. This cannon also fired shots weighing 136 kg, using gunpowder of 27.2 kg weight. There are three sets of handling rings and two sets of trunnions noticed on this marvellous cannon. The muzzle face shows the intricate engineering of this cannon (**Figure 3.34b**). Notice the twenty four staves, each of 1.5 inch thickness, which have been skilfully forged to produce the inner surface of the barrel. The massive trunnions, which are about 12 inches long and 17 inches in diameter, also deserve attention.

The *Fath Laskhar* cannon is seen in **Figure 3.35**. The *Tope-i-Haidari* located on the Lal Burj is shown in **Figure 3.36**. Its total length is 370 cm, the diameter of the muzzle being 79 cm and the bore 37 cm. There are two sets of handling rings noticed on the surface of this cannon. The other massive cannon, known as *Tope-i-Mahmud Shahi* at Munda Burj at Bidar, is seen in **Figure 3.37**.

That forge welding technology was refined in the Deccan area is clearly attested by the presence of numerous smaller forge-welded cannons all over the fort premises. In fact, these smaller pieces also deserve attention and need to be placed in proper locations

(a)

(b)

Fig. 3.33: *(a) Ali Barid on Mandu Gate and (b) close-up view of one of the trunnions of the cannon. (Photograph (a) courtesy: J. Deloche and (b) S. Jaikishan).*

(a)

(b)

Fig. 3.34: *(a)* Ali Barid *on Kala Burj and (b) muzzle face of this cannon showing the intricate engineering of the inner surface of the barrel using twenty-four staves. (Photographs courtesy: S. Jaikishan).*

Fig. 3.35: *Fath Lashkar on the north-west rampart of the Bidar Fort. (Photograph courtesy: J.Deloche).*

Fig. 3.36: *Tope-i-Haidari on Lal Burj in Bidar. (Photograph courtesy: S. Jaikishan).*

Fig. 3.37: Tope-i-Mahmud Shahi *at Munda Burj at Bidar.*

for their proper conservation. Two forge-welded cannons found lying in the Bidar Fort are seen in **Figure 3.38**. These smaller cannons also reveal all the intricate details that are revealed in the larger pieces.

Some of the cannons from the Bidar Fort have also been shifted to other places, and one notable example is the forge-welded cannon that is presently in Campal, Goa (see **Figure 3.39**) that originated from Bidar. Its length is 376 cm and the diameter of the bore is 41 cm.

Hyderabad

The Golconda Fort is a majestic monument, which lies on the western outskirts of Hyderabad, in the state of Andhra Pradesh. The construction of the fort in its present form by Mohammeḍ Quli Qutub Shah was started around 1525 CE. The Golconda Fort is fortified with two lines of defences. The inner rampart, about 5 km in circumference, protected the palaces and garrison located on the Golconda hill. The outer rampart, surrounding the entire township of Golconda, is about 11 km long, and this was also strongly fortified (see **Figure 3.40**). At regular intervals, the outer fortified wall was provided with *burjs* (bastions). At these bastions, iron and bronze cannons were strategically located (Deloche 2002: 39-106).

We shall look at two forge-welded cannons located on these bastions. After the fort fell into the hands of the Mughals in 1687, they located some of their wonderful cast bronze cannons at strategic locations along the outer fort wall. Therefore, the bronze cannons at Golconda Fort are from the time of Mughal occupation, while the iron cannons

(a)

(b)

Fig. 3.38: *(a) and (b) Small forge-welded cannons lying in Bidar Fort. The former is a hollow cannon lying in front of the Fort Museum showing twenty-two rings. (Photographs courtesy: S. Jaikishan).*

Fig. 3.39: *Forge-welded cannon that was originally from Bidar, now located at Campal, Goa.*

were present even before the Mughals took over Golconda. The iron cannons are not provided with trunnions, but with rings.

A massive forge-welded cannon is located on a bastion called *Bada Burj* (Big Bastion) (see **Figure. 3.41a**) (Balasubramaniam *et. al.* 2005c: 321-336). Its engineering drawing is seen in **Figure 3.41b**. It was manufactured in 1644 CE. The total length of the cannon, as measured from the front end to the back end, is 509 cm. The inner and outer diameters of the cannon are 31 and 69 cm, respectively. The conservative weight of the cannon is about 12 tonnes. The iron cannon was manufactured using three layers of pre-fabricated iron rings, hooped and forge-welded over twenty-one longitudinally placed iron staves, which have been flared out in the front end of the cannon (**Figure 3.41c**). There are two excellent decorative patterns near the front end of the cannon (**Figure. 3.41d**). The iron cannon had four sets of handling clamps, in which iron rings were originally located.

The second forge-welded cannon (see **Figure 3.42a**) is located near the Fateh Darwazah bastion (Balasubramaniam *et. al.* 2005d: 337-348). The date of construction of the cannon is not known with certainty. The total length is about 474 cm (see **Figure**

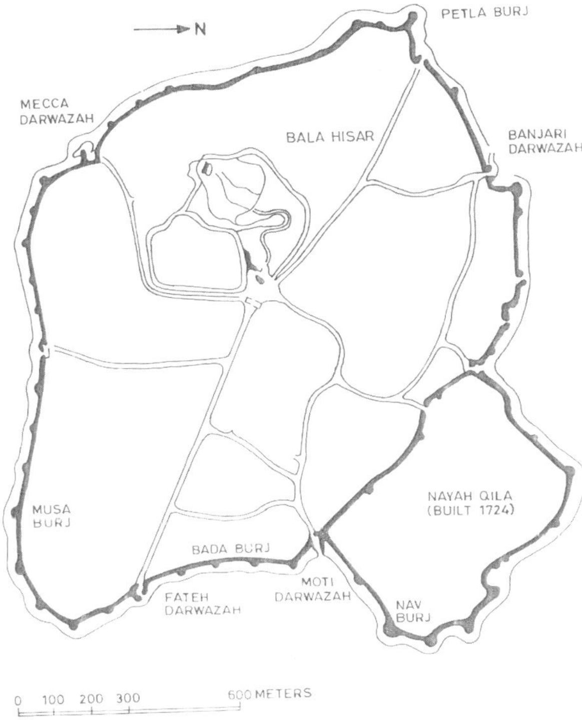

Fig. 3.40: *Plan of the Golconda Fort.*

3.42b). The outer diameter of the cannon at the rear end is 86 cm. The inner diameter of the cannon, measured on the front face, is 30 cm. The iron cannon was provided with ten handling rings, five on each side. The handling rings have been fixed on handling clamps, located at regular intervals along the length of the cannon (see **Figure 3.42a**).

In several instances, forge-welded cannons can also be found within the modern city and town premises. For instance, the Archaeology Department of Andhra Pradesh recovered two forge-welded cannons from a remote fort in the state, and it was placed in the premises of the State Archaeology Department at Hyderabad (see **Figure 3.43**). The total length of the larger cannon is 550 cm. with the diameter of the muzzle being 40 cm and that of the bore 25 cm. The other small sized cannon, noticed in the same picture, is a typical example of a howitzer, a cannon that was used for throwing cannon balls up into the air to reach targets deep inside fortifications.

It appears that each of these great cities of the past has so much to offer in terms of material that these wonderful metallurgical objects tend to be neglected. A typical

(a)

(b)

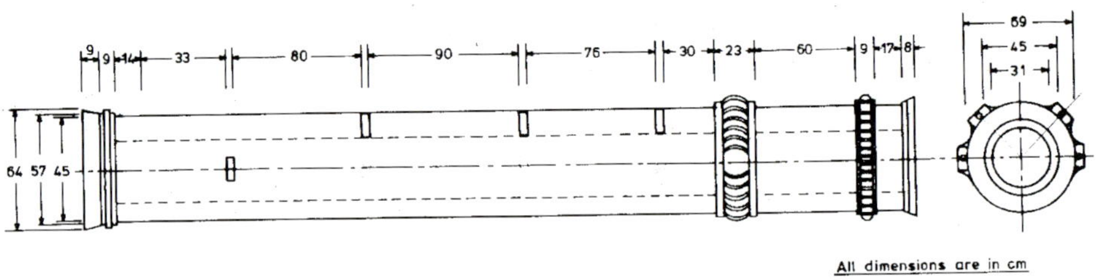
9
9
14
33
80
90
76
30
23
60
9
17
8
69
45
31
64 57 45
All dimensions are in cm

(c)

(d)

Fig. 3.41: *(a) The forge-welded cannon at Bada Burj of the Golconda rampart in Hyderabad, (b) its engineering drawing, (c) muzzle face and (d) decorative bands on the front end of the cannon.*

(a)

(b)

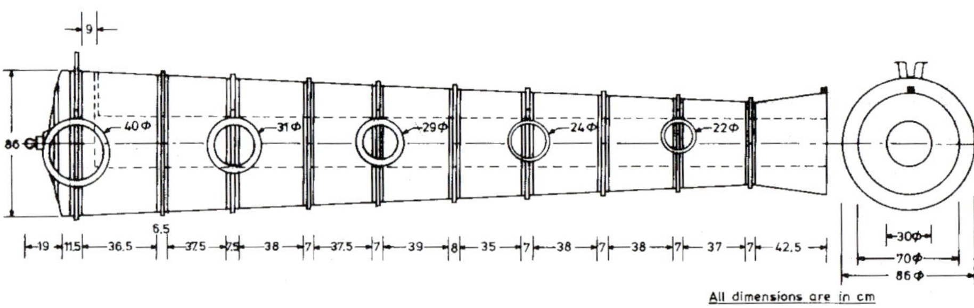

Fig. 3.42: *The forge-welded cannon near Fateh Darwazah of the Golconda rampart in Hyderabad, and (b) its engineering drawing.*

Fig. 3.43: *The forge-welded cannon discovered in the premises of the Andhra Pradesh Archaeology Department at Hyderabad. Notice a forge-welded howitzer at the bottom of the photograph.*

scene in one of the lanes within Golconda is shown in **Figure 3.44**, where half a buried cannon can be seen to co-exist peacefully with the vagaries of modern life.

Karimnagar District

The Deccan region was famous for the production of iron. We can still observe, even in remote locations and remote forts of the Deccan, a large number of cannons. Not much is known about these cannons. There are some dedicated people who are helping to catalogue these objects. One notable person is a historian of Andhra Pradesh, S. Jaikishan. He has located and described ninetten large forge-welded cannons at three remote forts (Ramagiri, Elgandal and Jagtial) in Karimnagar district of Andhra Pradesh (Jaikishan 2005: 487-502). One of the famous cannons at Ramagiri Fort is the *Pillala Firingi* cannon. It is currently broken into two pieces (**Figures 3.45a** and **3.45b**). There is an interesting custom practised by the local people of the region. Childless couples crawl through the barrel of the cannon, especially in the month of Shravan (rainy season), in the belief that they will be blessed with children. **Figure 3.45a** is a typical scene showing this. Several massive forge welded cannons at Ramagiri fort have been described by Jaikishan (2005: 487 502).

Fig. 3.44: *Cannon lying half buried in soil by the side of one of the lanes of the Golconda Fort.*

(a) *(b)*

Fig. 3.45: *(a) Front portion of the* Pillala Firingi *cannon at Ramagiri Fort showing people crawling through the cannon in the month of Shravan, and (b) second piece of the broken cannon. (Photographs courtesy: S. Jaikishan).*

The cannons located at Elgandal Fort are even more formidable (see **Figure 3.46**) (Jaikishan 2005: 487-502). One cannon is particularly interesting because it is known as *Kodimyal Tope.* Kodimyal is a *mandal* headquarter on the way from Karimnagar to Jagtial. This village is famous for its bronze and iron works since ancient times. Kodimyal was a well-known place known for iron smelting and wootz steel making during the medieval period. The name of the cannon being named after Kodimyal indicates that it must have been a centre for manufacturing forge-welded cannons. That this region was famous for iron-making is well-known from the travel records of Europeans.

While some of the cannons have been properly preserved most of the cannons are lying in a neglected condition.

Basava Kalyan

There are several interesting and massive cannons located at Basava Kalyan Fort (Deloche 2005a: 573-596). We shall look only into the forge- welded iron pieces. A forge-welded iron cannon, with very intricate details on the surface and the muzzle face, is located at the top of the fort (**Figure 3.47a**). The cannon is connected to the pivot by means of a swivel. Such is the arrangement that the cannon can be manipulated very effectively, even today. The length of the cannon is 340 cm, with the muzzle diameter being 29 cm and the bore diameter 14 cm. The diameter at the back of the cannon is 48 cm. It is locally called as the *Kadak Bijli* cannon. The very fascinating design of the muzzle resembles a dragon (**Figure 3.47b**). The entire surface of the cannon is decorated with *koftgari* (inlay) work. In this kind of work, bronze material is encrusted (pressing metal on to grooves) on to the surface in different floral designs. The details of the inlay work can be noted. The interesting design of the fuse hole must also be noted because it appears that a hollow rod has been introduced in to a drilled hole to create the vent hole of the cannon.

A massive-forge welded cannon called *Nav Gazi Tope* (Nine Yard cannon) is located at the top of the Basava Kalyan Fort (see **Figure 3.48**). We notice that the term *Nav Gazi* is frequently used to denote cannons of certain dimensions. Ideally, it meant 27 feet or 9 yards. In case of this cannon, the measured length was about 24 feet (precisely 716 cm long). The outer diameter of the cannon is 74 cm while that of the bore is 40 cm. This is truly a massive cannon. The cannon possesses seven sets of handling rings and massive forge-welded trunnions. Eight of the original fourteen rings are still present on the cannon surface. We do not know how much longer would these rings remain

Fig. 3.46: *One cannon located at the top of Elgandal Fort. (Photograph courtesy: S. Jaikishan).*

because of rampant vandalism of such objects placed in remote locations within the fort. It was noted that some of the rings have been already damaged due to vandalism. Interestingly, the damaged location provides valuable clues as to how the second layer of rings was placed over the first layer. From the appearance of the muzzle face, it appears that there are three layers of rings. However, the damaged portion indicates that only two layers of rings might have been present.

Udgir

A massive forge-welded cannon located on top of the Udgir Fort is seen in **Figure 3.49**. The length of this cannon is 260 cm, with the outer diameter being 33 cm and the bore diameter being 17 cm. A smaller forge-welded cannon, located at the entrance to the moat, is seen in **Figure 3.50**. It possesses an excellent finish, although it is smaller in size compared to the other cannon. Its length is 150 cm and the bore diameter is 20 cm. The interesting design of the muzzle face, shaped like a dragon, is worth noting (see **Figure 3.50**).

(a)

(b)

Fig. 3.47: *(a) Movable cannon on pivot at the top of the Basava Kalyan Fort (Photograph courtesy: J. Deloche). (b) Dragon-like design of the muzzle swell (Photograph courtesy: S. Jaikishan).*

Fig. 3.48: *A massive forge-welded cannon called* Nav Gazi Tope *is located at the top of Basava Kalyan Fort (Photographs courtesy: S. Jaikishan).*

Fig. 3.49: *A massive forge-welded cannon located atop the Udgir Fort. (Photograph courtesy: S. Jaikishan).*

Fig. 3.50: *Smaller forge-welded cannon at Udgir Fort showing interesting design of the muzzle face, shaped like a dragon.*

Khandhar

There are several forge-welded cannons in this fort. Of particular significance are the *Ambari Tope* (see **Figure 3.51**) and *Maghrabhi Tope* (see **Figure 3.52**). The *Ambari Tope* is 500 cm long, with a tapering shape. It is located at the Ambari Burj. The diameter at the muzzle end is 30 cm while at the rear end it is 40 cm. It is said that this cannon had a range of 3 km. The front of the cannon is shaped like a devil's head. The *Maghrabhi Tope* is located on the Maghrabhi Burj (see **Figure 3.52**). The front of the cannon is shaped like a crocodile. Two sets of handling rings are provided. There is a necklace around the neck. An interesting sight at Khandar fort is an upright forge welded cannon (see **Figure 3.53**). Finally, a small forge-welded howitzer from the same fort is seen in **Figure 3.54**. One can clearly see the touch hole in the middle of the cannon.

Kaulas

The Kaulas Fort in Nizamabad district of Andhra Pradesh is home to some wonderful forge-welded cannons. **Figure 3.55** shows one of these cannons. It is 150 cm in length, with the muzzle diameter being 29 cm and the bore diameter 11 cm.

Deccani Forts

Deloche found four large forge-welded iron cannons lying in Mudgal Fort (Deloche 2005b). One cannon located at the Fateh Darwazah is shown in **Figure 3.56**. The front portion clearly reveals that two layers of rings were forged over the staves. It is interesting to note that when only two layers of rings are used, the rings are relatively thicker. Two other forge-welded cannons at the Kati Darwazah are seen in **Figures 3.57** and **3.58**. The use of separate handling plates, placed over the barrel of the former cannon, must be noted.

Two massive cannons located at Parenda Fort are shown in **Figure 3.59**. They are almost 500 cm in length with bore diametre of 30 cm. The repair of the cannon in Fig. 3.59b is noteworthy. One located at the top of Raichur Fort is seen in **Figure 3.60**. It is almost 30 feet in length, a fairly long cannon. A forge-welded cannon from the Khammam Fort is seen in **Figure 3.61**. It is 220 cm long, with a 30 cm muzzle diameter and 15 cm bore diameter. The diameter at the rear is 48 cm. The forged trunnions are clearly visible. Forge welded cannons from Ausa, Gavilgarh, Malhar, Narnal and Naldurg forts are presented in **Figures 3.62 through 3.69**.

Fig. 3.51: Ambari Tope *in Khandar Fort.*

Fig. 3.52: Maghrabhi Tope *in Khandar Fort.*

Fig. 3.53: *Upright forge welded cannon at Khandar Fort.*

Fig. 3.54: *Forge-welded howitzer in Khandar Fort. (Photograph courtesy: S. Jaikishan).*

Fig. 3.55: *One of the several massive forge-welded cannon in Kaulas Fort. (Photograph courtesy: S. Jaikishan).*

Fig. 3.56: *Forge-welded cannon located at Fateh Darwazah of Mudgal Fort showing the front portion where two layers of rings are forged over the staves. (Photograph courtesy: J. Deloche.)*

Fig. 3.57: *One of the two forge-welded cannons located at Kati Darwazah at Mudgal Fort showing the use of separate handling plates placed over the barrel. (Photograph courtesy: J. Deloche.)*

Fig. 3.58: *The second of the two forge-welded cannons located at Kati Darwazah at Mudgal Fort. (Photograph courtesy: J. Deloche).*

(b)

(b)

Fig. 3.59: *(a) and (b) Large forge welded cannons at Parenda Fort.*

Fig. 3.60: *A forge-welded cannon at Raichur Fort. (Photograph courtesy: S. Jaikishan).*

Fig. 3.61: *A large forge-welded cannon at Khammam Fort. (Photograph courtesy: S. Jaikishan.)*

Fig. 3.62: *Cannon at Ausa.*

Fig. 3.63: *First cannon at Gavilgarh.*

Fig. 3.64: *Second cannon at Gavilgarh.*

Fig. 3.65: *Third cannon at Gavilgarh.*

Fig. 3.66: *Cannon at Malhar.*

Fig. 3.67: *Cannon at Narnal*

Fig. 3.68: *First cannon at Naldurg.*

Fig. 3.69: *Second cannon at Naldurg.*

Other Locations

Forge welded-cannons can also be found in establishments connected with the military and the police. For instance, a forge-welded cannon of the seventeenth century, now located at the District Police Headquarters in Pune is shown in **Figure 3.70**. Its length is 305 cm and bore diameter is 10 cm. Four handling rings are provided in addition to the trunnions.

Large forge-welded cannons are also found scattered in other parts of India in old forts. For instance, three massive forge-welded cannon in the famous Mehrangarh Fort at Jodhpur are shown in **Figure 3.71**. An inscription on the barrel of the cannon in **Figure 3.71a** indicates its name as *Nusrat Laskar* ("Glory of the Army"). Its length is 386 cm and its calibre 43 cm. Six holding rings and two trunnions are found on its barrel, the rear portion of which has four raised rings.

Fig. 3.70: *Forge-welded cannon located at the District Police Headquarters in Pune.*

(a)

(b)

(c)

Fig. 3.71: *(a), (b) and (c) Details of three of the massive forge-welded cannons located in Mehrangarh Fort in Jodhpur.*

TECHNOLOGY OF FORGE-WELDED CANNONS

Guns cast from non-ferrous alloys during the first half of the fourteenth century were small and expensive. Therefore, gun-makers soon began to try iron. In Europe, the technique of casting cast iron was then very much in its infancy. Therefore, blacksmiths began forging guns from wrought iron. They were called bombards from the Greek *bombos*, meaning a loud buzzing noise.

The construction of the basic bombard (that is, forge-welded cannons) is schematically shown in **Figure 3.72**. To construct a bombard, the smith first made a wooden cylinder called a mandrel of the same length as the desired piece, and of the same diameter as its bore. He then forged a number of iron bars of nearly rectangular section, which he fitted closely together around the mandrel. Next, a number of rings of internal diameter slightly less than the external diameter of the bars, as assembled on the mandrel, were forge-welded (**Figure 3.72**). The rings were heated to white heat and fitted over the bars so that on cooling they contracted, holding the bars very tightly together.

Before fitting the rings, the smith in some cases poured molten lead into the gaps between the bars to prevent the escape of propellant gas. We do not generally notice the use of lead in between the joints of the Indian forge-welded cannons. With heavier types, the rings were usually placed end-to-end. The term gun barrel derives from this method of construction because the bars and rings correspond to the staves and bands, respectively, of the common wooden barrel. In small pieces, instead of bars the smith sometimes bent a sheet of iron into a cylinder, welded the edges together and shrunk rings around it, as above. Bombards, especially those on which the rings were placed end-to-end, were thus pre-stressed in much the same way as built-up guns made five centuries later. It is not known if the makers realised this fact.

Design

As the piece was built on a mandrel, it was open at both the ends. Therefore, two possibilities existed for loading the gunpowder and shots. In the first method, the charge and shot could be loaded at the back and this was called breach loading. In the second method, the charge and the shot could be loaded from the front and this was called muzzle loading.

By the end of the fifteenth century, muzzle loading guns of cast non-ferrous alloys were fast superseding those of forged iron (Smith and Brown 1989). A few breech-loading

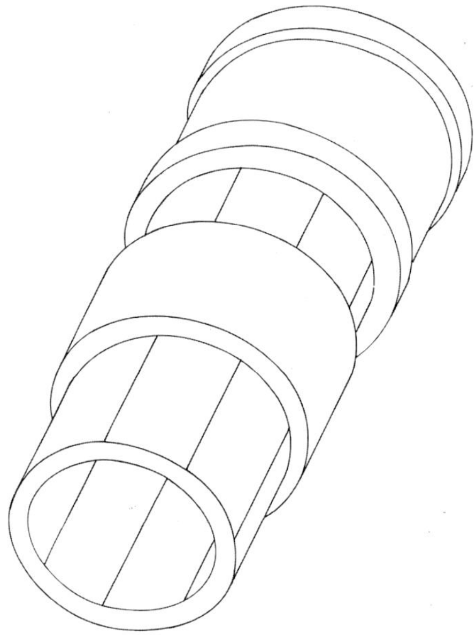

Fig. 3.72: *Basic construction of a wrought-iron cannon. Schematic illustration of hooping of iron rings over central staves, in order to produce the barrel of forge-welded cannons.*

pieces were made of these alloys but muzzle loading types predominated. No more forged iron guns were made after about 1520 in Europe, whereas the Indian blacksmiths excelled in making forge-welded cannon well into the next century. Although not easy to load, muzzle loading guns had no obturation problems (that is, escape of gases through the joints).

Initially, there were problems of offset bores in case of cast cannons, which was later overcome by casting in solid piece and machining the inside material out. While the bores of cast pieces were turned on a boring machine after manufacture, this was not the case with forged pieces. Thus cast pieces tended to be more accurate. Furthermore, trunnions could be cast integral with the piece, that is did not have to be made separately but was somehow attached to it.

Before we look into the engineering of these wonderful forge-welded cannon pieces, let us dwell on the general design characteristics of these cannons. We had noted earlier that most of the early forge-welded cannons are of uniform diameter throughout, very much reminiscent of the European "port pieces".

Two distinct types of cannons can be classified. We notice forge-welded cannons without any trunnions but with just handling rings (for instance, the massive *Rajagopala* cannon in Thanjavur seen in **Figure 3.10b**), and cannons that possess both trunnions and handling clamps (for instance, the long forge-welded cannon at Gulbarga seen in **Figure 3.20**). Forge-welded cannons were also fabricated similar in design to the bronze cannons in that they were provided with proper trunnions, without handling clamps (some examples being the massive forge-welded iron cannons at Bishnupur (see **Figure 3.13a**) and Jhansi fort (**Figure 3.14**).

It is quite possible that cannons that are provided with trunnions could be later specimens. Only limited information is available from inscriptional evidences because of lack of inscriptions on massive forge-welded cannons, unlike their bronze counterparts. The cannon at Bada Burj on the Golconda Fort ramparts in Hyderabad is dated to 1644 (see **Figure 3.41**), and this cannon was provided only with handling rings. In contrast, the more recent *Bhavani Shankar* cannon in Jhansi Fort, dated to 1725, is provided only with trunnions (see **Figure 3.14**). This line of reasoning cannot be strictly true because the provision of trunnions could also be indicative of the cannon being constructed for mobility in field warfare rather than placed on a fort bastion.

The massive forge-welded cannons that were placed on fort bastions also reveal two types of designs. In the first type, the cannons are provided only with handling rings and in the second type, the cannons are provided with both trunnions and handling rings. In the former type, the cannons appear to have been positioned on massive wooden logs. In all the locations where massive forge-welded cannons are located, the logs are no longer present. However, an idea of the kind of arrangement used can be had from the photograph of the massive *Malik-i-Maidan* bronze cannon at Bijapur (see **Figure 3.5a**).

In the case of the second type, the trunnions were used to connect to a curved fork, which was placed on a central iron pivot. The fork was also manufactured out of forged iron. A good example of this can be seen in the Gulbarga cannon (see **Figures 3.20**, where the swivel arrangement can be clearly noted).

Construction

There are different aspects of construction of forge-welded cannons, as related to different parts of the cannon, for example the barrel, the muzzle and the breech sections. We shall briefly discuss the salient features of the manufacturing methodology of these different parts. The skill of manufacturing the forge-welded cannon clearly rested in the ability to construct the main barrel of the cannon. Interestingly, the origin of the term "barrel" reflects the construction of the early cannons in a manner similar to wooden barrels, that is, long horizontal staves joined by circular rings. This is schematically illustrated in **Figure** 3.73.

The skill required to manufacture the barrel by the use of forge-welded iron rings must be appreciated because close dimensional tolerances were required apart from a good understanding of the thermal expansion and contraction properties of the material. When one considers the enormous number of rings used in the construction of each cannon, the excellent blacksmithy skills of the medieval Indian smiths becomes very evident.

The rings were first placed over the iron staves, that is, longitudinal plates that were placed horizontally over a mandrel such that they formed the inner surface of the barrel. In some cases, just one set of rings was used to close the staves. In other cases, we notice two or three layers of rings. The placement of rings with respect to the layers will be seen shortly.

The method used to place the rings was by shrink fitting. In order to accomplish shrink fitting, it is important to understand the principle. When iron is heated, it expands and on cooling, it contracts. When iron ring is heated, it assumes a larger diameter. It is then placed on top of the staves or the earlier ring layer. On cooling down, the ring contracts and in this manner closes the gap precisely. Another advantage is that when the rings contract, they are restricted from contracting completely, and therefore, the

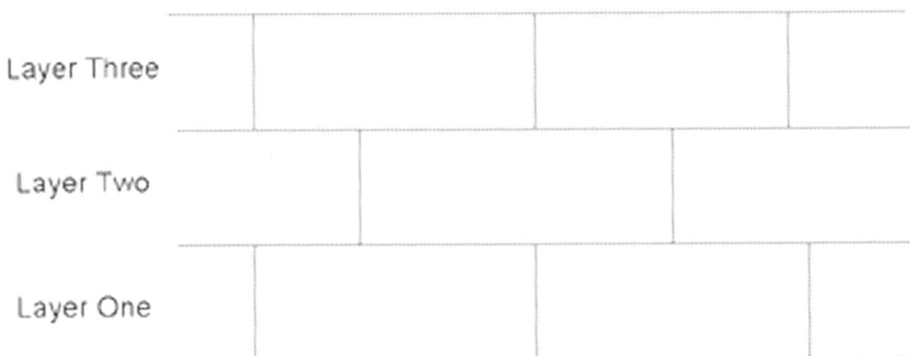

Fig. 3.73: *Schematic showing the placement of rings over each other. The layer of rings on the top generally closed the gaps in the layer of rings that came on the bottom.*

layer beneath is put in a state of compression. These compressive stresses are beneficial because they help in providing further toughness to the walls.

Tensile stresses usually cause damage, while compressive stresses are beneficial because they must first be overcome to result in damage. Therefore, the process of shrink fitting was very beneficial because it helped in producing tight joints as well as provided toughness to the wall thickness. It is no wonder that the Indian blacksmiths preferred forge-welded cannons because, based on simple engineering fundamentals, they were far superior to the cast iron cannons in terms of their strength and toughness.

There were doubts whether the rings were forge-welded after being shrunk fit. Radiography studies conducted on the *Mons Meg* cannon have established that the rings were just shrunk fit and they were not additionally forge-welded. Though similar studies have not been conducted on Indian forge welded cannons, to understand the technology of their production as well as fine details of its inner construction, it is reasonable to conclude that similar techniques must have been applicable because the interface between rings can be clearly distinguished in the Indian forge-welded cannon and does not show any evidence of further working.

Some fine points regarding barrel (and cannon) manufacture can be obtained by careful technical analysis of massive forge-welded cannons.

The barrel is an important part of the cannon. This had to withstand the pressure of the exploding gunpowder as well as ensure the smooth passage of the cannon ball to reach its destination. Therefore, the basic criteria for making a good barrel must have been the smoothness of the inner surface and the toughness of the barrel wall.

Let us first consider the technology for the construction of the main barrel. The basic method was as follows. Long flat iron rods were placed longitudinally over a mandrel to produce the inner surface of the cannon barrel. These iron plates are called staves in cannon terminology. Then, carefully pre-fabricated iron rings, of the required dimensions, were heated and placed over the staves such that the rings contracted on cooling and held the staves together. Usually, an additional one or two layers or rings were hooped (that is, shrunk fit) over the first layer of rings for further strengthening of the barrel. The additional layer of iron rings was placed such that the rings in this additional layer closed the gaps between the rings of the first layer. In case a third layer was used, the rings in this layer closed the gaps between the rings that made the second layer. This kind of placement of rings zis schematically shown in **Figure** 3.73.

It appears that either two or three layers of rings were generally provided. Three layers are noticed in the design of several cannons, for instance the *Rajagopala* cannon of Thanjavur. The relative positioning of the three layers can be clearly noticed in the cross-section of the broken piece of the *Pillala Firingi* cannon at Ramagiri Fort (see **Figure 3.45b**).

The *Kadak Bijli* cannon at Jhansi is a typical example where two layers of rings are used. The arrangement of the layers is noticed from the cross-section in the broken section (see **Figure 3.16a**). Another example is the massive forge-welded cannon located on Fateh Darwazah in Mudgal Fort, and this is shown in **Figure 3.56**. It is interesting to note that when only two layers of rings are used, the rings are relatively thicker.

Keeping in view the basic construction of the barrel, there was need to put additional rings at certain locations along the barrel, depending on requirements. One location was the front face of the cannon, where usually additional rings were provided to strengthen this location.

Additional rings were also provided along the body of the cannon in order to further strengthen the barrel. Such rings can be noted along the body of the *Rajagopala* cannon in **Figure 3.74**.

Another location that was frequently strengthened was the rear portion of the barrel because this had to withstand the force of the gunfire as in the case of the *Rajagopala* cannon and the, *Dal Mardan* cannon (**Figure 3.13a**). In several cases, we also notice that additional rings were added at the rear location, as seen in **Figure 3.75**, as in the case of the long *Gulbarga* cannon.

Secondly, there were rings that contained the trunnions, which were hooped over the barrel at the appropriate location (see **Figure. 3.33b** for a good example of the same in the case of the *Ali Barid* cannon at Haidar Burj at Bidar).

Thirdly, there were rings that contained the holding clamps (that is, containing provision for holes) through which circular handling rings were inserted. Several designs can be noted in this regard. The *Rajagopala* cannon shows a unique kind of plate arrangement on each of which two rings could be attached (see **Figure 3.76**). Another simpler way was to provide for clamps with holes on which the rings were attached. These rings must have been specially constructed before they were shrunk fit. This implies careful planning, design, engineering and construction of the forge-welded cannons.

Two contrasting arrangements of handling rings can be seen in **Figures. 3.39** (cannon at Campal, Goa) and 3.71 (Shivaji cannon at Pune). Notice the provision of pairs of rings

Fig. 3.74: *Additional rings provided along the barrel of the* Rajagopala *cannon to provide further strength to the cannon barrel.*

Fig. 3.75: *Rear portion of the long Gulbarga cannon. Notice additional rings provided in order to strengthen this location. (Photograph courtesy: S.M. Khened).*

Fig. 3.76: *Plates provided on top of the* Rajagopala *cannon on each of which two rings could be attached.*

with handling clamps, each containing two handling clamps, in the middle of the cannon on either side of the trunnion, in the case of the forge-welded cannon at Campal, Goa. Rings containing single handling clamps are seen in the front and rear end. This operation also involved careful planning as well as organisation in order to manufacture these cannons. In contrast, the forge-welded cannon in **Figure 3.71**, which is from Chattrapati Shivaji's arsenal, is provided with just two rings, each containing two handling clamps. The cannon is lying in the District Police Headquarters in Pune.

It must be noted that there were other innovative methods by which cannons were handled and manipulated. One was the use of separate handling plates placed over the barrel. A good example of this is shown in **Figure 3.57**, which shows one of the two forge-welded cannons at the Kati Darwazah of the Mudgal Fort. Interestingly, such designs were also used to manipulate the height of even bronze cannons, as can be seen in the example of **Figure 3.77**, a cannon located in the Andhra Pradesh State Museum at Hyderabad. Notice that an iron band has been placed over the cannon barrel.

It is interesting to note that the rings (attached to the clamps on the cannons) were placed along a line. This implies that rods must have been inserted through all of them so as to lift them up. The design of the iron rings also needs to be appreciated. The rings occur in pairs, and generally, are, also placed symmetrically and evenly along the length of the barrel.

The next aspect that needs to be addressed is the design of the inner smooth surface. As an exceptional case, we notice a smooth inner surface of cannon barrel in the case of the *Dal Mardan* cannon (see **Figure 3.78**). The method by which this was produced is not known. In contrast, the other more popular method noticed is the provision of staves. Some interesting feature regarding the use of staves can be discerned in the Indian forge-welded cannons. In several cases, the iron staves are flared out on the open muzzle end (see **Figure 3.41c** for the example of the cannon at *Bada Burj* at Golconda Fort). In other cases, the staves come to an abrupt end at the muzzle face (see **Figure 3.16a** which shows the damaged front portion of the *Kadak Bijli* cannon showing very many details of the staves where it meets the muzzle face).

There also appears to be no fixed number of plates used in the construction of the central circular section. The thickness of the iron staves is also not constant. However, it is clear that the thickness of the plates used was not constant along the length of the barrel. This can be noted by comparing the thickness of the staves on the front face (see **Figure 3.16a**) of the *Kadak Bijli* cannon and the thickness in the rear (see **Figure 3.16b**).

There was a third method by which the smooth inner surface was provided. This was by using a cylindrical plate, which was shaped in the form of a barrel. The iron rings were shrunk fit over this barrel and later, the entire assembly was cast over with bronze. This composite cannon manufacture was another innovation of the Indian cannon technologists. One good example of this kind of cannon is the *Azdaha Paikar* located at Musa Burj of the Golconda Fort's outer rampart. We shall shortly see more about the cannon while discussing composite cannon technology.

Out of these three methods of providing the smooth inner surface, the use of staves appears to have been the most popular. This could probably be due to evenness of the surface produced by this method, and the maintenance of this smoothness even after repeated firing. It is possible that the staves manufactured were of high carbon steel to provide additional strength to the material here.

Another important aspect of cannon construction is the method by which the iron staves were joined at the extreme end of the cannon. There is no possibility of understanding the methodology based on the existing complete cannons in the Indian subcontinent. However, there is one forge-welded iron cannon that has been opened out in the back portion, the *Kadak Bijli* cannon at Jhansi Fort. This open section in the rear provides valuable clues to how the staves were joined to the rear end of the cannon.

Fig. 3.77: *Circular plates provided on the barrel of the bronze cannon lying in the A.P. State Museum at Hyderabad. Iron plates used for the manipulation of the bronze cannon.*

Fig. 3.78: *Inner smooth surface of the* Dal Mardan *cannon, as seen in this photograph of its front face.*

The iron staves proceed all the way to the rear end. Another interesting feature that we notice is that the thickness of the staves also increases on going into the cannon. At the rear end, the staves are clamped to the rear block by the hooped iron rings (see **Figure 3.16c**). The iron staves from the front end of the cannon progress all the way up to the rear section, where they were connected to the rear block (see **Figure 3.16d**).

Some unique features of the powder chamber design of the *Kadak Bijli* cannon can also be seen in **Figure 3.16c**. It appears that the gun powder was loaded in another cylindrical barrel of smaller diameter. This cylinder is of smaller diameter (10 cm) compared to the inner bore of the cannon. This hollow cylinder is made up of six plates, each about 6.5 cm wide. The inner diameter of this cylinder is 10 cm and it protrudes 22 cm from the rear portion onto the barrel of the cannon. The gun powder was probably filled up in this smaller cylinder and lighted, using the fuse hole placed on the top of the rear section. Therefore, this smaller cylindrical barrel should proceed up to the location of the fuse hole (see **Figure 3.16e**).

The next section of the cannon that will be addressed is the cascable. The extreme rear portion of the cannon is known as cascable in western terminology. In Persian terminology, the rear portion was known as *dharu-khana*. This is not the cascable, but refers to the powder chamber.

Let us see how the rear portions of forge-welded cannons were designed and constructed. There are several noticeable designs. In the first case, the rear part of the cannon ends abruptly with the provision of a rear plate in several cases. One such example is shown in **Figure 3.57**, which shows one of the two forge-welded cannons that is located in Kati Darwazah at Mudhol Fort. In the second case, the rear section is manufactured by using forge-welded rings of differing diameters to produce the tapered end (see **Figure 3.10d**), showing the rear portion of the *Rajagopala* cannon. In the forge-welded cannons, dated to a later time, the cascable takes typical European cannon designs and this has been skilfully executed by forging (see **Figure 3.14a** that shows the marvellous design of the rear portion of the *Bhavani Shankar* cannon). Moreover, these designs also permit the incorporation of more advanced powder chamber designs, as noted in the *Kadak Bijli* cannon.

Another feature noticed at the back of certain cannons is the provision of sighting arrangement, using which the gunner could take aim before firing. This sighting device sometimes had a counterpart in the front of the cannon for further aiding the cannon sighting. These features are noticed in the forge-welded cannon in front of the Fateh Darwazah in Golconda Fort (**Figure 3.79**).

In addition to these basic design features, the forge-welded cannons were provided with several decorative designs. These designs were sometimes chiselled out on the surface, as noted in the case of the *Bhavani Shankar* (see **Figures 3.14**) and *Kadak Bijli* (see **Figure 3.16a**) cannons in the Jhansi Fort. This shows the skill of the ancient Indian blacksmiths. They had to first forge weld the iron rings, and on top of that the designs were intelligently carved out using chisels. Several striking examples of intricate muzzle design can be noted in the forge-welded cannons discussed in the last section. For instance, the design on the cannon on the pivot at Basava Kalyan is noteworthy (see **Figure 3.47b**). It appears that the design of similar dragon-like features were common for muzzle faces, as can be seen in the forge-welded iron cannon at the A.P. State Archaeology Museum at Hyderabad (**Figure 3.80**) and at the Archaeological Museum at Bijapur (**Figure 3.81**). The special muzzle designs noticed on forge welded cannon in Naldurg and Daulatabad are shown in **Figure 3.82**. The lion design of muzzle face is another cannon occurance like the cannon at Amritpol Gate at Mehrangarh fort (see **Figure 3.83**)

Special decorations were sometimes provided on the iron cannons. Notice the interesting carving work done on the whole body of the cannon now located at the Andhra Pradesh State Museum at Hyderabad (**Figure 3.79a**). We had noted the inlay work in the case of the Basava Kalyan cannon (see **Figure 3.47b**).

In several cases, decorative bands were provided by special forge-welded rings, meant specifically for this purpose. These have been described in literature as "necklace" of the cannons. These decorative bands appear at different locations on the barrel, that is, around the trunnions, in the front and back portion of the cannon. One typical example of a decorative design on the forge-welded cannon (the cannon at Bada Burj on the Golconda Fort rampart) is shown in **Figure 3.41d**. When observations of the cannon were made in November 2003, all the iron rods that made up the decorative design were intact. Sadly, when the same cannon was studied in September 2005, several of the rods had been vandalised. This example also clearly brings out the slow but steady vandalism and destruction of these wonderful forge-welded cannons because of the lack of appreciation of these marvellous pieces. Their remote locations, far removed from public view, also complicate their preservation. There is an urgent need to collect all these massive cannons located at remote bastions in fort ramparts, and to place them in a centrally protected location where they can be supervised constantly.

COMPOSITE WROUGHT IRON-BRONZE CANNONS

Analysis of the historical development of bronze and wrought-iron cannon technologies in the Indian subcontinent reveals that the nature of firearms in the Mughal, Maratha and Deccan states remained almost the same throughout the seventeenth and first half of the eighteenth century, similar to what evolved at the end of Akbar's reign (1556-1605) (Khan 2004b: 91-127). One notable failure was the non-adoption of cast iron technology for cannon and cannon ball manufacture by the Indian states, which resulted in the ultimate domination of India by the European colonial powers. It was not that the Indians were not experts in casting technology. They simply failed to adopt the casting methodology because they were well-versed in forge-welding technology for manufacturing iron objects.

In spite of stagnation in cannon technology, there were two notable innovations that were implemented during this period. These were the use of light cannons resting on swivels fired from the backs of camels (*shaturnal* meaning "camel barrel") and the strengthening of wrought iron cannon barrels by casting them over with bronze (which

Fig. 3.79: *Sighting device at the back portion of the cannon noticed in the forge welded cannon in front of the Fateh Darwazah in Golconda Fort.*

Fig. 3.80: *Iron cannon located at the Andhra Pradesh State Museum at Hyderabad. (Photographs courtesy: S. Jaikishan).*

Fig. 3.81: *Excellent design on the muzzle of the forge welded cannon in front of ASI Museum at Bijapur*

(a)

(b)

Fig. 3.82: *Interesting muzzle designs on forge welded cannon at (a) Naldurj and (b) Daulatabad fort.*

Fig. 3.83: *Typical lion design of the muzzle noticed in the cannon located at Amritpol gate at Mehrangarh fort in Jodhpur.*

we may define as a composite cannon) (Khan 2004b: 91-127). There are several examples of *shaturnal* in several museums of India, for example the Red Fort Museum at New Delhi, Indore Museum, Gwalior, Mehrangarh and Alwar Museums. We shall not discuss *shaturnals* here but concentrate on composite cannons.

The composite cannon innovation may have been an attempt to economise on the use of copper (a relatively expensive metal then and even now), without weakening the barrel. European visitors admired these composite cannons, particularly the excellent joint between the iron and bronze sections. One commentator notes that, "nothing but the different colour of the two metals indicated the joining" (Thorn 1896: 139). The Maratha and Rajput cannon-makers also appear to have manufactured composite cannons in the eighteenth century. The strengthening of wrought iron cannon barrels, by casting them with bronze, is unique in the annals of cannon technology (Khan 2004b: 91-127).

According to Khan (2004b: 91-127), the earliest surviving composite cannon is located at Narwar Fort. The inscriptions on this cannon reveal its name *Fathjang*, and that it was manufactured in the Samvat 1753 (1696 CE) for use by Raja Jai Singh Sawai, a Rajput chief in the services of the Mughal Empire (Cunningham 1872: 317).

There are several composite cannons dating to Aurangzeb's reign. The first example is the *Azdaha Paikar* cannon (see **Figure 3.84a**), located on the Musa Burj of the Golconda outer rampart (Balasubramaniam 2005c: 389-408). The name of the cannon translates as "Dragon Body". Such fancy names were often given to cannons in the Mughal period. The inscriptions on the cannon provide the year of manufacture as 1674, thereby proving that it is older than the composite cannon at Narwar. Moreover, the weight of the gunpowder (11.0 kg) and shot (33.5 kg) are precisely known. The complete history, dimensions and engineering design (see **Figure 3.84b**) of the cannon have been described elsewhere (Balasubramaniam 2005c: 389-408). The front face of the cannon clearly indicates that it was manufactured by casting bronze on an iron assembly consisting of shrunk-fit iron rings over a cylindrical iron barrel. The inner iron barrel has been constructed by curling over two iron plates. The bore diameter is 24 cm and the overall diameter of the front face is 70 cm. The length of the cylindrical barrel, excluding the back portion, is 414 cm. The back portion adds another 38 cm, thereby providing the overall length of the cannon as 452 cm. Assuming the shrunk fit iron assembly to continue till the end of the barrel, the weight of the iron assembly (iron barrel and shrunk fit rings) has been estimated to be 3.28 tonne. The weight of the remaining portions, assuming it to be composed primarily of copper, is 13.72 tonne. Therefore, the overall weight of the cannon is 17 tonne. The excellent designs on the surface are noteworthy.

A smaller composite cannon located on top of the Golconda Fort (**Figure 3.85a**) indicates that iron staves were cast over with bronze. The cannon was fabricated in 1666 and is called *Qila Kusha* ("Conqueror of the Fort"). Its length is 325 cm, its muzzle diameter 38 cm and bore diameter 18 cm (Balasubramaniam *et. al.* 2005f: 503-538). The back portion of the cannon (see **Figure 3.85b**) indicates a central iron rod at the extreme end of the cannon and smaller iron rods placed regularly along the circumference of the base plate. These iron rods must be related to the manufacturing methodology of the cannon, with the central iron rod acting as a support for the iron assembly inside.

A wonderful example of Aurangzeb's composite cannon that was constructed with iron staves hooped over with iron rings and the entire assembly cast with bronze, is the *Tope Zafarbaksh* cannon located at Fort William (**Figure 3.86a**). The inscriptions on the cannon indicate that this was constructed in 1674 by one Mihir Das. This wonderful cannon is therefore the handiwork of the Hindu engineer employed by Aurangzeb. The cannon was used in the siege of Asir fort, as revealed by one inscription. The front face of the cannon indicates that the inner bore is composed of iron staves. *Tope Zafarbaksh* also shows the existence of iron chaplets on the body of the cannon. The provision of chaplets clearly indicates that the inner iron assembly, consisting of the iron rings hooped over the irons staves, were held in position in a vertical direction and fixed to the mould with the aid of chaplets. Molten bronze was then poured into the mould, and this resulted in the final composite cannon. There are several cannon marks on the surface of the cannon and several locations on the surface that have been damaged. One such location in the middle of the cannon indicates that the iron staves were hooped over with iron rings, and bronze was poured over the entire assembly. Indications are that a major portion of the cannon must be composed of iron. The rear portion of the cannon is also designed with intricate carvings (**Figure 3.86b**). This portion also provides valuable clues about the manufacturing technology. It appears that iron rods were also used in the rear end, as seen in the case of the other Mughal composite cannons. The wonderful designs found on the surface of the cannon must be appreciated.

We possess several other composite cannons of Aurangzeb. One located at Daulatabad is called *Qila Shikan* (Breaker of Forts) (see **Figure 3.87**). The composite cannons at Parenda fort are named *Malik Maidan* (Master of Battlefield) and *Azdaha Paikar* (Dragon Body). These two cannons are shown in **Figure 3.88**.

The design and construction of composite cannons is fascinating, and this reveals the skill of the medieval Indian metalsmiths in engineering such wonderful devices. This

(a)

(b)

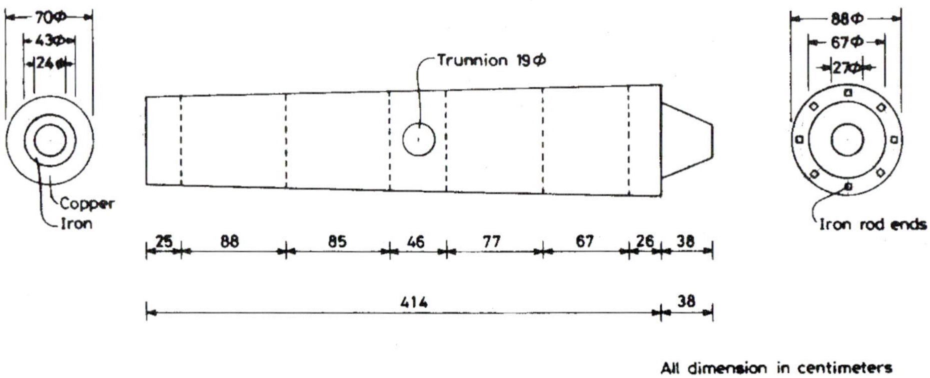

Fig. 3.84: *(a)* Azdaha Paikar *cannon located on the Musa Burj of the Golconda Fort rampart in Hyderabad and (b) its engineering design.*

(a)

(b)

Fig. 3.85: *(a) The composite iron-bronze Mughal cannon, named* Qila Kusha *located on top of the Golconda Fort in Hyderabad, and (b) rear portion showing iron rods used in its construction.*

(a)

(b)

Fig. 3.86: *(a) Mughal cannon of Aurangzeb's period called* Tope Zafarbaksh, *now located at Fort William in Kolkata and (b) rear side of cannon.*

Fig. 3.87: *The* Qila Shikan *cannon at Daulatabad Fort.*

would have required a very good understanding of metallurgy and also metallurgical operation of wrought iron manufacture and bronze casting technology.

UNSOLVED QUESTIONS

There are numerous massive cannons scattered all over the forts of India that are begging for attention. There is a great need for scholars from different disciplines to study these wonderful pieces and highlight the metallurgical aspects of forge-welded cannon technology practised in India. There is only limited technical literature on how the cannons were fabricated (both iron and bronze ones) and, therefore, this exercise would help in understanding the history of science and technology, a very important aspect of Indian society during the medieval times. There are several other unresolved questions related to cannon technology in India that need to be resolved like the kind of cannon balls used, the effectiveness of the cannons in breeching fortifications, the estimate of cannon ball travel and thrust based on available cannon dimensions, cannon ball weight and gunpowder weight, the manufacture, storage and use of gunpowder, details of gun carriages, handling of the large cannons, procedure adopted for firing the cannons, details of accessory and special complementary equipment, the organisation of the artillery, the depiction of cannons in Indian miniature paintings from all available sources, the cannon

(a)

(b)

Fig. 3.88: *Massive composite cannons at Parenda Fort: (a)* Malik Maidan *and (b)* Azdaha Paikar.

technology as practised by different powers (Mughals, Marathas, Sikhs, Rajputs), the European gunners and foundry personnel who were in the service of Indian monarchs, the locations of foundries and workshops where the cannons were fabricated, the influence of European cast iron technology on Indian forge-welded cannon technology, and information about forge-welded cannons that were deliberately destroyed by the Europeans. The last point may seem surprising because the European powers took great efforts to destroy the numerous forge-welded cannons from the Indian forts that they captured. Dupliex mentions that an enormous number of forge-welded cannons were taken from Senji fort to Pondicherry and melted there (Deloche 2000). Therefore, there is a great need to study the history, evolution, epigraphy and social impact of cannon technology, apart from detailed technical study of cannon manufacture, material characterisation and both destructive and non-destructive testing (like radiography) to determine the inner construction details.

These marvellows cannon pieces, which once decided the fate of dynasties, have long gone silent. They are either lying uncared for in fort ramparts or residing as mute spectators in museums. The sight of **Figure** 3.89 of a lonely cannon atop Medak fort in Andhra Pradesh is common in the Indian sub-continent. If one focuses attention on these cannons, approaches them with wonder and hears them out in patient silence, these pieces of Indian metallurgical skill will spew forth their nostalgic memories.

Fig 3.89: *Lonely cannon atop Medak fort in Andhra Pradesh*

4

WOOTZ STEEL

EARLY IDEAS ABOUT THE INTRODUCTION OF IRON TRADITION INTO INDIA FROM THE West have now been proven incorrect. There are firm early dates for the advent of iron in the Indian subcontinent. The independent origin of iron in the Indian subcontinent has been convincingly argued by Chakrabarti (1992) and Tripathi (2007) in the complemantary volume in this series. Agrawal and Kharakwal (2002) have compiled all radiocarbon dates of excavated iron manufacturing sites in the Indian subcontinent. The earliest available date at present is from Raja-Nal-Ka-Tila in Uttar Pradesh. The radiocarbon dating of iron-making sites has been updated by Tripathi (2007).

One of the greatest material discoveries to originate from the Indian subcontinent is Deccani wootz steel, often referred to as "the wonder material of the orient" (Sachse 1994, Srinivasan and Ranganathan 2004). This was the material from which the famed Damascus blades were made. The high-quality wootz swords, knives and armour were artistically embellished with carvings and inlays of brass, silver, and gold. These were specially made for important persons, for ceremonial functions, etc. A separate book dealing with wootz steel will appear as a complementary work. The description given below is only an introduction to wootz steel.

APPLICATIONS OF WOOTZ STEEL

Swords

Swords in ancient times were the equivalent to the firearms of today. Therefore, they were basically functional and well-made equipment. It was the cutting quality that was most treasured. The best swords and warfare objects were designed for absolutely critical life-and-death situations in the battlefield and not meant for display purposes. Such arms were not ornately gilded and silver-chased. The best swords were, at the most, coated with blood from the battlefield! Such was the greatness of blades made of Deccani wootz. **Figure 4.1** shows some typical swords made of wootz steel, while smaller blades are seen in **Figure.** 4.2.

There is no way that the technology of wootz steel and making swords from wootz originated outside the Indian subcontinent. It was only after the entry of Islam into India that the technology for manufacturing swords out of wootz steel was learnt from the local artisans. However, the best wootz steel cakes were still produced in India, although we also hear of their production in some central Asian centres. There is historical evidence to back the claim of primacy of Indian skill in making wootz steel and manufacturing excellent swords out of them.

One contemporary manual provides the testimony of weapons of battle from the Sultanate period (Digby 2001). This manual of war was called *Adab al-harb wa'l-shaj'a*, written by Fakhr-i Mudabbir during the reign of Iltutmish from CE 1210-36. The most commonly employed weapon of close combat was the sword. The bow was the primary weapon of the horsemen and they could be deployed from a distance. The terror and the majesty of the sword were greater than those of the other weapons and, therefore, when a kingdom was taken by force of arms, it was said to have been won by the sword. While his evidence regarding the superiority of the Muslim bows over the Indian ones is indecisive, he is clear that the Indians had superior techniques or material for the manufacture of the sword. Swords of different kinds are quoted in this text, namely Chini, Rusi, Khazari, Rumi, Firangi, Yamani, Bilamani (read Saylamani), Shahi, Slai, Hindi and Kashmiri. First, this implies that there was a great trade in arms extending through the medieval Islamic world from Europe to China. All the varieties that the author encountered are famous swords, but he states that the best among them all was the *Hindi* sword and the most lustrous (*gawahar-dartar*). Many other references reveal the high esteem in which *Hindi* swords were held throughout the medieval Islamic world, rightly attested by their exports to such distant areas as Umayyid Spain and Seljuq Anatolia.

Fakhr-i Mudabbir further identifies several varieties of *Hindi* swords, whose names are not readily identifiable. The most costly and choicest of them all was the one called *mawj-i-darya* (waves of the sea, identifying the watering of the blade). He also mentions that of all the other varieties that he had named, none was made outside India. Moreover,

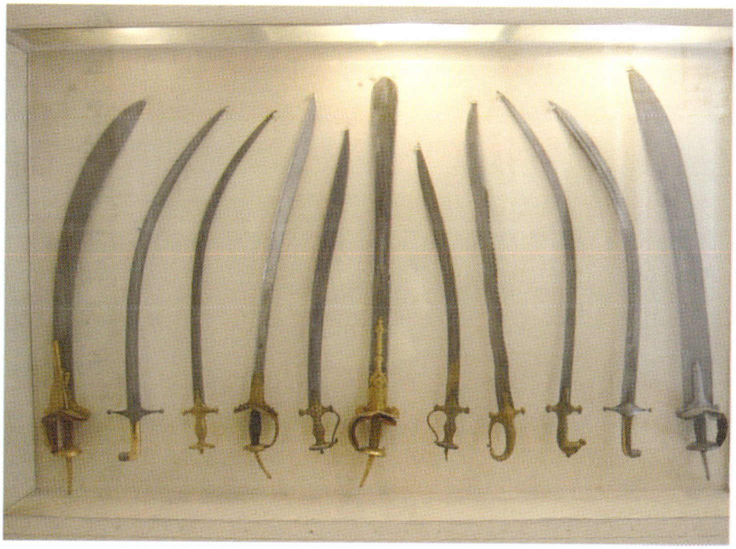

Fig. 4.1: *Typical long swords made from wootz steel from the Mehrangarh museum, Jodhpur. Notice the different varieties based on their shape and design of the hilt.*

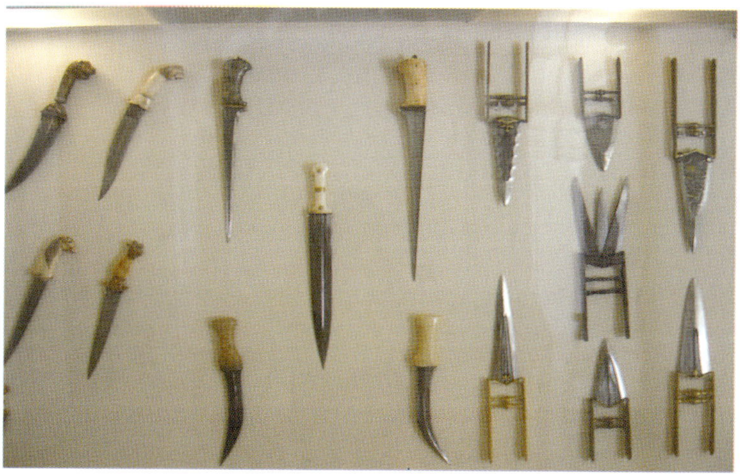

Fig. 4.2: *Typical small blades made from wootz steel from the Mehrangarh museum, Jodhpur.*

the *Hindi* swords possessed the hardest blades of all swords. Fakhr-i Mudabbir also mentions another kind of sword used in Hindustan in which silver and copper are added to soft iron. On account of silver, it was supposed to be more pliable and if one was wounded by this sword, the wound did not heal easily.

Another interesting fact that Fakhr-i Mudabbir states is about a city on the banks of the Sindh, where the ironsmiths were masters of the craft and produced by their process of forging, a blade watered like a date palm leaf. He also quotes that these blades were cherished by the Ranas, Thakurs and men of the tribes, and they were very sharp for wounding. This makes it clear that the best swords were in the hands of the Rajputs and not the invaders (Digby 2001).

The wootz steel was legendary because it was used in making excellent blades, which were highly prized in the Middle Eastern bazaars during the middle ages. The Europeans procured these blades from Damascus, a large trading centre in the Middle Ages. These were among the best swords available in Europe at that time. The Damascus blades were known to be extremely hard and tough, and could retain their cutting edge for a long time. The Damascus blades were distinguishable from other inferior blades by the distinctive and beautiful watery patterns, called the *damask*, obtained on the surface of the blade after polishing and etching with a mild vegetable acid (**Figure 4.3**). The Arab traders used to baffle their customers about the fineness of the edge by slicing a gauze handkerchief in mid-air with the sharpened blades. This added to the saga of the Damascus blades.

The wonderful swords from Persia were much appreciated throughout the world. They were traded and known in Europe through the trading centre of Damascus in modern-day Syria. Therefore, the Europeans called these swords as Damascus blades. A typical Indian sword wrought from Deccani wootz is shown in **Figure 4.4**. This sword can be classified as a typical Indian *talwar* based on the design of its hilt, which is of iron covered by a thick layer of yellow gold. The blade is of wootz steel and bears a gold inlaid Arabic inscription on its spine. An inscription made as a series of small punched marks is translated as "the work of Kalb 'Ali, son of Assadullah of Isfahan." Isfahan was a major centre of sword-making in Persia, ancient Iran.

Where did the Isfahan blacksmiths obtain the raw material used for forging? Voysey (1832) in his article on the "Description of the Native Manufacture of Steel in Southern India" writes:

(a)

(b)

Fig. 4.3: *(a) Details of one blade at Mehrangarh museum, Jodhpur and (b) another blade showing more clearly "Mohammed's Ladder" pattern.*

> The export, however, of the metal to Persia must be profitable, as it is sufficient to bring dealers from that country and to defray the cost and risk of travelling. We found at the village (named Kona Samundram, 12 miles south of the Godaveri and 25 miles from Nirmul, celebrated for its manufacture of steel), in 1820, Haji Hussy, from Ispahan, engaged in the speculation; and it must have answered his purpose, as he was here again in 1823, having returned in the interval to Persia and disposed of the venture. He informed us that the place and the process are both familiar to the Persians and that they have attempted to imitate the latter without success.

It should also be noted that in spite of the large costs involved in the transportation of the wootz cakes from India to the Middle East, its transformation into swords, and then its further travel to Europe, it was still a profitable enterprise. This speaks volumes about the premium the blades used to fetch in the European markets.

The *damask* pattern was a sign of quality. These macroscopic watermarks resulted because of thermomechanical processing of wootz ingot in a particular manner. The ingenuity resided in the skilful manner in which the wootz cakes were forged by the Indian and Middle Eastern blacksmiths. The legend of the steel grew when the European smiths tried, often without success, to make such implements.

Of more basic concern was the starting material – wootz cakes. Numerous attempts were made by the Arabs and the Europeans to produce wootz steel. Several commissions were established in Europe to reproduce wootz steel. Brilliant minds were engaged in understanding the mystery of Wootz. The works of Faraday in England, Anossoff in Russia and Breant in France are noteworthy (Wadsworth and Sherby 1980, 1985). A large number of elements, including precious metals such as gold, silver, and platinum, were added to iron to obtain the material which would result in the *damask* pattern. These attempts proved to be largely unsuccessful and this added to the mystery of the Damascus blade.

Armour

It is also known that wootz steel was used in other applications related to warfare equipment. Wootz steel, with a texture similar to that noted in Damascus swords, was also used in shields and armour. There are several fine examples in museums of India. Wootz steel was usually employed in the form of plates of a simple shape inserted in

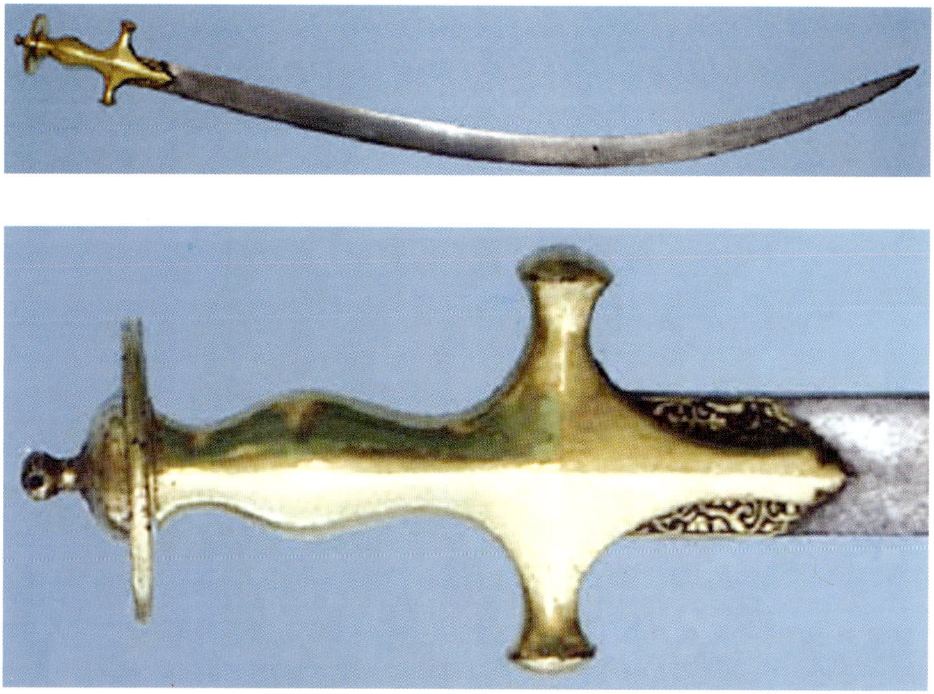

Fig. 1.1: *A typical Indo-Muslim hilt of* Delhishahi *form, likely in the eighteenth century. Many authorities would classify this as a* talwar *based upon this hilt, which is of iron covered by a thick layer of yellow gold. A false ricasso, in the form of two plates with an embossed and gilded intertwined floral pattern, may be seen behind the langets covering the root of the blade. The blade is of wootz steel and bears a gold inlaid Arabic inscription on its spine, likely to be a religious invocation or prayer. A cartouche with an inscription made as a series of small punched marks is present and is illustrated. Overall length: 92.5 cm (36.2 inches); blade length: 80 cm (31.2 inches). The inscription is executed in a very different manner as a series of very small punches and may be translated as "the work of Kalb 'Ali, son of Assadullah of Isfahan". Text and photographs courtesy: Lee Jones.*

larger structures. Several examples can be found in the collection of National Museum, New Delhi (Pant and Sharma 2001). Smith (1965) mentions a cuirass of a north Indian set of armour (ca. CE 1700) possessing a rectangular piece of watered steel about 12 x 15 inches, riveted (almost invisibly) into a plain steel surround, now located at the Metropolitan Museum of Art in New York. Pant and Sharma (2001) provide some excellent examples of Indian swords and armour from the National Museum, New Delhi.

One example of wootz steel used in helmets is seen in **Figure 4.5**, while the use of wootz for body armour is illustrated in **Figure 4.6**. Pant was a renowned expert on Indian arms and has authored several books on this subject. The evolution, origins and classification of various types of sword blades and hilts have been researched in detail by Pant (1980).

Firearms

Another major application of wootz steel was in the manufacture of small firearms. The advent of gunpowder and its use for projecting objects at great velocities led to the development of other technologies. Apart from cannons, development of guns (i.e. firearms) was a major development. *Sukraniti*, a sixteenth century Sanskrit text, has mentioned these small arms in addition to cannons (Bag 2005: 657-662). In this treatise, *khudra-nalika* stood for small guns or matchlocks and *brihan-nalika* for big guns or cannon. The *Sukraniti* also mentions that the matchlock was 2½ cubits long with a longitudinal bore of the thickness of the middle finger and provided with two raised points in order to take aim. The gunpowder was ignited by means of a fuse, the fire being originated by either a fuse wire (match-locks) or percussion of powdered stone struck with a hammer (flintlock). The matchlocks had wooden handles and were used by the infantry and the cavalry. This was in contrast to the big guns which were carried in carriages. The range of guns depended on the thickness of the metal-plate and bore, their length and size of balls.

The medieval army employed a variety of projectile devices, apart from cannons. The terms used for these light arms were slightly different among the Mughals, Sikhs and the Marathas. Matchlock and flintlock guns were called *tufangs* and were used by the Mughal infantry. An example of a *tufang*, preserved at the Golconda fort, is shown in **Figure 4.7**. Notice the relatively long barrel made of iron attached to the wooden stock. Such arms were used in the defence of fortifications as well as in field battle.

There are several Mughal miniature paintings where firearms have been depicted. One typical example showing the use of firearms in field battle (here in naval battle) is seen in **Figure 4.8**, in an illustration from the *Akbar Nama*. The use of handheld muskets in defending fortifications can be noted from **Figure 4.9**, which shows again a Mughal miniature painting from *Akbar Nama* (c. 1600). In this painting, gunners can be seen firing light cannons and muskets from the rampart of a fort. In this case, the barrels of the muskets are supported by the crenels on the fort ramparts. However, it was also possible for the barrels to be supported by a tripod that facilitated shooting.

Fig. 4.5: *A typical helmet fabricated out of wootz steel.*

Fig. 4.6: *Typical body protection gear wrought out of wootz steel.*

Fig. 4.7: *Medieval period matchlocks, known as* tufangs, *in this example from the Golconda Fort in Hyderabad.*

Fig. 4.8: *Mughal miniature painting from* Akbar Nama *showing the use of firearms in field battle.*

Fig. 4.9: *Mughal miniature painting from* Akbar Nama *showing the use of firearms in defending fortifications.*

The matchlocks were of different sizes. Akbar's matchlocks were of two sizes, 66 inches and 44 inches. They were made of rolled strips of wootz steel with two edges welded together. The barrel was damascened and decorated with gold or silver wires. The barrel was sometimes provided with inscriptions. The wooden stock was sometimes inlaid with ivory. The heavier matchlocks were mounted on tripods and called *sakh-i-tufang*. In the early days they were loaded with muzzle loading rods. The flintlock guns (called as *chaqmaki* or *toredar*) were introduced later.

The flint gun was not common. In his memoirs, Jahangir writes, "I had in my possession a certain fowling piece, for which I understand Mirza Rustum had offered to the former owner the sum of Rs 12000 and 12 horses, without success. As this appeared to me an extravagant price I wrote to enquire what were the peculiar excellences of the piece and I was informed in reply that if fired 100 times successively without intermission, it was never inconveniently heated, and secondly, that that was a flintlock and not a matchlock, being self-igniting, thirdly, a ball discharge from it never missed the mark."

There were several other Indian states that adopted the use of firearms on a large scale. The Sikh infantry, especially during the time of Ranjit Singh, who took special interest in the development of artillery and infantry, included matchlock guns (consisting of a long barrel of wrought iron which was attached to a wooden belt and wrapped with metal bands) known as *bandook toradar*. It was fired by a *fatila* (slow light match). In its operation, the gunpowder was loaded from the muzzle end using a muzzle-loading rod. On triggering, the *fatila* was brought in contact with the powder in the flash pan and the gun was fired. The name *toradar* derives from fibre stalks of elephant creeper called *tor* or *taur*, which was used for the slow matches after drying. This was commonly used in the seventeenth century by the Mughals. They were very impressive and it has been mentioned that they struck men at a distance of nine hundred paces.

Flintlocks were of European origin and they reached in the late sixteenth century, but could replace the matchlocks and wheel locks only in the eighteenth century. The Sikhs were the first to realise their importance and used them on a large scale. Flintlock was a long barrelled piece, firing with flint and pan. It was called as *bandook pathar kala* or *bandook chaqmaq*. There was no lighted match but it contained a self-contained ignition mechanism in which a hammer striking a piece of flint produced a spark that ignited the gunpowder placed in the pan. Sometimes, *sangins* (bayonets) were attached to the front part of the barrel. These Indian flintlocks were praised by the British who placed them at par with their pieces.

We again notice the use of wootz steel for the barrel of the flintlocks. The wonderful pieces of medieval Indian firearms indicate barrels covered with elaborate damascened patterns, thereby indicating that wootz steel was used in their construction. Moreover, the surfaces were often embossed with metal work with various designs inscribed either in lacquer or painting or by inlaying different materials. The most fancy of them were engraved with gold and the butt built of ivory or ebony cap. The bands that were used to hold the barrel with the stock were made of gold, silver, brass or steel. Sometimes they were of perforated design and also chased.

Bagnold (1826: 1-3) has provided an account of manufacture of gun barrels from wootz steel. The pistol was introduced sometime in the early eighteenth century in India. It was called *tamanchah* or *tameanchah* (meaning a sharp blow). These were essentially used by higher ranked people. The Indian pistols followed the British design, which was highly developed. Here again we find that the material used for the barrel was wootz steel.

Musical Strings

Wootz steel was used in other applications where exceptional soundness and hardness were necessary, for instance, in cutting implements of various kinds. Another application where it was probably important was in the manufacture of fine steel wires for use in musical instruments. For this purpose, structurally sound ingots with very few non-metallic inclusions are necessary. Channapatna, near Mysore, was famous for manufacturing these wires for musical instruments.

WHAT IS WOOTZ?

Wootz steel is primarily iron containing a high percentage of carbon (1.0-1.8% C). It should be mentioned that the term steel used in modern parlance normally means an alloy of iron and carbon. By this definition, most of the bloomery iron, after being refined and carburised in the smithy, has enough carbon to be called steel. The term wootz should therefore be used only for the high carbon alloy produced by the crucible melting process.

In terms of modern metallurgical parlance, wootz steel is a hypereutectic ferro-carbon alloy with partially and heterogeneously spheroidised cementite, with carbon contents between 1.3% – 1.8%. In order to process wootz steel cakes into fine swords, the wootz discs were cut open longitudinally. They were then skilfully worked through several stages by beating, tempering, sharpening and finally etching the surface. This required very careful control of metallurgical parameters. The metallurgy of this material and its subsequent processing into blades will be addressed in brief here. It is important to show that ancient Indians mastered the complexities involved in both special steel production and their processing into fine cutting edge objects. The high-carbon containing wootz steel cakes were manufactured in the Deccan in large amounts and were shipped to centres of sword production in India and all over the Islamic world during the medieval period. The exceptionally long and localised monopoly of the smelters in the Deccan in the production of wootz cakes must be appreciated (Panseri 1962: 29-30).

The surface of the blade showed an intricate wavy pattern, the best *jauhar* (pattern) being the circles and waves popularly called the *lahriyadar*. There also exist complete manuals on this craft, called the *Shamshernamas*. Thus, from the time of Alexander, Herodotus, Pliny, Al-Biruni, Fakhr-I-Mudabbir, we constantly come across superlatives being used to describe the Indian swords. There are separate sections in the *Adab al-harb wa'l-shaj'a* and in the various *Jawaharnamahs* on the Indian swords.

The English word wootz is a corruption of the basic word for steel found in Indian languages, especially the ones spoken in the South. A simple approach to the problem is the linguistic one. Most of the South Indian languages have a specific word for steel. We therefore notice *uruku/uruki* in Tamil, *urku/ukku* in Kannada, *ukk/urukku/ukku* in Malayalam and *ujk/ukku/ukki/karc* in Kodagu (*karc* means very hard brittle steel). There are several other intricacies regarding etymology (Toussaint 2002: 39-46), but we shall not discuss them here.

EARLY EUROPEAN ENCOUNTERS

The Europeans first came into contact with the swords wrought of Deccan wootz steel cakes during the crusade wars. The use of Damascus swords was immortalised by Sir Walter Scott in his 1871 fictional book *The Talisman*. In this famous book, Scott narrates a meeting between Richard the Lionhearted and the Saracen King Saladin in the twelfth century CE. The two adversaries were showing off the virtues of their swords. Richard cleaved an iron mace to demonstrate the strength and toughness of his heavy, two-handed, straight blade. In reply, Saladin took a silk cushion and "drew [his] scimitar across the cushion . . .with so little apparent effort that the cushion seemed rather to fall asunder than to be divided by violence . . ." This demonstrated the sharpness of his blade. To further prove that this was not a magic trick, Saladin then sliced through a limp cloth veil in midair. This really startled the Europeans. Interestingly, Scott describes Saladin's marvellously sharp and wieldy weapon as a curved and narrow blade, which "glittered not like the swords of the Franks, but was, on the contrary, of a dull blue colour, marked with 10 millions of meandering lines." He was certainly referring to a sword exhibiting *damask* pattern made out of Deccani wootz. *The Talisman* was made into two movies and a BBC television mini-series, and this revived the fame of Deccani wootz and Damascus swords in modern times.

The fame of Damascus swords was for real. European crusaders received a fright when they encountered wootz-based Damascus swords in action. A swinging blow with a Damascus sword made of "*telingana*" steel could cut a man in two even if he was protected with the best European armour. Crusader helmets were of no use against these swords. Remarkably, the swords never shattered or broke even with very rough use. And the best part was that the swords retained the sharp edge even after continuous use. These famed stories of the Damascus blades have been so much quoted in literature that it cannot just be a myth, but has to be a fact.

These highly prized swords were also traded in Europe from Damascus in Syria. Therefore, these swords were called as Damascus blades by the Europeans. The use of "Damascus" while referring to the blades does not provide proper appreciation for the origin of such swords from the Indian subcontinent. The manufacture of wootz cakes, and fabrication of swords from these cakes, were known even prior to the arrival of Muslims in India. The Indian blacksmiths were very intelligent smelters as well as blacksmiths. This is attested by the large number of iron and steel weapons discovered routinely by archaeologists in Andhra Pradesh and Karnataka. The Deccani Kakatiyas were renowned for their swords and skilled swordsmanship. Wootz steel was transported all over India to centres of excellent sword manufacture in Rajasthan, Bihar, Punjab, etc. Later, with the arrival of Muslim rule in India, a large amount of wootz cakes was traded to the Arab world. Swords fabricated from wootz were traded in Damascus, a city in modern-day Syria. Damascus was a trading and manufacturing centre, quite similar to what Singapore is today. The semi-finished wootz swords and blanks were imported from the Deccan, and they were worked upon by the artistic swordsmiths and armourers of Syria, Iran, Armenia and Caucasus to manufacture the so-called Damascus blades. Apart from swords, the blanks were also worked into knives and high-class armour. These were sold at Damascus.

There is another interesting origin for the word Damascus sword. The typical pattern noticed on the surface of Damascus sword was called "watered silk" or damask cloth. European importers bought damask cloth at Damascus. If two thin silk cloths of plain weave are held close together against a light, a characteristic pattern is seen. This is technically called *moire* interference pattern.

The manufacturers of wootz steel and skilled swordsmiths were equally responsible for the most prized category of swords in the medieval world. It was a hi-tech material of the ancient world. There was really nothing mysterious or magical about it. It was a material that was developed with a great deal of intelligent hard work, empirical observation, and by trial and error pounding away at the anvil.

PRIMACY OF DECCANI WOOTZ

What is the evidence for the use of such high carbon steels in the Indian subcontinent? We shall first look at literary and then archaeological evidence.

Quintus Curtis mentions that a present of steel cakes was made to Alexander of Macedonia (323 BCE) by Porus, an Indian chief, whose country he had invaded. This shows that the material was much valued, and as Neogi (1914) comments, "we can hardly believe that a matter of about thirty pounds weight of steel would have been considered a present worthy of the acceptance by the conqueror of the world, had the manufacture of that substance been practiced by any of the nations of the West in the days of Alexander".

A world famous metallurgist, Sir Robert Hadfield (1912), has mentioned the possibility of the use of Indian steel chisels and craftsmen in the construction of the Egyptian pyramids. The so-called earliest steel piece to have been discovered from the Gizeh pyramid and dated to 2750 BCE (El Gayar and Jones 1989: 75-83) has been shown to belong to a much later period (Craddock and Lang 1993: 57-59). Iron must have been a prized object because daggers of both gold and iron were found on Tutankhamen's mummy, which is dated to 1350 BCE.

Neogi noted that there is no evidence to show that any of the nations of antiquity, besides the Hindus, were acquainted with the art of making steel. He stated that the references to iron by the Greek and Latin writers reveal their ignorance and not understanding. Although they frequently refer to the qualities of steel, they never refer to the method by which it was prepared from iron. It is now established that a maritime intercourse was maintained from the remotest antiquity between the Malabar Coast, the Persian Gulf, the country about the mouths of the Indus and the Red Sea (Ratnagar 1981: 157-200). Therefore, the proposal that the steel from Deccan found its way by these routes to the country of Porus, to the nations of Europe and to Egypt is not unreasonable. In the fourth-fifth century BCE, in the Persian Court, Ktesias was presented with two swords of Indian steel by the Malloi. According to *Periplus of the Erythrean Sea,* Indian steel was being exported to Abyssinia.

Coming to archaeological evidence, we note Hadfield's (1912) finding of high carbon in the samples analysed from Taxila and from the Sri Lankan region, and therefore attesting to the existence of high carbon steel and the idea of carburisation of iron in order to manipulate its properties. Neogi (1914) proposed that the numerous Ashokan pillars, which have been stone cut in a faultless manner from large blocks of stone, must have been possible with the use of the finest steel saws and steel chisels in India in the fourth century BCE. The use of a large number of surgical instruments quoted in the *Sushruta* (third century BCE), some of which "could bisect a hair longitudinally", also points out to the use of steel in India in making cutlery and surgical instruments in pre-Christian times.

Carburisation was known to Indians quite early in history. Ghosh and Chattopadhyay (1982) have reported an iron sickle found at Barudih in Bihar dated to 810 BCE. It contained 0.35% C, 0.2% Si, 0.2% S, 0.5% P and 0.04% Mn. Metallographic examination has shown the presence of 40% pearlite phase, and at some places tempered martensite at the sharp edge. Hadfield (1912) has analysed several iron objects from Taxila and found them to contain 1.3 to 1.5% C. According to him, the main feature of these specimens, belonging to first and second century BCE, was their high carbon percentage, namely 1.23% in one of the samples. He found that a chisel showed distinct signs of carburisation varying on the two faces "from saturation point (.9 per cent) to about .2 per cent carbon on the outside edge". Hadfield further remarked that "The presence of martensite and hardenite suggests the important information that the chisel has been quenched". The hardness and microstructure of two other samples indicated the presence of high carbon but these samples did not show the presence of martensitic structure. Hadfield concluded that he had never earlier come across any other specimen with such high carbon elsewhere and that the Indians in Taxila at this time made high carbon steel deliberately. Sir Robert concludes, "the author believes this to be the first time there has been put up on record evidence of the art of cementation having been known 1500 to 2000 years ago, as shown by these specimens; probably therefore, such knowledge could be traced back still further".

Abundant evidence is forthcoming to testify to the fact that India supplied iron for the famous Damascus blades. Sir George Birdwood (Neogi 1914: 32-40) says:

> Indian steel was celebrated from the earliest antiquity, and the blades of Damascus which maintained their pre-eminence even after the blades of Toledo became celebrated, were in fact of Indian iron. Ctasian mentions two wonderful Indian blades which were presented to him by the king of Persia and his mother. The Ondanique of Marco Polo's travels refers originally, as Col. Vule has shown, to Indian steel, the word being a corruption of the Persian Hundwany, i.e. Indian steel. The same word found its way into Spanish in the shape of "Al-hinde" and "al-finde" first with the meaning of steel and then of a steel mirror and finally of the metal foil of a glass mirror. The Ondanique of Kirman, which Marco Polo mentions, was so called from its comparative excellence, and the swords of Kirman were eagerly sought after in the fifteenth and sixteenth centuries CE by the Turks who gave great prices for them. Arrian mentions steel as imported into

the Abyssinian ports, and Salmasius mentions that the surviving Greek treatises was one on the tempering of Indian steel.

Feuerbach (2002) agrees that there is evidence suggesting that Wootz steel was produced earlier in India. Pliny (died 79 CE) wrote,"But of all the varieties of iron the palm goes to the Seres with their fabrics and skins. The second prize goes to Parthian iron; and indeed no other kinds of iron are forged from pure metal, as all the rest have a softer alloy welded with them" (Pliny, XXXIV translated by Rackham 1995: 232-233, 143-146). The Seres are the Tamil Cheras of South India (Juleff 1996). Bronson (1986) has argued that there is no evidence that the Cheras were producing and exporting wootz to Rome. However, the large number of Roman coins found in the Chera territory attests to the robust trade of the Deccanis with the Romans. The Tamil Cheras of South India are known to have been wootz steel producers from at least the third century BCE based on recent archaeological finds (Rajan 1989-90: 111-113 and 1990: 93-102; Craddock 1998: 41-66; Srinivasan and Griffiths 1997: 111-125).

That sword manufacture from wootz steel was practised widely in the Indian subcontinent is proved by noting the locations in medieval India where swords were manufactured. *Yuktikalpataru*, a manuscript of the eleventh century, mentions that swords were manufactured in Benares, Magadha, Ceylon, Nepal, Anga, Mysore, Surat and Orissa (Kalinga), and describes the qualities of the swords manufactured in the various places (Neogi 1914: 32-40). A similar reference is found in *Sharangadhar-Padhati*, a work undoubtedly composed in the fourteenth century by the alchemist Sharangadhar. In the fourteenth century, the following places were noted for the manufacture of swords—Khatikhattara, Rishi, Banga (Bengal), Shurporaka, Videha (Mithila or Tirhut), Anga (Bhagulpur), Madyama-gram, Bedideaha, Sahagram, and Kalinjar. It also refers to swords manufactured in China being "faultless and pure". (Neogi 1914: 32-40). In *Sharangadhar Padhati* as well as in *Yuktikalpataru*, long chapters on the dimensions and qualities of swords as well as on varieties of iron and their different colours have been inserted (Neogi 1914: 32-40). A Telugu text of the medieval period, *Kadaga Lakshana Shiromani*, provides qualities of different varieties of swords and this implies that the blacksmith was well- versed with different types of wootz steel and their processing (Balasubramaniam 2006: 587-589).

It is interesting to note that while the investigators of wootz, during the time when the British ruled India, highly praised wootz, the scholars are not so forthcoming in their praise after Indian independence. This also applies to several other technologies of the past in which India excelled. What is the reason for this grudge when India is a free country? Maybe the same psychology is at work as propounded by Macaulay to denigrate anything that is Indian so that the Indian people are not made to feel proud of their heritage and keep thinking that whatever is best always had to come from the West. Let us look at one recent example. Bronson (1986) in her review on this celebrated steel has questioned the origin of this Indian technology, and tried to give credit to this material to the Arabian countries. However, the Arabians possessed only knowledge of the qualities of this steel and considered it worthwhile to journey all the way to India to procure it.

Prakash (1989b: 95-96) refuted Bronson's claim by showing the antiquity of wootz steel in the Indian subcontinent as revealed by the detailed classification of iron-carbon alloys. Prakash (1989) provided circumstantial evidence, like the texts of *Brhatsamhita* of Varahamihira and *Rasaratnasamuccaya* and others to prove that India was indeed the pioneer in producing different kinds of wootz and malleable steel. Bronson (1986) grudgingly concedes that "India may have invented or perfected from the second century CE the idea of crucible steel making, but that should not be accepted as given in medieval studies".

It is known that *Rasaratnasamuccaya's* 'bluish black' *Kalayasa* (5.82), which had been mentioned much earlier in Kautilya's *Arthasastra* (2.17.14), corresponded beautifully with the Damascus sword, 'the sharpened edges of which do not get spoiled by hammering', and thus establishes India's primacy not only in wootz but also in finished steel. Fuerbach has analysed the origin of the term *"pulad"*, which is commonly used in Central Asia to denote crucible steel. She concluded that it did indeed originate from a Sanskrit based language, and used the proposed etymology to support the hypothesis that crucible steel originated in a region where a Sanskrit language was spoken. She proposes that crucible steel might have developed somewhere between northern India and eastern Persia/ Central Asia during the first half of the first millennium BCE. However, this will have to await the discovery of crucible making sites from this region and their accurate dating. Till then, the earliest evidence of crucible steel making is from the Deccan. It is therefore the Deccan where the story of wootz begins.

Feuerbach (2002) agrees that information regarding the spread of the technology, ingots and/or finished objects by trade is sparse. She quotes, "Al-Kindi and other Islamic writers provide some information on production and distribution centres, however the picture of the spread of the material and/or technology is incomplete. Apparently, over the next thousand plus years beginning the 4th century CE, crucible steel spread to the

Middle East, Africa, and Europe as far as Spain with Islamic armies, into Austria with Ottoman Turks, and occasionally as far west as England through trade. Crucible steel objects also spread northeast to Siberia and possibly as far east as China, Korea, and perhaps Japan. However, it seems that the technological know-how remained restricted to Central Asia and India."

Very few excavations of wootz production sites have been conducted in India. The few studies indicate crucibles dated 250 BCE in Tamil Nadu. The site at Kodumanal is dated to the third century BCE — third century CE. It is the earliest dated site containing crucibles that were used for wootz steel production (Rajan 1989-90: 111-113 and 1990: 93-102; Craddock 1998: 41-66; Srinivasan and Griffiths 1997: 111-125).

EUROPEAN ATTEMPTS TO DUPLICATE

Over the centuries, therefore, the wonderful surface pattern of the true wootz-made swords led to many attempts at similar fabrications in Persia, Central Asia, Far East, Europe and within India itself. One useful method of producing cutting objects with wavy surface patterns was by lamination of different grade steels. A good review of laminated cutting objects from around the world has been written by Wadsworth and Lesuer (2000). In Rajasthan, smiths heat-welded strips of wrought iron and steel which were twisted and beaten so as to eventually produce a wavy surface. This was known as welded damascus or *sakela* (Panseri 1962: 29-30) There were artisans who even tried to forge the entire wavy pattern by etching the swords with acids (Smith 1965). But none could match the property exhibited by swords made of true wootz steel. We shall learn about the European attempts to duplicate wootz steel, and their comments about the property of wootz.

Attempts are being made even at present to mass-produce this type of ferro carbon alloy (ultra high carbon steels) because of its combination of good flexibility and high hardness. The Russians tried to copy it in the ninetteenth century (Wulff 1966: 8-9), and it was the subject of numerous studies by the Europeans in the nineteenth and twentieth centuries. Anossoff reproduced this at his factory in Zlatonst with the help of Central Asian artisans, while another method was reported by Massalaski from the Bukhara region. Attempts by Anossoff to study surface manifestations of these structures microscopically also led to the birth of metal crystallography. Attempts at duplication have been conducted well over two centuries. Owing to the large varieties of steels, their classification itself had become quite an interesting problem (Wadsworth and Lesuer 2000: 289-313). Piaskowski (1981) has provided one set of scientific criteria to rationalise this system.

One of the most competent authorities in inorganic chemistry, Mellor (1932), comments:

> The Hindoo steel... appeared on the European markets in the seventeenth century, as wootz or wooz... This is the most prized variety, and forms the Persian *kirk narduban* – the forty steps of Mahomet's ladder. The steel is extremely ductile, so that P. Anossoff could say that a blade of good damascene steel [Wootz steel] cannot be broken by bending, but can yet be bent to such an extent as to lose its elasticity. When bent in the usual fashion the blade flies back and retains its original shape; and when bent more forcibly, say at a right angle, it does not break or lose its original elasticity when straightened out again. D.K. Tschernoff considered this kind of steel to be "the best ever made".

By the end of the eighteenth century, it was known that true Damascus blades were made form Indian wootz steel. Therefore, one finds several accounts of the process of making the steel at different places in India. Most of these accounts are by European travellers. These accounts will be described in not here.

European blacksmiths and scientists have been trying, since the Crusades, to reproduce the wootz blade. That they never really succeeded is attested by historical evidences. However, the inquisitive nature of European scientists and blacksmiths to understand what went into the making of patterned wootz steel blades laid the foundation of modern metallurgy. In spite of a number of studies conducted in reproducing the typical pattern of the wootz steel swords, the Europeans were not successful in obtaining swords of the same quality as forged by the Indian smiths. The fascination of Europeans with wootz, and its subsequent processing into blades, faded with the advent of modern steel-making technologies (like Bessemer converter, etc.) and attention was diverted to developing steels based on their experiments and experience of working with crucible steel production.

There were innumerable attempts made by European technicians and metallurgists to duplicate wootz steel. The activities undertaken in this regard make for a fascinating reading. The details of these attempts have been reviewed in great detail by Smith (1965),

Piaskowski (1978,1981), Wadsworth and Sherby (1980), Yater (1983, 1983-84), Thomsen (1987), Kedzierski and Stepineski (1987), Antieny (1987) and many others. Piaskowski (1978) has concluded that "Although the research on Damascene steel did not lead to its widespread production but the extent of interest shown by the research workers has enriched the imagination of scientists and has had a decisive influence on the development of science and technology".

It is hard to imagine now that the secret of wootz was much sought after by the Europeans. Wootz steel and damascened blades had a profound effect on European metallurgy. The Europeans were aware that the tough swords were forged from Indian steel known as wootz. The secret of both their structure and their superiority was intensely debated nearly two hundred years ago. However, wootz steel was regarded as almost unworkable by European smiths. Porta (1588) mentions that it can be worked after it has been annealed in calcined gypsum (that is, lime), and very slowly cooled. Reaumur (1722) was highly critical of Parisian artisans, because none of them succeeded in forging a tool out of a cake of Indian steel. It is interesting to note that wootz steel cakes were worked first in India and then sent to Europe. The large number of damask-patterned sharp blades, swords, etc. now on display at the Musee de Arms de Paris, must certainly have been worked in the Deccan and brought into the European continent and not forged in Europe. Moxon (1677) specifically mentions that wootz steel "very rarely came unwrought into England". The production of wootz steel was in full swing up to the early twentieth century, and an estimate of its demand in western countries can be had from the fact that in the seventeenth century, one Dutch consignment of this steel consisted of twenty thousand ingots shipped from India (Joshi 2002: 47-59).

The comments of a European blacksmith, quoted by Smith (1965), are most interesting: "It is the most difficult of any steel to work at the Forge, for you shall scarce be able to strike upon a blood heat but it will *Redsear*; in so much that these Symeters are by many workmen thought to be cast Steel; but when it is wrought it takes the finest and keeps the strongest edge of any other Steel. Workmen set almost an inestimable value on it, to make Punches, Cold Punches..."

A discussion of the early interest in wootz, those who studied it, and its etymology can be found in Hadfield (1931), Smith (1965), and Wadsworth and Sherby (1980). Europeans were very eager to unravel the mystery of Deccani wootz from which the tough blades were fabricated. Their interest in the metallurgy of wootz reads like a mystery novel. The following material has been summarised from a discussion provided originally by Smith (1965).

The European interest in wootz was aroused ever since they encountered it during the Crusades. The spirit of scientific inquiry was kindled in the European continent in the eighteenth century, and several notable scientific discoveries were made in this century. The approach of scientific research by experimentation was also established. Wootz did not escape the scientific minds of Europe.

Pearson (1795) reported the first chemical examination of wootz in 1795. Around this time, Mushet (1804) presented his investigation on wootz and correctly concluded that the critical property was the higher carbon content of wootz steel. Wootz was a much-researched enigma and one of the major scientific efforts of Europeans was in duplicating wootz steel. James Stodart, an expert cutler, was the first to initiate serious work on this subject. In a long letter written in 1814 to Benjamin Heyne, he noted that wootz was highly variable (Stodart 1814). He commented that when wootz was melted again and cast into bars like English steel, it was of superior quality, "decidedly the best I have yet met with". He advised the East India Company to teach the Indians to melt wootz and adopt tilt hammering, suggesting that it would become a source of considerable revenue. Stodart also wrote on wootz in 1819. Stodart later commenced scientific studies on wootz in collaboration with the famous scientist, Michael Faraday. These two collaborators incorrectly attributed the unique properties of wootz to its alumina and silica content (Stodart and Faraday 1820: 356-364).

Faraday was a son of a blacksmith, and it is natural that he took interest in understanding the production of patterned blades from wootz cakes. Faraday, in 1819, analysed wootz (with unsatisfactory results) (Faraday 1819: 288-290). In 1820, he made alloys with wootz-like *damask* (Stodart and Faraday 1820: 319-30). This was performed in collaboration with Stodart. They were sure that the Indian *damask* was the result of crystallisation. However, their steel was different in composition compared to Indian wootz. In another paper published in 1822, Faraday and Stodart described many alloys that showed good damask. However, they did not really appreciate the beauty of the simple Indian high carbon cast steel. Nevertheless, these experiments paved the way for alloy steel development.

When the French heard of Faraday's work, a commission was set up to investigate wootz. This was headed by Jean Robert Bréant, who was an Inspector of Assays at the Paris mint. The mandate of the Commission was to repeat Faraday's work. Bréant conducted over three hundred experiments in six weeks by adding Pt, Au, Ag, Cu, Sn, Zn, Pb, Bi, Mn, U, As and B to steel. It must be noted that his Commission also received

100 kg of wootz from the East India Company. He went on to draw the conclusion, similar to Mushet (1804), that it was the higher carbon percentage that was responsible for the typical damask pattern. His publication in 1823/34 is acknowledged as the first one to understand the nature of wootz. He is credited to be the first to successfully make blades similar to the one in India.

The paper by Bréant, in 1823, set out the principles of alloy formation in iron-carbon alloys, for the first time. Smith (1965) has summarised his paper thus:

> Breant's paper is one of the minor classics of metallurgy. In it he applies to steel Berzelius' principles of chemical combination, and suggests that carbon added to iron, at the proper temperature, first forms increasing amounts of steel, as a separate 'compound,' and that as more carbon is added beyond the ideal composition of steel, iron carbide commences to form. On slow cooling a steel of very high carbon content, the 'steel' and the carbide will crystallize separately, the crystals being larger the slower the cooling. The details of the *damask* depend on the manner of forging, being in the form of longitudinal streaks if forged in only one direction, crystalline if forged equally in all.

Bréant's procedure was adopted by a Russian major-general named Paul Anossoff, the Engineer of Mines and Director of Zlatoust Steel Works in the Urals (Anossoff 1841: 192-236). He established a factory for manufacturing blades. The biography of Anossoff makes for interesting reading (Proshkin 1971: 180-250). Sadly, Anossoff did not give credit of the procedure to Bréant. Belaiew (1918) concluded that Anossoff succeeded in making touch blades of high quality. Smith (1965) comments that the blades made by Anossoff did not match the quality of the blades wrought from Deccani wootz, based on a photograph of one of Anossoff's blades given in Lenz (1906/8). Anossoff performed several experiments with different compositions and added a number of elements to steel like Ag, Au, Pt and diamond (Savitsky and Kliachko 1978: 6-7). He finally settled upon a method of manufacture that involved melting iron with graphite and a flux, slowly cooling, and finally forging and etching (Anossoff 1841: 192-236). The metallographic interest of Anossoff's paper was commented on by Belaiew (1914).

Around the same time, Luyens (1844) analysed some swords as well as several cakes of Persian and Turkish cast steel. Based on his analysis, he concluded that an alloying element was needed to give a good *damask*, and preferred manganese. His sword production method required cutting of markings on the surface of the nearly finished blade.

A Swiss metallurgist, J.C. Fischer displayed in 1851 a high-nickel, low-carbon steel that he had developed, called *Meteor* steel (Schib and Gnade 1947), which he claimed showed damask in the interior part. However, the steel did not display a pattern visible to the naked eye.

From the middle of the nineteenth century, interest in Deccani wootz and Damascus blade declined in Europe. This was primarily due to the introduction of large-scale steel manufacturing processes of Bessemer and Siemens. These developments provided steel of more homogenous composition and were adaptable to large-scale production. Another factor responsible for the decline in interest was the advent of efficient firearms by 1850s. This made wootz redundant for the purpose of war.

In 1860s, a professor by the name of Tschernoff visited Zlatoust and rediscovered Anossoff's work. He returned to Petrograd and manufactured some high carbon steel at Oboukhof works. His lectures at the Michael Artillery Academy inspired Belaiew to repeat the work of Anossoff in 1904. Belaiew published a historical account of high carbon steels in 1906 (Belaiew 1906), followed by a publication in 1918 of his own studies on high carbon steel (Belaiew 1918: 417-37). His work recognised the malleability of this variety of steel to the globular nature (that is, spherodised) of the forged steel due to forging at red heat (~ 700-800°C).

Belaiew's method was adopted by Harnecker of Solingen, Germany, in 1924, to make a number of blades (Harnecker 1924: 1409-1411).

The microstructures of real Damascus blades were examined by Zschokke (1924). He also tried to understand the structural changes that resulted due to various quenching and tempering heat treatments. Wadsworth and Sherby (1980) refer to Zschokke's work to emphasise the importance of correct heat treatment in order to produce the *damask* pattern. It must be noted that Captain Bagnold (1918) wrote about this steel in 1831. However, he was not able to explain scientifically the extraordinary properties of this kind of steel.

Interest diminished in wootz steel after the 1920s, till the 1960s when Smith published his reviews on the history of metallography (Smith 1965). With the decline in the study of wootz steel blades, the factors controlling the ultra high carbon steel's capability of exhibiting *damask* were not researched in the middle part of the twentieth century. This was the situation before interest was revived again in America about fifty years ago.

The processes of producing wootz steel, practised in medieval India, and its processing into usable objects are not discussed in detail here. We shall only look at some of the aspects in a cursory manner.

PROCESS

The basic process of producing wootz steel consisted of heating iron from the bloomery with other ingredients, contained in a closed clay crucible. In this manner, the iron picked up appreciable amounts of carbon and melted. The crucibles were then cooled so that the metal after solidification took its shape in the bottom. This solidified ingot was the wootz cake. There are several differences noted by observers and these differences mentioned relate to the crucible material and size, the way the crucible is closed, ingredients charged into it, the number of crucibles heated at a time, the duration of firing, and the way the crucible is cooled afterwards.

The wootz steel-making process has been classified into two groups by archaeometallurgists based on significant differences noted (Yater 1983:2; 1983-84; Bronson 1986; Prakash 1997; Rao 1989: 1). The first classification is the so-called South Indian process practised in Karnataka, Tamil Nadu and Sri Lanka. Prakash mentions that this process was also being practised in Gujarat and Varanasi. This corresponded to carburisation of wrought iron in crucibles. The second is the so-called Hyderabad process, practised in Konasamudram and its surroundings. This process involved decarburisation of white cast iron by co-fusion of wrought iron and white cast iron.

It is interesting to note that these two methods were not practiced at the same place and it is likely that they were developed independently. The charcoal fuel necessary for these processes was prepared from the wood of *Aalbizzia amara*, *Acacia catechu*, *Xylia dolaberi formis* and *Sethia indica*. All these plants of South India yielded dense and strong charcoal (Prakash 1997).

South Indian Process

In the South Indian process, the crucibles were charged with pieces of wrought iron together with 5 to 10% of wood charcoal (by weight) of *Cassia auriculata*, and 1 to 2% of leaves of *Calotropis gigantica* (called *avaram* in Tamil) and the mouth was sealed with clay. In most of the accounts, the charge was covered with one or two leaves of plants like *Convolvus laurifolia* or *Asclepias gigantea*. In terms of actual weights used, the total charge varied between 250-500 gm (Balasubramaniam *et. al.* 1993: 165). In the account of CVB (1820), there is no mention of wood chips. But he mentions the addition of the creeper *vooganabalee* (in Kannada) or *tandra tegga* (in Telugu) with leaves and rice husk. The crucible is then sealed with a sun-dried clay lid or a ball of moist clay. Coomaraswamy (1908) mentions a small hole at the centre of the cover for the gases to escape. Others do not mention this. The closed crucibles were allowed to dry and then heated in a charcoal fire. The drying of crucibles took place typically in one day in the shade and one day in the sun. Buchanan (1807) gives details of the furnace with illustrations. The crucibles are arranged in an arched dome fashion. One of the crucibles opposite the blow tube is kept empty and can be removed periodically for replenishing charcoal below the crucible in the fireplace. The crucibles are then covered with charcoal and the fire started. Air is blown with large hand bellows, usually made from full buffalo skins. Coomaraswamy's report however shows foot operated drum bellows as used in the smelting furnaces of central India. Sometimes, two goatskin blowers were connected to the furnace, a short distance above the contracted neck, and the crucibles were heated by vigorous combustion of charcoal. The fire is kept going for about five to six hours, till the contents are molten.

The number of crucibles fired at a time varied between six and fifty nine. Normally, twenty to twenty five such crucibles were heated in a big charcoal hearth heated to a temperature of 1450^0-1550^0 C. Twenty-five such crucibles, when dry, were placed with their pointed ends downwards on the furnace, forming a flat arch and extending across a circular saucer shaped pit about 450 mm in diameter and 1050 mm deep. Before putting the crucibles, the pit was packed with straw. Prakash (1997) supposed that these acted as a receptacle for the slag formed during melting. From time to time the crucibles were shifted to charge charcoal and adjust the temperature of the crucibles. Charcoal was replenished periodically both above and below the crucibles. The bellows and the workers were protected from the sparks by a thick mud wall.

The whole operation took about six hours, and during this process the crucibles were gradually shifted to the hottest zone of the furnace where the carburised iron became molten and separated from the molten slag floating over its surface. This condition was judged sometimes by shaking the crucible during shifting to feel the movement of the liquid metal inside the crucible. Prakash (1997) specifically mentions that after about two hours of continuous blast, the twelve central crucibles, which had been subjected to a greater temperature, were removed and replaced by the others. He assumes that during this period, iron was generally sufficiently carburised and fused.

There are reports that the crucibles were laid flat when they were relocated within the furnace. One of the most distinguishing features of the Mawalgaha crucibles from Sri Lanka is that the crucible has two slag fins (Wayman and Juleff, 1999: 26-42). The first runs around the internal circumference, about a third of the way along the height of the crucible; the second is at right angles to this fin, running along the length of the crucible. This indicates that while the metal was molten, the crucible was placed on its side. This is also corroborated by Coomaraswamy's (1908) ethnographic report. The result was an elongated steel ingot.

There could be ideas of phase transformations also embedded in the operation of shifting of crucibles. Solidified wootz ingots typically reveal thick plates of cementite in a matrix of transformed ledeburite and pearlite. At the stage when the crucible containing molten steel was shifted to the lower temperature zone, the metal will solidify at a slow rate, producing coarse-grained structure containing thick needles/plates of cementite in a matrix of transformed ledeburite and pearlite.

After the crucible cooled to room temperature, the wootz ingot was removed by breaking the crucible. The ingot was then removed from the adhering slag. The contents of the crucible solidified inside the crucible taking its conical shape.

At the end of the operation, the crucibles are allowed to cool down. This is also an important step because there were several possible ways by which the cooling down of the crucible has been suggested. These include cooling in the furnace itself, in dry sand heap, in moist clay, or by quenching (that is, throwing water over them). These conditions represent increasing rates of solidification, with the furnace cooling being the slowest. Solidification is an important issue in wootz steel manufacture, and this has not been quite well understood. When cooled within the furnace, the grain sizes would be coarser, if the crucible was quenched, the grain sizes would be finer. Therefore, the rate of solidification dictates the structure and this has a bearing on the final property, namely the forging behaviour.

Feuerbach (2002) noted that the final pattern formed on blades from the ingots would be different in Central Asian and Indian wootz. In India and Sri Lanka, ethnographic reports state that ingots were removed from the furnace while the metal was liquid, quickly cooling the metal. The examination of an ingot by Wayman and Juleff (1999) revealed primarily Widmanstätten cementite, with a lesser amount of prior austenite grain boundary cementite, indicating rapid cooling, thus supporting the ethnographic reports. On the other hand, the remains of crucible steel ingots from Central Asia primarily have austenite, grain boundary cementite, with a small amount of cementite needles indicating that the ingots were cooled slowly. According to Verhoeven and Jones (1987), their replication experiments indicate that the quality of the final pattern would be "strongly influenced by both the morphology of the Cm (cementite) before the forging and the time/temperature cycle employed in forging". Hence, the pattern which would appear on blades made from the fast cooled Indian ingots would be finer than the pattern made from slow cooled Central Asian ingots. Whereas, the slow cooled ingots could be forged to create a fine pattern, a quickly cooled ingot could not produce a coarse pattern.

It is certain that the ancient wootz steel makers were aware of these fine differences, and they could have produced wootz steel with different forging capabilities based on the requirements of the blacksmiths. The wootz steel makers would not have shared these secrets when the Europeans were making the observation.

Digressing briefly from the main theme, let us critically view the observations on the local Indian technologies by the early European observers. First, they were not scientists but keen observers and ethnographers. Therefore, they must not have been aware of the fine points of the local method of manufacture. Moreover, the wootz steel makers must have closely guarded the wootz technology from the foreigners. On the other hand, there are examples of popular Indian metal technology being copied and patented in Europe. One famous example is the so-called Champion method for extraction of zinc metal. The story of zinc technology is really fascinating, and the primacy of zinc production in India is now clearly recognised the world over (Biswas 1996). However, let us see how this technology was transported to England. The British copied the Indian method and established trial plants next to the Indian furnaces in India, while at the same time duplicating similar furnaces in England. The extraction of zinc was then perfected in England by correcting any mistakes based on the Indian prototype, set up next to the Indian manufacturing furnace. This is an interesting example of reverse engineering. Once the extraction of zinc was perfected in England, based on the experience in the trial plant next to the Indian zinc furnace, the British went about systematically dismantling the local zinc industry. However, such a situation does not seem to have occurred with wootz steel manufacture. This could probably be due to the closely guarded secrets of the Deccani wootz steel smelters. They must have been aware of the power and fame of their "wonder" material, the world over, in fabricating famous swords and warfare objects. In one way, this closely guarded secret also led to its demise from the Indian subcontinent, fuelled by the ban imposed on wootz steel manufacture by the British.

The chemical action that takes place, as suggested by Heath (1839), is that during the application of heat to the closed crucible, the dry wood and green leaves would yield charcoal as well as an abundant supply of hydrocarbons. The joint action of carbon and hydrocarbons on the iron greatly facilitates the formation of steel as the European method of cementation by means of charcoal alone used to take six or seven days, and sometimes even fourteen to twenty days, while the Indian process took only four to six hours. Though cementation has been mentioned by Agricola in his *De re Metallica*, and though Reaumur in 1722 described the process of converting bar-iron into "blistered steel", it was only in 1800 that D. Mushet took out a patent for converting malleable iron into cast-steel by fusing it in a closed crucible in contact with carbon. "Now this specification," says Mr Heath, "unquestionably comprises the principle of the Indian process which adopts the use of dry wood, which is a substance containing the coaly or carbonaceous principle". This opinion is confirmed by Percy who says, "It is curious that Mushet's process, so far as it relates to the use of malleable iron in the production of cast-steel, should in principle, and I may add even in practice too, be identical with that by which the Hindoos have from ancient times prepared their Wootz. I cannot discover any essential difference between the two".

Percy did not take into consideration the action of carburetted hydrogen gas produced by the destructive decomposition of wood in the Indian process. In the year 1825, Mackintosh obtained a patent for converting malleable iron into steel by exposing it to the action of carburetted hydrogen gas in a closed vessel, at a very high temperature, by which means the process of conversion into steel is completed in a few hours, while by the old method it took fourteen to twenty hours.

The top surface of the cooled down wootz ingot showed striations indicating crystallisation from the liquid state. These were annealed and then forged into bars before being sold in the market. The molten metal when solidified produced typical structures which were later worked into tough swords, warfare items, cutting objects, wires for musical instruments, etc. **Figure 4.10** gives a macro-photograph of wootz steel ingot published by Tylecote (1962). These structures and their changes will be discussed in the next section while addressing the physical metallurgy of Decanni wootz steel.

Hyderabad Process

Voysey (1832), observed the process of wootz ingot making at Konasamudram near Hyderabad when the industry was still vibrant. This is evidenced by the fact that at the time of his visit, the place was also visited by the Persian trader Hoseyn (Husain). The process, as described by Voysey (1832); differs from the South Indian process in some significant details. The crucible was made from granitic clay with ground pieces of fired crucible and furnace (grog), rice husk (stabiliser) and oil, indicating that the crucible making had attained a certain state of sophistication. The crucible is said to be pine-shaped. The size of the crucible was larger. Though the crucible is closed with a ball of clay, the lid is perforated.

The major difference between the two processes is in the charge to the crucible. Voysey clearly mentions that two kinds of iron were charged in the crucible. One was a highly porous reddish grey product typically obtained from iron sands in a bloomery. The other was in the form of a partially consolidated iron which had a brilliant white fracture. This iron was obtained from iron clay and was dirty brown in colour and very

Fig. 4.10: *A cross-section of one of the ingots presented by Sir Thomas Holland at the end of the nineteenth century to the Royal School of Mines, clearly showing that the steel had been completely melted, based on the appearance of a well-defined large dendritic structure.*

fragile. This has been interpreted to mean that this is high carbon iron or, maybe, white cast iron. Some small amount of slag is also added. No organic matter, like wood chips or leaves, are mentioned among the ingredients by Voysey. Many have interpreted this to mean that the carbon was derived from the high carbon pieces. Bronson (1986) interprets this process to be analogous to the co-fusion processes practised in China. Opinions have also been expressed that the carbonaceous matter in the crucible wall contributes to the carbon in the steel (Rao 1982: 468).

Voysey (1837) reported that the crucible charge contained "*kanch*" and two different types of iron. The first is described as a "porous reddish grey bloom", while the second was "moderately compact and of a brilliant white fracture". These have been understood by Allan and Gilmour (2000) to be "small pieces of fused glassy furnace waste together with pieces of white cast iron and pieces of bloomery iron". Voysey (1832) also reported that the crucibles were heated for twenty four hours, then slowly cooled in the furnace and repeatedly annealed three to four times until soft. Lowe (1989b), however, states that the crucibles were removed from the furnace while molten. The resulting ingot is reported by Lowe (1989b) to be a white cast iron ingot, which exhibits a dendritic structure of cementite, lamellar pearlite, interstitial steatite, and shrinkage porosity.

Another significant variation in the process is the time duration. Voysey clearly mentions a twenty four hour-operation as against three to six hours for the South Indian process. It is not clear whether this is due to the lack of hydrogenous ingredients in the charge. It is known that hydrogenous gases significantly increase the rate of carburisation due to higher diffusivity.

Voysey also mentions long and repeated annealing operations (of twelve to sixteen hours) being carried out before the ingot is sold. Interestingly, the ingots are covered with clay or other earthen materials, like iron ore before being annealed. This may have been performed for avoiding decarburisation. Schwarz (1899) indicates that the annealing temperature was a light red heat.

Prakash (1997) has proposed that in the Hyderabad process, steel was produced by refining white cast iron (2.5% C) prills or small pieces by chemical interaction with a highly oxidising fayalite slag. The refining process involved reaction of iron carbide (Fe_3C) with FeO in the slag to remove C as CO, as per the following reaction:

$$Fe_3C + FeO \rightarrow 4Fe + CO$$

He also suggested that phosphorous was removed from cast iron by the reaction

$$2Fe_3P + 8FeO \leftarrow 3\ FeO.P_2O_5 + 11Fe$$

Prakash pointed out that when the white cast iron was decarburised, some dephosphorisation also took place at the same time. Other impurities like Si and Mn were also easily oxidised by this slag. Prakash noted that both these reactions are exothermic and they are self-sustaining once begun in the molten state. The heat produced by these oxidation reactions as well as the heat generated by the combustion of carbon and CO produced sufficient heat to separate the molten metal into a separate layer.

Prakash mentions that these reactions were carried out in a double chambered furnace made below the ground level (that is, pit furnace). For this, a hole was dug in the ground about 300 mm in diameter. This was divided into two parts with the help of a soft clay wall, and the smaller part served as a crucible for making steel. The bottom of this was first covered with the powder of quartz and magnetite mixture. A molten pool of highly oxidising molten slag was prepared from magnetite sand and quartz which had a melting point between 1170 to 1205°C. Sometimes, bloomery furnace slag was also used. The powdered mixture of magnetite and quartz was filled with charcoal and two bellows were fixed at forty-five degrees. Once sufficient molten slag was collected in the bottom of the furnace, well-cleaned prills or pieces of highly carburised iron were charged on top of the charcoal fire. These highly carburised and melted shots of iron were obtained by smelting magnetite ore. These carburised shots were first pounded in a mortar with a wooden pole to remove the adhering slag and then charged into the furnace. The high carbon iron became molten as it passed through the red-hot charcoal bed and reacted with the molten slag present in the bottom of this chamber, and it was tapped in the second pre-heated chamber by making a hole in the partition wall. The process was run based on the experience of the operator and at the end of melting, the furnace was cooled and the clay wall was broken to remove the steel. Prakash comments that these processes had been followed even during the early nineteenth century till the modern methods of steel making were developed.

The molten metal was allowed to solidify in the furnace itself. After solidification, a circular pancake shaped steel ingot or thick steel plate was obtained. This was cleaned. It was tested for its quality by making a 'V' shaped cut. This was sold to the blacksmiths. These steel disks or plates of wootz steel 'loaves' were exported to the West (Yater 1983: 2; 1983-84; Bronson 1986). Its microstructure was similar to that of steel produced by the South Indian process, but it was heavier and could be used for making swords without forge-welding. A typical analysis of wootz steel made by this process was quoted by Prakash to contain Carbon 1. 68%, Silicon 0.43%, Phosphorus 0.02% and Sulphur 0.2%.

THERMOMECHANICAL PROCESSING

The thermomechanical processing step to manufacture the blade from wootz was an important operation. We shall try and understand the metallurgy behind this operation in this section. Information on the processing of wootz ingot to produce blade is scarce and scattered. They are also often difficult to interpret, since the language is archaic. Temperatures are seldom mentioned. Most of the time one has to infer the temperatures from the colour of the heated specimen that has been reported.

Some typical features of wootz blades were noted by Smith (1965). First, no good wootz blade has a structure that indicates very extensive working. Secondly, they are all remarkably free from slag. Welding was not much used.

Later in this section, an eyewitness account of the typical way in which a wootz cake was worked in order to produce a blade will be provided. In the ancient times, the knowledge gained was more by experience and empirical observations.

The last two decades have seen extensive discussion on the working of wootz steel. The debate was started after a combined group (from the University of California at Berkeley, USA, and Stanford University) claimed that they had succeeded in deciphering the mystery behind producing *damask* patterns from high carbon steels (Wadsworth and Sherby 1980). Another group at Iowa State University at Ames, USA, also started detailed studies on microstructural aspects of high carbon blades. This led to a flurry of experimental activity. Though some of the controversies surrounding the Deccani wootz conversion to blade remain, the body of material that has been published recently has thrown considerable light on the physical metallurgy of wootz. A very brief review is presented below.

Using the iron-carbon phase diagram and applying the lever rule, a typical steel containing about 1.5 % carbon would have about ten to fifteen percent proeutectoid cementite by the time it is slowly cooled to the eutectoid reaction temperature. If cooling in the range between 950^0 and 727^0C has been done slowly, this cementite would appear as massive precipitates at the austenite grain boundary. On further cooling down the steel to room temperature, the austenite would convert to pearlite, bainite or martensite depending on the cooling rate.

In the presence of a massive network of cementite at the prior austenite grain boundaries, the steel will be extremely difficult to work, even at high temperatures. If, however, it is worked carefully with very low rates of strain (moderate forging blows), at about 700^0 – 800^0C (that is, in cherry red hot ~750°C condition), the cementite network can be slowly broken down into a dispersion of granular/spheroidised particles. The spheroidisation treatment converted the cementite plates into spherical massive cementite. This was the step that needed very intelligent blacksmithy skills. In the hands of an expert smith, the forging operation distributed the cementite particles in such a fashion as to result in the beautiful pattern of the *damask*. During this operation, the basic shape of the sword was wrought. Later, the resultant steel was etched to reveal the pearlite/bainite grains as a dark background. This treatment was followed by cold forging of the sharp edge and low temperature annealing (~800°C). The forged sword blade was cleaned and given proper surface finish before it was hardened.

We had noted above that there are two schools of thought regarding how the final pattern was obtained from forging ultra high carbon steels. Let us look at these alternate views below in more detail.

Wadsworth-Sherby Mechanism

Wadsworth, Sherby and co-workers opine that the critical factor deciding the appearance of the *damask* pattern is the heat treatment cycle, and they proposed a typical cycle (**Figure 4.11**) that would produce the so called *damask* pattern in ultra high carbon steel (Taleff *et al* 1997: 189-198; 2001: 19-23). This schematic illustrates four possible steps used in producing *damask* in ultra high carbon steel material. The first step relates to homogenisation annealing of the ingot. In this step, all the iron-carbide is dissolved and a large austenite grain size is obtained. In the second step, the ingot is hot worked to homogenise the casting, refine the microstructure and obtain a billet of suitable size for additional mechanical processing. The third step is an austenite grain coarsening treatment involving a long-time soak at 1093°C, followed by furnace cooling to develop a continuous proeutectoid cementite network at austenite grain boundaries. The proeutectoid carbide network will create a pattern visible to the unaided eye. The fourth step is a thermomechanical process, which Wadsworth and Sherby termed as Divorced Eutectoid Transformation With Associated Deformation (DETWAD) (Sherby *et. al.* 1976). In this step, the billet is first heated to about 40°C above the A1 transformation temperature. At this temperature, the eutectoid carbides are mostly dissolved and the continuous proeutectoid network remains essentially intact. The material is weak (soft) because the diffusion rate of iron in austenite is enhanced by the presence of dissolved carbon. It is also very ductile, and during deformation, continuous cementite in the network breaks

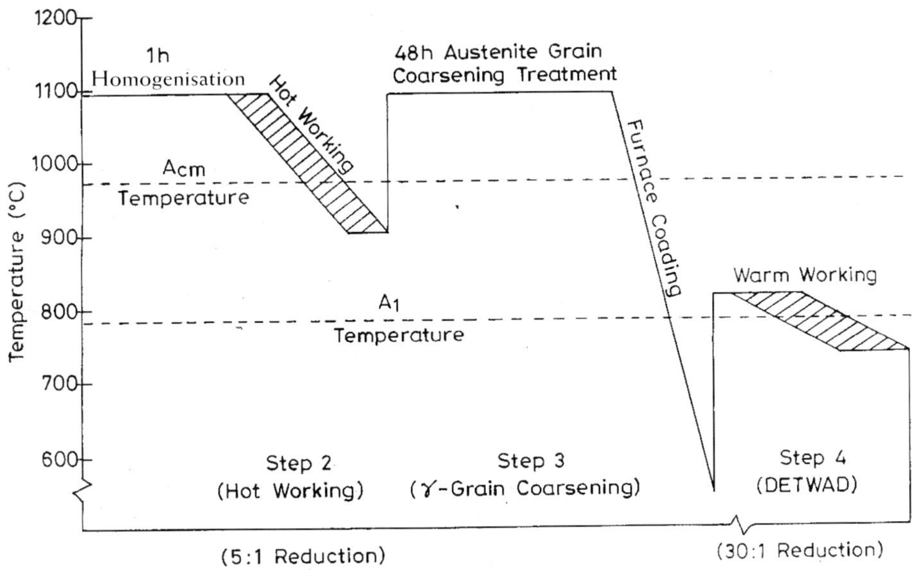

Fig. 4.11: *The Wadsworth-Sherby heat treatment schedule for producing the so-called damask pattern in high carbon steel. The schematic illustrates the four thermal + mechanical steps used in producing a damask in ultra high carbon steel material. Step 1 is the homogenisation annealing of the ingot. Step 2 is the hot working to homogenise the casting and obtain a billet of suitable size. Step 3 is an austenite grain coarsening treatment involving a long-time soak at 1093°C, followed by furnace cooling to develop a continuous proeutectoid cementite network at austenite grain boundaries. Step 4 involves a DETWAD treatment. This later procedure leads to a fine-grained ferritic matrix with fine spheroidised cementite particles and a visible discontinuous network of proeutectoid carbides.*

up. The result is elongated, but visible, prior-austenite grains outlined by a discontinuous network of carbides. The temperature of the billet decreases rather slowly during repetitive mechanical working, because of adiabatic heating. When the temperature descends below the A1 transformation point, austenite transforms into a structure which is partially pearlitic and partially spheroidised, the latter from a divorced eutectoid transformation (DET). The last step leads to a fine-grained ferritic matrix with fine spheroidised cementite particles and a visible discontinuous network of proeutectoid carbides.

Based on their mechanism, Wadsworth and Sherby hypothesised the possible way by which the master blacksmiths forged Decccani wootz cakes to *Damascus* blades. A hypereutectoid steel ingot (wootz) is first upset forged below a white heat, 800°C to

1200°C, to height reductions in the range of 3:1 to 8:1. This first step helps to homogenise the casting and develop a discontinuous proeutectoid cementite network at austenite grain boundaries. The steel is then forged by complex folding and twisting at a medium to bright cherry-red heat, 650^0 – 850°C, further refining the microstructure until the desired shape is produced. The final blade may be quenched from about 800°C to achieve a high hardness.

It must be understood that in all these operations, the blacksmith had precise control of the manner in which the wootz cake was worked in order to produce the final sword. This was very important in determining the orientation of the *damask* patterns and, therefore, the toughness of the sword.

Let us take a look at a typical way in which a wootz cake was worked in order to produce a blade. This is based on actual observation of such a process by Abbot (1847) in the middle of the nineteenth century, which goes on to show that the blacksmith's skills were much required in order to produce blades of topmost quality. Abbot goes on to describe the operation of forging of blade from wootz cake as follows:

> The substance is a small cake of cast steel weighing about 2 lbs and exhibiting manifest symptoms of the fluid condition in which it acquired its plano-convex shape. That is, the lower or convex surface, bears the impression of the coarse gravely mould into which it was poured. And the upper or flat surface, has those concentric wrinkles and radiations, which all metals take in crystallising after fusion. This cast steel (*fowlahd*) is purchased at Umritsur in the small cakes above noted. The natives know not its origin, but only that it comes from the south, and can be purchased at Delhi, in large as well as in small cakes.
>
> The accompanying sketches 1 and 2 (**see Figure 4.12**) represent the plan and profile of a mass lying upon the table before me. Now, upon considering the internal structure of this, we are aware that is a bundle of concentric needles crystallized around a porous centre, the vesicles of which are coarse and apparent, formed by the splash of the metal as it fell fluid into the mould. These I have rudely represented in dots in sketch 12 (**see Figure 4.12**). It is also manifest that the most solid portions of the mass are the lower or convex surface. And, accordingly, in beating it out into a bar, great care is taken to preserve each surface distinct from the other, in order that the edges of the lenticular mass may become the sides or flat surfaces of the blade; that the convex surface may become the

edge; and the flat, porous surface, the back. Under any other disposition, the damask figures would be confused and unseemly and, as cast steel cannot be welded, by any art known in Asia, the porosity of the centre of crystallisation in the mass, would either offer a jagged, flawed edge, or one of the sides must be disfigured and weakened by it. And thus the arrangement pursued in the fabric of the simple *damask* blade is suggested by sound sense. The elegance and symmetry arising from the arrangement is the accidental but necessary consequence.

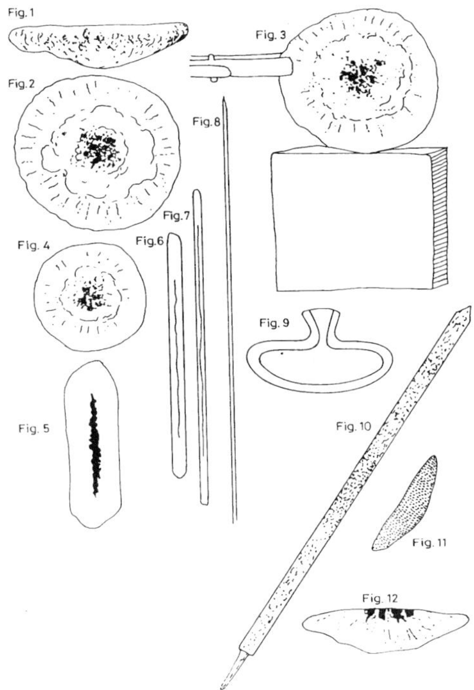

Fig. 4.12: *Typical account of how wootz cake was processed into a blade, based on real time account of the process by Abbot (1847).*

The mass of cast steel being brought to red heat and held, as represented in sketch 3 (**see Figure 4.12**), edge-wise upon the anvil, is beaten into a square prism or bar-an operation of about two hour's duration. When the requisite length is attained, the bar is fattened under the hammer, those sides in the bar, which had been the edges, being placed, the one above the other below, so as to become the flat surfaces of the blade. The blade, being shaped with the hammer and file and roughly burnished, is brought to a dull red heat in a long charcoal fire; a long vessel of common oil is placed within reach, and the blade is plunged by successive drawing cuts edge-foremost, into the oil; so that the edge becomes the most highly tempered part, and the back remains the softest. The excessive temper is abated in the usual manner by laying the blade over a slow charcoal fire. It is then burnished, and ground, and being carefully cleansed from grease in wood ashes, white vitriol (*kussces*) dissolved in water is rubbed over all the surface excepting the edge. This, eating deepest between the interstices of the crystals, exhibits their arrangement which constitutes the *damask* of the blade.

In following the mass of cast steel through all the changes of figure produced by the action of the hammer (sketches 1, 5, 7, 8 in **Figure 4.12**) we perceive that, as it cannot be welded, the pores in the centre of crystallisation must remain, although immensely elongated under the extension of the mass. These accordingly exhibit themselves in an irregular and ugly seam in the back of the blade, impairing both its elegance and its solidity. And hence it is manifest, that in order to the production of a blade without flaw, either the porous heart of the mass should be ground out previous to the action of the hammer, or the blade should be forged of excessive breadth, and the unsound back be ground away. But the necessity of either precaution would not exist were necks made to the moulds (sketch 9 in **Figure 4.12**) in which the steel is originally cast; so that there might be a surplus of metal (as in casting bullets and guns) – to give solidity by pressure to the incumbent mass.

We further observe, that as the flat surfaces of the blade (sketch 10 of **Figure 4.12**) are formed of the edges of the lenticular mass (sketch 11 of **Figure 4.12**); they present a section across the crystallisation; rectangular in the centre, but of various obliquity toward either end. It follows, that the less the original mass is altered by hammering, the more nearly lateral will be the disposition of the dots representing the ends of crystals – and hence the various figures presented by the same metal under slightly different treatment. It is also apparent that these figures will materially alter, according to difference in the shape of the original mass – and it may be reasonably doubted, whether the shape in which the cast steel is brought to India, be the most conducive to symmetry of *damask* or to soundness of fibre.

> As the *damask* of a blade is the map of its crystallisation, so it is probable that the figures alter according to the purity of the iron of which the steel is formed, the quantity of carbon contained in it, or to both these circumstances combined. Nay, the degree of heat of the fused metal at the time of casting, and the temperature of the mould in which it was formed may both contribute to differences in the crystallisation.

It is no wonder that making swords was considered an art rather than a simple metallurgical operation. Sadly, this aspect is never borne in mind when traditional technologies are discussed, and this is very readily apparent in the scientific writings of the western scholars, which show a distinct reluctance to accept the skills of the Indian blacksmiths, especially the technology of forging swords out of wootz cakes.

Verhoeven-Pendray Mechanism

Although in 1987, Verhoeven and Jones (1987) concluded that the "Wadsworth-Sherby mechanism was probably the major mechanism" producing genuine wootz steel patterns, by 1990 Verhoeven *et. al.* (1990) stated that the "Wadsworth-Sherby technique is probably not the technique used by ancient blacksmiths to produce the Damask pattern in their blades". Verhoeven (2001) states, "At first we tried to produce blades using the method put forward by Wadsworth and Sherby, but we failed to produce either the internal microstructure or the surface Damascene patterns".

Verhoven and co-workers have raised some simple objections to the mechanism of Wadsworth and Sherby (Wadsworth and Sherby 1980, Taleff *et. al.* 2001: 189-198) and to the claim that the W-S mechanism "contains a likely explanation for the surface markings found in Damascus steels". (Taleff *et. al.* 2001: 189-198). Verhoeven and Peterson (1992) pointed out that one of the outstanding characteristics of genuine wootz blades is that the cementite particles that produce the surface *damask* are planar arrays of particles. They concluded this comparison of the microstructure on the short and long transverse sections of the blades. They noted that the geometric constraints associated with the Wadsworth-Sherby mechanism are not consistent with this requirement, and will inherently produce a surface pattern having the appearance of an elongated grain structure. Based on a detailed examination of numerous examples of high-quality wootz blades catalogued by Verhoeven (1991), Verhoeven and Pendray (2001) argued that such surface patterns are not a characteristic of wootz blades. Verhoeven *et. al.* (1993)

conducted experiments on two genuine wootz blades in which the carbides were completely removed by dissolving into austenite above the Acm temperature and then quenching to martensite and retained austenite. It was shown that the planar arrays of carbide particle could be made to return, along with the surface pattern, by thermal cycling (Verhoeven *et. al.* 993: 187-200). Pointing out that the Wadsworth-Sherby mechanism requires cementite particles formed on the boundaries of the large austenite grains to be retained during deformation, Verhoven and Pendray (2001) concluded that the pattern present on at least these two genuine wootz blades could not have been formed by the Wadsworth-Sherby mechanism. Verhoven (2000) has therefore emphasised that the surface patterns formed on genuine wootz steel blades resulted from a type of microsegregation-induced carbide banding that requires thermal cycling.

The Verhoeven group advocates that the critical element that provides banding is vanadium (Verhoeven *et. al.* 1998). They provided evidence to support their theory that the distinct patterns on the blades resulted due to the carbide-banding phenomenon. They propose that this was produced due to microsegregation of minor amounts of carbide-forming elements present in wootz ingots from which the blades were forged. Their argument was that the blades with the distinct damascene patterns were produced only from wootz ingots supplied from those parts of India which contained the necessary impurity-containing ore.

This interesting debate has been continuing for some time now. The refutation of the Wadsworth-Sherby mechanism was rebutted by the authors Wadsworth and Sherby (2001) in a subsequent reply to Verhoeven and Pendray's (2001) objection. Similarly, Wadsworth and Sherby (1992) replied to the objections raised by Verhoeven *et. al.* (1992). These kinds of exchanges are important because this is the way science progresses, by questioning and logical reasoning.

DEATH OF DECCANI WOOTZ

Once the strength and properties of iron and steel were known, the use of non-ferrous metals and alloys were confined only to domestic and other areas of human needs. The Indian metal craft was flourishing during the Mughal period, but after the spread of the British Empire and the restrictions imposed by them in the form of production taxes and ban on export, this industry died down. This disappearance of the ancient technology during the eighteenth to the nineteenth century was supported by the discovery of new alchemical principles and the development of new industrial process of metal production in Europe.

The process of wootz steel had reached its zenith during the eighteenth century CE when it was banned by the British Government. However, there was significant interest in its properties. The importance of wootz steel totally declined after the advent of the processes for making liquid steel in large scale in the middle of the nineteenth century, and alloy steels towards the end of that century. The export trade from India declined and the practice became extinct by the beginning of the twentieth century. Even the existence of the industry is not known to the present day artisans. The study of the process and its reconstruction, therefore, has to be based on the written records alone.

The British Government made attempts to work on iron ores on a large-scale by modern methods. Several iron and steel works were set up in the country. For instance, the Bengal Iron Company was established at Barakar in 1874. It was able to employ eight hundred and twenty one people in 1891 and produce 12,000 tonnes of pig iron (Jaggi 1989: 135-136). However, these iron works depended on the availability of charcoal, and this necessarily meant the destruction of forests and depletion of charcoal supplies. Another factor was also at play. By the end of the century, the indigenous iron ceased to be produced because of the import of iron.

The industries of the villages that had no competition from outside had to face a challenge. The introduction of large-scale manufacturing techniques by British rulers, made an important impact in the industrial and technological system in India. As a result of this impact, some of the manufacturing techniques have totally vanished, while some were preserved with some improvements.

There is an ironic end to the story of wootz. During the eighteenth and nineteenth centuries when wootz steel research was being undertaken in Europe, to discover how the pattern was formed from wootz cakes, the traditional technology was dying out in the Indian subcontinent and elsewhere in Central Asia. Feuerbach (2002) proposes that this is probably because of the availability of cheap imported European steel. She cites some of the last known records of crucible steel production in Central Asia (Massalski's report from Bukhara during the nineteenth century (Allan and Gilmour 2000)) and India (Abbots's (1847) account from north India during the mid-nineteenth century). By the beginning of the twentieth century, the glorious tradition of more than two thousand and four hundred year-old wootz steel technology died a sad death.

There is a saving grace here. It is mentioned that the rigorous research conducted to understand the metallurgy of wootz steel, and its subsequent processing, laid the foundation of alloy steels in Europe. These steels were initially developed during the eighteenth and nineteenth century as an offshoot of research delving into mechanisms that produced the wootz steel pattern. With the advent of large-scale production of iron in Europe, the development of different grades of steel laid the foundation for the Industrial revolution. In all this process, India lost out because of the lack of innovation, partly caused by imperialist suppression. There were several advantages in using mass produced steel. Moreover, wootz steel was expensive. The sad and unfortunate matter is that the techniques of the art have been lost. One reason is the ban imposed on production of wootz by the British in India.

Another factor was that certain essential steps were not shared by the master smiths with anybody except their favoured apprentices. Traditional artisan communities in India never revealed full details to outsiders, and when the communities disappeared, so did the methods. We note the prevalent system in India of handing over the process secret and experiences from generation to generation within the family and the religious dogma attached to the processing.

Metalwork, particularly smelting ore, was always kept a closely guarded secret by the metalworkers in the Central Himalayas. Not all members of the smith communities knew the smelting technology. That is why even in a small region like the Central Himalayas; copper - and iron-smelting activities remained confined to a few pockets, and to the select families of the smiths thereof. We do not know to what extent the smiths were faithful in revealing the secrets of their knowledge of metallurgy to outsiders. Even today when their primitive technology has become outdated and hopelessly uneconomical, the tradition-bound smiths are not willing to reveal it to the outsiders. This probably explains why Atkinson's account of wootz steel production is at variance in details with what we have recorded concerning metallurgy (Atkinson 1884: 262-275).

Other factors include the use of same age-old furnaces, processes and blowers (*bhatthi*) by many tribes even today, which is a proof that these process secrets were well-guarded and any change in the process or equipment was considered as a bad omen. This probably is one of the reasons for the loss of metal technology and its reintroduction by the Europeans.

In the twentieth century, the condition has worsened so much that the memory of ancient glory remained only in the form of stories narrated by old men, and after its independence in 1947, India had to borrow modern technology from western countries to set up steel plants.

The wishful thinking of Neogi, in 1914, is worth recollecting. "We hope we have been able to give a trustworthy account of the process of the manufacture of Indian steel, which was an object of envy of all nations but successfully imitated by none and which supplied the materials of many a true blade of warriors both in the East and the West. It is sad to reflect that an ancient indigenous industry which attracted merchants from Persia, as narrated by Dr Voysey, barely hundred years ago, is on the point of extinction; but as even the darkest cloud is not without a silver lining, a distinct ray of hope is visible in the not very distant horizon presaging that India will yet regain her lost iron industry under modern scientific conditions together with other attendant industries depending upon iron."

The worst casualty of the traditional practice of maintaining secrecy was the knowledge of producing crucible steel so far as ironworking is concerned. We do not know if we have lost this knowledge for good, or does it still remain, howsoever faint it might be, in the mind of someone whose ancestors once practised it. It is for this and similar other reasons that it is important to conduct research on traditional technologies with an ethno-archaeological perspective.

What scientists explained in theory, and experimented in sophisticated laboratories, the illiterate smith practised in the familiar *āphara* (forge) with perfect ease time and again. It is important to explore research using these traditional knowledge sources because these so-called illiterate people can explain in simple, unsophisticated, vernacular language, how iron is subjected to different types of treatment, (which in scientific terminology are termed as carburisation, tempering, etc) to render iron suitable for making different items. Joshi (2002) is very positive in commenting that "without being philosophical, let me add folk wisdom has infinite dimensions, and scientists have yet to decipher the secrets of the knowledge of illiterate".

REVIVAL OF INTEREST

There has been renewed interest in understanding the materials science behind wootz steel. This primarily has been taken up by American scientists. Based on research conducted over the last three decades, two mechanisms for the appearance of the typical *damask* patterns from ultra high carbon steels have been proposed. The Wadsworth-Sherby mechanism attributes the formation of the structure to specific heat treatments, while the Verhoven-Pendary mechanism attributes the appearance of the pattern to the presence of critical carbide forming elements, notably vanadium, in the original ore from which the Deccani wootz was manufactured. These trace elements are supposed to have been present in iron ore body found in the Deccan. The theory holds that when this particular ore deposit was depleted, the steel made from other ores did not show these characteristics. However, this needs to be critically viewed because wootz steel was made at several different centres far removed in distance from each other in South India. In such circumstances, it is difficult to believe that one particular source of ore was used in making wootz steel. There may be more to the mystery of wootz than revealed by the recent scientific investigations.

There is sadly no research by Indian metallurgists into aspects of wootz manufacture and the making of blades from Decanni wootz. It is certain that if research is taken up in earnest, the secrets of the master steelmakers of Telangana, their process of making *ukku* by repeated heating and cooling for days on end to red heat at a particular temperature, their blacksmithy skills by hand hammering small globules of steel into ingots, the related heat treatments during and after shaping the lumps into shaped blanks, and the final etching of the *damask* pattern will be rediscovered.

It is also sad that despite the extensive number of reports that claim the importance of India in producing vast quantities of wootz, only a few archaeological sites have been investigated. There are many ethnographic accounts of Indian crucible steel production (Bronson 1986:13). Scientific investigations of wootz steel remains have only been published from four regions: three in India and one in Sri Lanka (e.g. Rajan 1989-90 and 1990; Craddock 1998; Srinivasan and Griffiths 1997; Anantharamu *et. al.* 1999, Freestone and Tite 1986, Rao *et. al.* 1970; Wayman and Juleff 1999; Lowe 1989a, 1989b, 1991). There is great need for scholars to take up archaeological investigations on wootz steel manufacturing sites in the Deccan.

It is possible to revive the ancient Indian method of making crucible steel and the process of converting them to sharp cutting objects, such as knives, blades, etc. The same practices can be adopted but for the laborious blowing of air by bellows, which can be automated. Once the steel is produced by the traditional method, it can be worked to produce objects with high value. If the products can be made with artistic skill and brilliance, then a niche market can be found for this type of products which can rake in profits for all the people involved. This will also bring back the glorious tradition of Indian blacksmithy to the main focus and help revive the glory of iron and steel-making practice of the Indian subcontinent.

BIBLIOGRAPHY

Abbot, J. 1847. Process of working the Damascus blade of Goojarat. *Journal of the Asiatic Society of Bengal* 16: 417-423.

'Abd al-Rahim. 1921. *Memoirs of Zahir-Ed-Din Muhammad Babur, Emperor of Hindustan*: Written by himself in the Changtai Turkish, Persian version translated by William Erskine, annotated by Lucas King, London: Oxford University Press, p. 187.

Ágoston, G. 2005. *Military Power and the Weapons Industry in the Ottoman Empire*. London: Cambridge University Press.

Agrawal, D.P. and J.S. Kharakwal. 2002. Outstanding problems of early Iron Age in India: Need of a new approach. In *Tradition and Innovation in the History of Iron Making: An Indo-European Perspective* (Eds.) Girija Pande and Jan af Geijerstam, Nainital: PAHAR Parikrama. Pp. 3-20.

Agricola, G. 1556. *De re Metallica*. Basle, 1556; English Translation, London, 1912, reprinted New York, 1950.

Akhbarat. 1694. *Akhbarat-i-Darbar-i-Mualla*. Calcutta: J.N. Sarkar Collection, 38th R.V. p. 29.

Al-Hassan. A.Y. 1978. Iron and steel technology in medieval Arabic sources. *Journal for the History of Arabic Science* 2: 31-43.

Allan, J.W. and B. Gilmour. 2000. *Persian Steel: The Tanavoli Collection*. Oxford: Oxford University Press.

Alvi, M.A. and A. Rahman, 1968. *Fathullah Shirazi: A Sixteenth-Century Indian Scientist*. New Delhi: Indian National Science Academy. Pp. 4-13.

Anantharaman, T.R. 1996. *The Rustless Wonder – A Study of the Iron Pillar at Delhi*. New Delhi: Vigyan Prasar.

Anantharaman. T.R. 1999. The iron pillar at Kodachadri in Karnataka. *Current Science* 76: 1428-1430.

Anantharamu, T.R., P.T. Craddock, R.K. Nagesh, S.R.N. Murthy and M.L. Wayman. 1999. Crucible steel of Ghattihosahalli, Chitradurga District, Karnataka, Southern India. *Journal of Historical Metallurgy*, 33: 13-25.

Anossoff, P. 1841. On the Bulat. First Published in *Grony Journal* in 1841. Later reprinted as "Mémoire sur l'acier damassé". In *Annuaire du Journal des Mines de Russie,* 1843. pp. 192-236.

Antieny, A. 1987. Results of metallographic examinations of pattern welded swords and lance heads in the Baltic area. *Symposium on Archaeometallurgy of Iron*, Liblice, Oct. 1987.

A.P. 1984. *Guntur District Kaifiyaths*, Vol. III, Hyderabad: Andhra Pradesh State p. 204

Atkinson, E.T. 1884. *The Himalayan Gazetteer*. Volume 1, Part I. pp. 262-275.

Babur Nama. 1979. Translated by A.S. Beveridge, reprinted in 1979. Delhi. pp. 469, 536, 547.

Bag, A.K. 2005. Historical Notes: Sukraniti on Guns, Cannons and Gunpowder. *Indian Journal of History of Science* 40: 657-662.

Bagnold, M.E. 1826. On the Indian methods of working iron and steel, for the Damascus gun-barrels and sword-blades. *The Franklin Journal* 2: 1-3.

Bagnold, M.E. 1918. *Bereitung des kunstlichen Damasts in Ostindien*. London.

Bajwa, F.S. 1964. *Military System of the Sikhs during the Period 1799-1848*. New Delhi: Motilal Banarasidas. p. 6.

Balasubramaniam, A.V., 2006. *Current Science* 90: 587-589.

Balasubramaniam, A.V., N.B. Ballal, B. Prakash, P. Krishna Rao and S. Waghulde. 1993. *Indigenous Iron and Steel Technology of India.* Bombay: IIT Bombay. p. 165.

Balasubramaniam, K. 1994. *Thanjavur (600 AD—1850 AD)* (in Tamil). Thanjavur: Anjana Publications. pp. 312-337.

Balasubramaniam, R. 1995. Studies on the corrosion resistance of the Delhi Iron Pillar. *National Metallurgical Laboratory Technical Journal* 37: 123-145.

Balasubramaniam, R. 1997a. Mixed potential theory analysis of the corrosion resistance of the Delhi Iron Pillar. *Transactions of the Indian Institute of Metals.* 50: 23-35.

Balasubramaniam, R. 1997b. New insights on the corrosion of the Delhi Iron Pillar based on historical and dimensional analysis. *Current Science* 73: 1057-1067.

Balasubramaniam, R. 1998a. Decorative bell capital of the Delhi Iron Pillar. *JOM* 50(3): 40-47.

Balasubramaniam, R. 1998b. On the presence of lead in the Delhi Iron Pillar. *Bulletin of the Metals Museum* 29: 19-39.

Balasubramaniam, R. 1999a. Elucidation of the manufacturing technology employed to construct the body of the Delhi Iron Pillar. *Bulletin of the Metals Museum* 31: 42-65.

Balasubramaniam, R. 1999b. Some aspects of lead presence in the Delhi Iron Pillar. *Current Science* 77: 681-686.

Balasubramaniam, R. 1999c. Delhi Iron Pillar rust characterization by X-ray diffraction analysis. *National Metallurgical Laboratory Technical Journal* 41: 13-20.

Balasubramaniam, R. 2000a. Identity of Chandra and Vishnupadagiri of the Delhi Iron Pillar inscription: numismatic, archaeological and literary evidence. *Bulletin of the Metals Museum* 32: 42 61.

Balasubramaniam, R. 2000b. On the corrosion resistance of the Delhi Iron Pillar. *Corrosion Science* 42: 2103-2129.

Balasubramaniam, R. 2002a. *Delhi Iron Pillar – New Insights*. Shimla: Indian Institute of Advanced Studies and New Delhi: Aryan Books International.

Balasubramaniam, R. 2002b. A new study of the Dhar Iron Pillar. *Indian Journal of History of Science* 37: 115-151.

Balasubramaniam, R. 2002c. On the growth kinetics of the protective passive film of the Delhi Iron Pillar. *Current Science* 82: 1357-1365.

Balasubramaniam, R. 2003a. Effect of material inhomogeneity on protective passive film formation on the Delhi Iron Pillar. *Current Science* 84: 534-541.

Balasubramaniam, R. 2003b. On the origin of non-uniform surface electrochemical potentials on the Delhi Iron Pillar. *Current Science* 85: 378-382.

Balasubramaniam, R. 2005a. On the first catalogue of forge-welded iron canons by Neogi. *Indian Journal of History of Science* 40: 259-268.

Balasubramaniam, R. 2005b. Kadak Bijli – the forge-welded iron cannon at Jhansi fort. *Indian Journal of History of Science,* 40: 371-388.

Balasubramaniam, R. 2005c. Azdaha Paikar – the composite iron-bronze cannon at Musa Burj of Golconda fort. *Indian Journal of History of Science* 40: 389-408.

Balasubramaniam, R. 2005d. Fath Raihbar – the massive bronze cannon at Petla Burj of Golconda fort. *Indian Journal of History of Science* 40: 409-430.

Balasubramaniam, R. 2005e. Catalogue of massive forge-welded iron cannons of India – I. *Journal of the Ordnance Society* 17: 67-90.

Balasubramaniam, R. 2005f. Development of cannon technology in medieval India. *Indian Journal of History of Science* 40: 503-538.

Balasubramaniam, R. 2005g. European mercenary artillerymen in the Indian subcontinent (1500-1800). *Indian Journal of History of Science* 40: 673-678.

Balasubramaniam, R. 2005h. *Story of the Delhi Iron Pillar*. New Delhi: Foundation Books.

Balasubramaniam, R. 2005i. *The World Heritage Complex of the Qutub.* New Delhi: Aryan Books International.

Balasubramaniam, R. 2007. *The Saga of Indian Connons*, New Delhi: Aryan Books International.

Balasubramaniam, R. and M.I. Dass. 2004. On the astronomical significance of the Delhi Iron Pillar. *Current Science* 86: 1134-1142.

Balasubramaniam, R., M.I. Dass and E.M. Raven. 2004b. On the original image atop the Delhi Iron Pillar. *Indian Journal of History of Science* 39: 177-203.

Balasubramaniam, R. and S. Jaikishan. 2005a. Saltpetre manufacture and marketing in medieval India. *Indian Journal of History of Science* 40: 663-672.

Balasubramaniam, R., K. Mondal and A.K. Nigam. 2005c. Dal Mardan – the medieval forge-welded iron cannon at Bishnupur. *Indian Journal of History of Science* 40: 295-320.

Balasubramaniam, R. and V.N. Prabhakar, 2007. On technical analysis of characters of the oldest Delhi Iron Pillar inscription. *Current Science* 92: 1709-1719.

Balasubramaniam, R. and A. V. Ramesh Kumar, 1998. Corrosion product Analysis of ancient corrosion resistance Indian iron. Corrosion Science 40: 1169-1178

Balasubramaniam, R. and A. V. Ramesh Kumar 2000. Characterization of Delhi Iron Pillar rust by X-ray diffraction, Fourier enfrared spectroscopy and Mössbauer spetroscopy *Corrosion Science* 42: 2085-2104.

Balasubramaniam, R. and A.V. Ramesh Kumar. 2003. Corrosion resistance of the Dhar Iron Pillar. *Corrosion Science* 45: 2451-2465.

Balasubramaniam, R., S. Sankaran and M. Surender. 2005e. The forge-welded iron cannon near Fateh Burj of Golconda fort rampart. *Indian Journal of History of Science* 40: 337-348.

Balasubramaniam, R., A. Saxena and T.R. Anantharaman. 2005b. Rajagopala – the massive iron cannon at Thanjavur in Tamil Nadu. *Indian Journal of History of Science* 40: 269-294.

Balasubramaniam, R., A. Saxena, T.R. Anantharaman, S. Rigeur and P. Dillmann. 2004a. A marvel of medieval Indian metallurgy: Thanjavur's forge-welded iron cannon. *JOM* 56(1): 17-23.

Balasubramaniam, R., S. Srinivasan and S. Jaikishan, 2005g. *Qila Kusha – The Composite Iron-Bronze Cannon at Golconda fort*. Unpublished research.

Balasubramaniam, R., K. Gayathri Subramanyam and J. Kedareswari. 2005f. *The Forge-welded Cannons at Gun Foundry in Hyderabad*. Unpublished research.

Balasubramaniam. R., M. Surender and S. Sankaran. 2005d. The forge-welded iron cannon at Bada Burj of Golconda fort rampart. *Indian Journal of History of Science* 40: 321-336.

Banerjea, J.N. 1956. *The Development of Hindu Iconography*. New Delhi: Munshiram Manoharlal. p. 93.

Banerji, R.D. 1911. Inscribed Guns from Assam. *Journal and Proceedings of the Asiatic Society of Bengal* VII: 44-46.

Bardgett, W.E. and J.F. Stanners. 1963. Delhi Iron Pillar – A study of the corrosion aspects. *Journal of the Iron and Steel Institute* 210: 3-10 and *National Metallurgical Laboratory Technical Journal* 5: 24-30.

Beglar, Y.D. 1874. Report for the Year 1871-72. *Archaeological Survey of India Annual Reports* IV: 28-30.

Belaiew, N.T. 1906. *On the Bulat, Thesis*. St. Petersburg: Michael Artillery Academy.

Belaiew, N.T. 1914. Les précurseurs de la métallographie. *Revue de Métallurgie* 11: 221-227.

Belaiew, N.T. 1918. Damascene steel. *Journal of Iron and Steel Institute* and 97: 417-37.

Belaiew, N.T. 1921. Damascene steel, part II. *Journal of Iron and Steel Institute* 104: 181-186.

Belaiew, N.T. 1950. Sur le 'Damas' Oriental et les lames damassées. *Métaux et Civilization* 1: 10-16.

Bernier, F. 1668. *Travels in the Moghul Empire 1656-68*. Translated by A. Constable. New Delhi: New Asia Publications (1995). pp. 73, 93, 217.

Beveridge, H. 1968. *The Tuzuk-i-Jahangiri* (The Memoirs of Jahangir). New Delhi: Munshiram Monoharlal. Vol. I. pp. 406-408.

Bhatt, S. 1971. Inscriptions on the cannons conserved in Central Museum, Indore. Translated from the original article in Hindi titled *Kendriya Sangrahalaya Indore Mein Sarankshit Topoein Par Utkeern Lekh. Ahilya Smarika.* 2: 52-55.

Biringuccio, V. 1540. *De la Pirotechnia*. English Translation, New York (1950).

Biswas, A.K. 1996. *Minerals and Metals in Ancient India.* New Delhi: D.K. Printworld.

Biswas, A.K. 2005. Epic of Saltpetre to Gunpowder. *Indian Journal of History of Science* 40: 539-572.

Breant. J.R. 1823. Description d'un procédé àà l'aide duquel on obtient une espèce d'acier fondu, sembable à celue des lames damassées Oreintales. *Bull Société d'Encouragement pour l'Industrie Nationale* 22: 222-227. Reprinted in *Annales de Mines* 9 (1824) 319-328.

Bronson, B. 1986. The making and selling of wootz, a crucible steel of India. *Archeomaterials* 1: 13-27.

Brown, P. 1976. *Indian Architecture (Buddhist and Hindu Periods)*. Bombay: D.P. Taraporevala and Sons, Seventh Reprint, 1976. pp. 11-49.

Buchanan, F.A. 1807. *Journey from Madras, Through the Countries of Mysore, Canara and Malabar*. London: East India Company.

Campbell, J. 1895. *J. Bombay Branch of the Royal Asiatic Society*, XIX: 157.

Carleton, N. 2002. The lion's teeth: the artillery of Maharaja Ranjit Singh. *Soldiers of the Queen* 109: 3-7

Carleton, N. and M. Buck. 2004. Guns of the Rajahs: Indian artillery from the Mughals to the Sikhs. *Journal of the Ordnance Society*. 16: 57-66.

Chakrabarti, D.K. 1992. *The Early Use of Iron in India*. New Delhi: Oxford University Press. pp. 15-116.

Chatterji, S.K. 2001. *Vintage Guns of India*. New Delhi: Macmillan.

Chattopadhyay, P. 2005. Cannons of Eastern India. *Indian Journal of History of Science* 40: 465-486.

Choudhary, G.C. 1963. *Political History of Northern India from Jain Sources (650 AD to 1300 AD)*. Amristar: Sonalal Jaindharma Pracharak Samiti. Pp. 96-115.

Clark, G.T. 1873. *Archaeological Journal* 30: 265, quoted in C. Singer *et. al.*, (Eds.). History of Technology. Oxford. Vol. III, 1957, p. 363.

Cole, H.H. 1872. *The Architecture of Ancient Delhi, Especially the Buildings around the Kutb Minar*. London.

Coomaraswamy, A.K. 1908. *Mediaeval Sinhalese Art*, Chapter XI, New York.

Cooper, R.G.S. and N.K. Wagle. 1995. Maratha artillery: from Dabhoi to Assaye. *Journal of the Ordnance Society* 7: 58-78.

Cousens, H. 1902. The Iron Pillar at Dhar. *Archaeological Survey of India Annual Reports* (1902-03). 205-212.

Cousens, H. 1916. *Bijapur and its Architectural Remains, with a Historical Outline of the Adil Shah Dynasty.* Bombay. pp. 29-33 and pl. III and IV.

Craddock, P.T. 1995. Early metal mining and production. In *Early Metal Mining and Production.* Edinburgh: Edinburgh University Press.

Craddock, P.T. 1998. New light on the production of crucible steel in Asia. *Bulletin of the Metals Museum* 29: 41-66.

Craddock, P.T and J. Lang. 1993. Gizeh iron revisited. *Journal of the Historical Metallurgy Society* 27: 57-59.

Cunningham, A. 1872. *Archaeological Survey of India Annual Reports* 2: 317.

CVB. 1820. Method of making steel in Mysore. *Asiatic Journal* 9: 441.

Dass, M.I. 2001. *Udayagiri – Rise of a Sacred Hill, Its Art, Architecture and Landscale – A Study.* Ph.D. Thesis. Leicestershire: DeMontfort University.

Dass, M.I. and R. Balasubramaniam. 2004. Estimation of the original erection site of the Delhi Iron Pillar at Udayagiri. *Indian Journal of History of Science* 39: 54-71.

Datta, P.K. 1968. Guns in Mughal India. *Bulletin of the Victoria Memorial* II.

Datta, P.K. 1969. Cannon in India during the Mughal days. *Bulletin of the Victoria Memorial* III-IV.

Datta, P.K. 1972. *Deg:* arm of the Mughal period. *Bulletin of the Victoria Memorial* VI-VII.

Deloche, J. 2000. *Senji (Gingi), ville fortifiée du pays tamoul,* Paris/Pondichery, 2000.

Deloche, J. 2001. Études sur les fortifications de l'Inde: III. La fortification hindoue dans le Sud de l'Inde (VIc-XVIIIc siècle). *Bulletin de L'École Française D'Extrème-Orient* 88: 77-134.

Deloche, J. 2002. Études sur les fortifications de l'Inde: IV. La fortification musulmane dans le Dekkan méridional (XVc-XVIIIc siècle). *Bulletin de L'École Française D'Extrème-Orient* 89: 39-106.

Deloche, J. 2005a. Gunpowder artillery and military architecture in South India (fifteenth–eighteenth century). *Indian Journal of History of Science* 40: 573-596.

Deloche, J. 2005b. Personal Communication. Four cannons were located at the Mudgal fort located in the Lingasugur Taluk of Raichur District in Karnataka. The first one was on Fateh Darwazah, the second on Ali Burj; both these were long wrought iron cannons. The last two cannons were found inside the walls, north of Kati Darwazah, "a short one of large diameter and a long one surrounded by strange rings kept in position by hooks".

Digby, S. 2001. The Problem of the Military Ascendancy of the Delhi Sultanate. In *Warfare and Weaponry in South Asia 1000-1800* (Eds.) Jos J.L. Gommans and D.H.A. Kolff. New Delhi: Oxford University Press.

Dillmann, P. and R. Balasubramaniam, 2001. Characterisation of ancient Indian iron and entrapped slag inclusions using electron, photon and nuclear microprobes. *Bulletin of Materials Science* 24: 317-322.

Dillmann, P., R. Balasubramaniam and G. Beranger. 2002. Characterisation of protective rust on ancient Indian iron using microprobe analyses. *Corrosion Science* 44: 2231-2242.

Dishalkar, D.B. 1944. Some old guns in the Indore Museum. *Journal of Indian History* XXIII, Part I: p. 40.

Dube, R.K. 1990. Aspects of powder technology in ancient and medieval India. *Powder Metallurgy* 33: 119-125.

El Gayar, E.S. and M.P. Jones. 1989. Metallurgical investigation of an iron plate found in 1837 in the Great Pyramid at Gizeh, Egypt. *Journal of the Historical Metallurgy Society* 23: 75-83.

Evans, U.R. 1926. *Corrosion of Metals*. London: Edward Arnold. p. 266.

Faraday, M. 1819. An analysis of Wootz or Indian steel. *Quarterly Journal of Science* 7: 288-290.

Feuerbach, A.M. 2002. *Crucible Steel in Central Asia: Production, Use, and Origins*. Ph.D. Thesis. University of London.

Forbes, F. 1840. Great brass gun at Bijapur. *Asiatic Journal and Monthly Register for British and Foreign India, China and Australasia* New Series XXXII: 84-85.

Freestone, I.C. and M.S. Tite. 1986. Refractories in the ancient and pre-industrial world. In *Ceramics and Civilization* (Ed.) W.D. Kingery. III: 35-64.

Friend, J.N. and W.E. Thorneycroft. 1924. Examination of iron from Konarka. *Journal of the Iron and Steel Institute* 110: 313-315.

Führer, A. 1893. *Annual Report of the Archaeological Survey Circle, North-Western Provinces and Oudh for the Year ending 30th June 1893*. Rourkee: Thomson College Press. p. 21.

Ghosh, A.L. and P.K. Chattapadhyaya. 1982. *Masca Journal* 2: p.63

Ghosh, M.K. 1963. The Delhi Iron Pillar and its iron. *National Metallurgical Laboratory Technical Journal* 5: 31-45.

Gillet,C., M.H. Lefebvre and J. Galloy. 2004. A technological success in the fifteenth century: Jehan Cambier's Mons Meg. *Journal of the Ordnance Society.* 16: 19-26.

Graves, H.G. 1912. Further notes on the early use of iron in India. *Journal of the Iron and Steel Institute* 85: 187-202.

Guilmartin, J.F. 1974. *Gunpowder and Galleys: Changing Technology and Mediterranean Warfare at Sea in the Sixteenth Century*, Cambridge: Cambridge University Press.

Guilmartin, J.F. 1974b. Appendix 3: The design and construction of bronze cannon in the sixteenth century. In Chapter 4: The weapons of sixteenth century warfare at sea. In *Gunpowder and Galleys: Changing Technology and Mediterranean Warfare at Sea in the Sixteenth Century*. Cambridge: Cambridge University Press.

Hadfield, R. 1912. Sinhalese iron and steel of ancient origin. *Journal of the Iron and Steel Institute* 85: 134-174.

Halder, S., G.K. Gupta and R. Balasubramaniam. 2004. On the role of environment on the corrosion resistance of the Delhi Iron Pillar. *Current Science* 86: 559-566.

Harnecker, Von K. 1924. Beitrag zur Frage des Damanzenstahls. *Stahl Eisen* 44: 1409-1411.

Heath, J.M. 1839. On Indian iron and steel. *Journal of Royal Asiatic Society* 5: 390-397.

HMSO. 1963. *Catalogue of the Museum of Artillery in the Rotunda at Woolwich*, Pt. 1, Ordnance. London.

Hudson, J.C. 1953. The Delhi Iron Pillar. *Nature* 172: 499-500.

Irvine, W. 1962. *The Army of the Indian Moghuls*. Originally published in 1894 and reprinted in 1962. New Delhi: Eurasia Publishing House. p. 152.

Jaggi, O.P. 1989. *Science and Technology in Medieval India*. New Delhi and Lucknow: Atma Ram and Sons. pp. 135-136.

Jaikishan, S. 2005. Forge-welded cannons in the forts of Karimnagar district in Andhra Pradesh state. *Indian Journal of History of Science* 40: 487-502.

JCPDS. 1996. JCPDS Powder Diffraction Files. *PCPDFWIN Software*, Joint Committee on Powder Diffraction Standards—International Centre for Diffraction Data, Swarthmore, USA.

Joshi, M.P. 2002. Some aspects of ironworking in antiquity vis-à-vis Central Himalaya. In *Tradition and Innovation in the History of Iron Making: An Indo European Perspective* (Eds.) Girija Pande and Jan af Geijerstam. Nainital: PAHAR Parikrama. pp. 47-59.

Juleff, G. 1996. *Early Iron and Steel in Sri Lanka: A study of the Samanalawewa Area*. Ph.D dissertation. University of London.

Kannan, R. and R. Balasubramaniam. 2000. *Documentation on the Cannons in the Government Museum Chennai (Madras)*. Chennai: Government Museum.

Karim, Abdul. 1992. *Corpus of the Arabic and Persian Inscriptions of Bengal, Dhaka*. pp. 387-388.

Kedareswari, J. 2005. *Catalogue of Cannons in the Andhra Pradesh State Museum*, Hyderabad: Andhra Pradesh Archaeology Department Publications.

Kedzierski, Z. and J. Stepineski. 1987. *Symposium on Archaeometallurgy of Iron*. Liblice, October 1987. p. 387.

Khan, I.G. 2000. *Metallurgy in Medieval India – 16th to 18th centuries*.

Khan, I.A. 2001. Early use of cannon and musket in India: AD 1442-1526. In *Warfare and Weaponry in South Asia 1000-1800* (Eds.) J.J.L. Gommans and D.H.A. Kolff. New Delhi: Oxford University Press. pp. 321-336.

Khan, I.A. 2004a. *Gunpowder and Firearms: Warfare in Medieval India*. New Delhi: Oxford University Press. pp. 17-91.

Khan, I.A. 2004b. Artillery in Mughal India: 1556-1739. Chapter 3 in *Gunpowder and Firearms: Warfare in Medieval India*. New Delhi: Oxford University Press. pp. 91-127.

Khan, I.A. 2004c. European artillery in India during the fifteenth century. Chapter 2 in *Gunpowder and Firearms: Warfare in Medieval India*. New Delhi: Oxford University Press. pp. 41-58.

Khan, Q. 1971. *Adab-i-Alamgiri*. Lahore. Vol. I. pp. 528-532.

Kulkarni, D.A. 1969. *Rasa Ratna Samuccaya*. New Delhi: Meher Chand Lakshmandas.

Kumar, V. and R. Balasubramaniam. 2002. On the origin of high P contents in ancient Indian iron. *International Journal of Metals, Materials and Processes* 14: 1-14.

Lahiri, A.K., T. Banerjee and B.R. Nijhawan. 1963. Some observations on corrosion-resistance of ancient Delhi Iron Pillar and present-time Adivasi iron made by primitive methods. *National Metallurgical Laboratory Technical Journal* 5: 46-5.

Lal, B.B. 1996. In *The Delhi Iron Pillar: Its Art, Metallurgy and Inscriptions* (Eds.) M.C. Joshi, S.K. Gupta and Shankar Goyal. Jodhpur: Kusumanjali Book World. pp. 22-58.

Lenz, E. von. 1906/8. Uber Damast. *Zeitschrift fuer Historische Waffenkunde* 4: 132-142.

Lowe, T.L. 1989a. Refractories in high-carbon iron processing: A preliminary study of the Deccani Wootz-making crucibles. In *Ceramics and Civilization* (Ed.) P.E. McGovern. The American Ceramics Society. IV: 237-251.

Lowe, T.L. 1989b. Solidification and the crucible processing of Deccani ancient steel. In *Proceedings of the Indo-US Conference on the Principles of Solidification and Materials Processing* (Eds.) R. Trivedi, J.A. Sekhar and J. Mazumdar. New Delhi: Oxford and IBH. pp. 729-740.

Lowe, T.L., N. Mark and G. Thomas. 1991. An historical mullite fibre-reinforced ceramic composite: characterization of the 'Wootz' crucible refractory. In *Materials Issues in Art and Archaeology II* (Eds.) P.A. Vandiver *et. al.*, Washington: Materials Research Society, 185: 627-632.

Luyens, H.T.P.J. 1844. Mémoire sur la fabrication de l'acier fondu et damassée. Paris. German extract in *Polytechnische Centralblat* 1: 315-321.

Mahamud, S.J. 1988. *Metals Technology in Medieval India*. Daya Publishing House.

Manucci, N. 1906. Storia do Mogor. 4 vols. *History of the Moghuls 1653-1708*. Translated by W. Irvine 1906. London: John Murray. Vol. II. p. 365.

Mazumdar, R.C. 1994. The use of guns in medieval India. In Appendix to Chapter XIV in The Delhi Sultanate. Vol. VI. In *The History and Culture of the Indian People* (Ed.) R.C. Majumdar. Bombay: Bharatiya Vidya Bhavan. pp. 460-463.

Mellor, J.W. 1961. *A Comprehensive Treatise on Inorganic and Theoretical Chemistry*. 1932. London: Longmans. Vol. XII. pp. 853-854.

Misawa, T.T., K. Asami, K. Hashimoto and S. Shimodaira. 1974. The mechanism of atmospheric rusting and the protective amorphous rust on low alloy steel. *Corrosion Science* 14: 279-289.

Misawa, T., T. Kyuno, W. Suetaka and S. Shimodaira. 1971. The mechanism of atmospheric rusting and the effect of Cu and P on the rust formation of low alloy steels. *Corrosion Science* 11: 35-48.

Moore, J.J. 1990. Slag Chemistry. In *Chemical Metallurgy*. Oxford: Butterworth-Heinemann. Pp. 152-192.

Moxon, J. 1677. *Mechanick Exercises, or the Doctrine of Handiworks*. London. Vol. I: No. 3.

Mushet, D. 1804. Experiments on Wootz or Indian steel. *Philosophical Transactions of the Royal Society* 95: 175. see also *Philosophical Magazine* 1805 22: 40-48. Reprinted in Mushet's *Papers on Iron and Steel*, London, 1840, pp. 650-78.

Narasimha, R. 1999. Rocketing from the galaxy bazaar. *Nature* 440: 123-125.

Nath, R. 1984. *Monuments of Delhi—Historical Study*. Jaipur: The Historical Research Documentation Center Programme. Illustration 18.

Needham, J. 1986. *Science and Civilisation in China*. Vol. 5 Chemistry and Chemical Technology, Part 7: Military Technology; The Gunpowder Epic. Cambridge: Cambridge University Press. pp. 367-373.

Neff, D. and R. Balasubramaniam. 2005. Bhavani Shankar – the forge-welded iron cannon at Jhansi fort. *Indian Journal of History of Science* 40: 349-370.

Neogi, P. 1914. *Iron in Ancient India*. Calcutta: Indian Association for Cultivation of Science. Pp. 32-40.

Oberhoffer, P. 1915. Über das Gefüge des Damazenersahls. *Stahl und Eisen* 35: 140-141.

Okada, H. 1968. Atmospheric corrosion of steels. *Journal of the Society of Materials Science Japan* 17: 705-7709.

Okada, H., Y. Hosoi, K. Yukawa and H. Naito. 1969. Structure of the rust formed on low alloy steels in atmospheric corrosion. *Journal of the Iron and Steel Institute Japan* 55: 355-365.

Paludan, A. 1994. The Tang dynasty iron oxen at Pujin bridge. *Orientations*. May: 61–68.

Panseri, C. 1962. Damascus steel in legend and in reality. *Armi Antiche*. pp. 29-30.

Pant, G.N. 1980. *Indian Arms and Armour: Volume II, Swords and Daggers*, New Delhi: Army Educational Stores.

Pant, G.N. and K.K. Sharma. 2001. *Indian Armours in the National Museum Collection—A Catalogue*. New Delhi: National Museum.

Parker, G. 1988. *The Military Revolution*. London: Oxford University Press. p. 129.

Partington, J.R. 1999. *A History of Greek Fire and Gunpowder.* Cambridge: Cambridge University Press.

Pearson, G. 1795. Experiments and observations to investigate the nature of a kind of steel manufactured at Bombay and there called wootz. *Philosophical Transactions of Royal Society Series A* 85: 322-346.

Percy, J. 1864. Direct Extraction of Iron in the Malleable State from the Ore. *Metallurgy (Iron and Steel)*. London.

Piaskowski, J. 1978. Mettallographic examination of two Damascene steel blades. *Journal of Historic Arabic Science* 2: 3-30.

Piaskowski, J. 1981. Classification of the famous Damascene swords. In *Proceedings of the First International Conference on the History of Turkish Islamic Science and Technology*. Istanbul. Vol. III. pp. 155-161.

Pleiner, R. 1971. The problem of the beginning of Iron Age in India. *Acta Praehistorica et Archaeologica* 2: 5-76.

Poona Residency. 1800. Poona Residency Correspondence. Vol. 4: p. 298.

Porta, G.B della. 1588. *Magiae naturalis libri XX*. Naples 1588. English Translation, London 1658. Reprinted New York 1958.

Prakash, B. and V. Tripathi. 1986. Iron technology in ancient India. *Metals and Materials* 2: 568-579.

Prakash, B. 1989a. Archaeometallurgical study of Iron Pillar at Dhar. *Puratattva* 20: 111-122.

Prakash, B. 1989b. (and reply by B. Bronson) *Archaeomaterials* 3: 95-96.

Prakash, B. 1991. Metallurgy of iron and steel making and blacksmithy in ancient India. *Indian Journal of History of Science* 26: 351-371.

Prakash, B. 1997. Metals and Metallurgy. In *History of Technology in India* (Ed.) A.K. Bag. New Delhi: Indian National Science Academy. Vol. I.

Proshkin, D.A. 1971. *Pavel Petrovich Anossoff*. Moscow: Izdatelsvo Nauk. pp. 180-250.

Puri, V. R. Balasubramaniam and A.V. Ramesh Kumar. 1997. Corrosion behaviour of an ancient fifteen hundred-year old Gupta iron. *Bulletin of Metals Museum* 28(II): 1-10.

Rackham, H. 1995. *Pliny Natural History XXXIV-XXXV*. Cambridge: Harvard University Press. pp. 232-233, pp. 143-146.

Raj, B., P. Kalyanasundaram, T. Jayakumar, C. Babu Rao, B. Venkataraman, U. Kamachi Mudali, A. Joseph, A. Kumar and K.V. Rajkumar. 2005. Nondestructive evaluation of the Delhi Iron Pillar. *Current Science* 88: 1948-1956.

Rajan, K. 1989-90. Iron and gemstone industries as revealed from Kodumanal excavations. *Puratattva* 20: 111-113.

Rajan, K. 1990. New light on the Megalithic culture of the Kongu region. *Man and Environment* 15: 93-102.

Ramesh Kumar, A.V. and R. Balasubramaniam. 1998. Corrosion product analysis of ancient corrosion resistant Indian iron. *Corrosion Science* 40: 1169-1178.

Ramesh Kumar, A.V. and R. Balasubramaniam. 1999a. Delhi Iron Pillar rust characterisation by Fourier transform infrared spectroscopy analysis. *National Metallurgical Laboratory Technical Journal* 41: 37-41.

Ramesh Kumar, A.V. and R. Balasubramaniam, 1999b. Delhi Iron Pillar rust characterisation by Mössbauer spectroscopy analysis. *National Metallurgical Laboratory Technical Journal* 41: 57-61.

Randhawa, M.S. 1983. *Paintings of the Babur-nama*. New Delhi: Indian Publications Division, p. 121, Plate XVIII.

Ratnagar, S. 1981. *Encounters: The Westerly Trade of the Harappa Civilization*. New Delhi: Oxford University Press. pp. 157-200.

Rao, K.N.P, J.K. Mukherjee and A.K. Lahiri. 1970. Some observations on the structure of ancient steel from South India and its mode of production. *Historical Metallurgy* 4: 12-17.

Rao, K.N.P. 1982. Iron and steel technology in India in ancient and medieval periods. *The Metallurgist and Materials Technologist* p. 468.

Rao, K.N.P. 1989. *Metal News*, 1(3): 1.

Ray, P.C. 1909. *History of Hindu Chemistry*, Vols. I and II. Calcutta: The Bengal Chemical & Pharmaceutical Works Limited.

Reaumur, R.A.F. 1722. *L'Art de convertir le fer forgean acier*, Paris. English Translation, Chicago: Chicago University Press (1956).

Rennel. 1793. *Memoir of a Map of Hindoostan; or the Mogul Empire: With an Examination of some Positions in the Former System of Indian Geography; and some Illustrations of the present one: And a Complete Index of Names to the Map*. London: Brown. p. 61.

Ritter von Schwarz. C. 1901. Uber die Eisen und Stahlindustrie Ostindiens (About the iron and steel industry of East India). *Stahl und Eisen* 21: pp. 209-211, 277-283.

Ritter, K. 1938. Aufbau und Herstellung der schmiedeeisernen Steinbüchsen des Mittelalters. *Technische Mitteilungen Krupp: Technische Berichte* Fried. Krupp AG Essen 6(5): 113-129.

Roessler, K. 1995. The non rusting Iron Pillar at Dhar. *National Metallurgical Laboratory Technical Journal* 37: 143-154.

Roessler, K. 1997. The big cannon pipe at Tanjavur. *Metal News* 19(1): pp. 1.

Rostoker, W. and B. Bronson. 1990. *Pre-Industrial Iron, Its Technology and Ethnology*. Philadelphia: Archaeomaterials Monograph No. 1.

Roy, K. 2005. Rockets under Haidar Ali and Tipu Sultan. *Indian Journal of History of Science* 40: 635-656.

Sachse, M. 1994. *Damascus Steel: Myth, History, Technology, Applications*. Wirtschaftseverk: N.W. Verl. Fur Neue Wiss.

Sarkar, J.N. 1979. *The Life of Mir Jumlaa, the General of Aurangzeb's Reign*. Kolkata.

Savitsky, E.M. and B.S. Kliachko. 1978. *Metals of the Space Era*. Moscow: Metallurgica. pp. 6-7.

Schib, K. and R. Gnade. 1947. *The Metallurgist, J.C.Fisher, and His Relations with Britain*. Schaffhausen. See also by the same authors Johann Conrad Fischer, 1773-1854, Schaffhausen, 1954.

Schwarz, C von. 1899. Correspondence on Syed Ali Bilgrami's Iron Industry in Hyderabad. *Journal of Iron and Steel Institute* 56(2): 89.

Shastri, H.P. 1890. *Proceedings of the Asiatic Society of Bengal* 1890. p. 167.

Sherby. O.D. *et. al.* 1976. *Superplastic UHCS*. US Patent 3951697. Stanford University. 20 April 1976.

Smith, C.S. 1965. *A History of Metallography – The Development of Ideas on the Struture of Metals Before 1890*. Chicago: The University of Chicago Press.

Smith L.E. 1805. *A Sketch of the Rise, Progress and Termination of the Regular Corps formed and Commanded by Europeans in the Service of the Native Princes of India*. Kolkata. pp. 6-7, 47, 72-73, 387-388.

Smith, R.D. 1993. Port pieces: the use of wrought iron guns in the sixteenth century. *Journal of the Ordnance Society* 5: 1-10.

Smith, R.D. 2005. Monster cannon: wrought iron bombards of Europe. *Indian Journal of History of Science* 40: 451-464.

Smith, R.D. and R.R. Brown. 1989. *Bombards Mons Meg and Her Sisters*. Royal Armouries: The Dorset Press.

Smith, V.A. 1898. The Dhar Iron Pillar. *Journal of the Royal Asiatic Society of Great Britain and Ireland* (1898) 143-146.

Sohoni, S.V. 1990. Historical Background of Iron Industry in Malwa of Bhoja's Period. *Society and Science* 10: 104-109.

Srinivasan, S. and D. Griffiths. 1997. Crucible steel in South India – preliminary investigations on crucibles from some newly identified sites. *Material Issues in Art and Archaeology* 5: 111-125.

Srinivasan, S. and S. Ranganathan. 2004. *Wootz Steel – Legendary Material of the Orient*. Bangalore: Indian Institute of Science.

Stirling. 1824. *Asiatic Researches*. XV: 330.

Stodart, J. 1814. Account of the method of making steel in Mysore country. Letter quoted by Benjamin Heyne in *Tracts Historical and Statistical of India*. London. 1814. pp. 356-364.

Stodart, J. 1818. A brief account of Wootz or Indian steel. *The Asiatic Journal and Monthly Register* 5: 570-571.

Stodart, J. and M. Faraday. 1820. Experiments on the alloys of steel, made with a view to its improvement. *Quarterly Journal of Science* IX: 319-30.

Subbarayappa, B.V. 1971. Chemical Practices and Alchemy. In *A Concise History of Science in India* (Eds.) D.M. Bose, S.N. Sen and B.V. Subbarayappa. New Delhi: Indian National Science Academy. Pp. 274-349.

Taleff, E.M. B.L. Bramfitt, C.K. Syn, D.R. Lesuer and O.D. Sherby. 1997. Mechanical behavior of an ultrahigh-carbon steel exhibiting a damask surface pattern. In *Thermomechanical Processing and Mechanical Properties of Hypereutectoid Steels and Cast Irons* (Eds.) D.R. Lesuer, C.K. Syn and O.D. Sherby, Warrendale, TMS. pp. 189-198.

Taleff, E.M., B.L. Bramfitt, C.K. Syn, D.R. Lesuer, J. Wadsworth, and O.D. Sherby. 2001. Processing structure, and properties of a rolled ultrahigh-carbon steel plate exhibiting a damask pattern. *Materials Characterization* 46: 19-23.

Thomsen, R. 1987. Pattern welded swords from Illorup land Nydam. *Symposium on Archaeometallurgy of Iron*. Liblice. October 1987. p. 37.

Thorn, W. 1896. Memoirs of War in India, 1803-06. p. 117: cited by W. Irvine. *The Army of the Indian Moghuls: Its Organization and Administration*. Originally published from Kolkata 1896. New Delhi: Eurasia Publishing House. 1962. p. 139.

Toussaint, F. 2002. Iron and steel in ancient India. In *Tradition and Innovation in the History of Iron Making: An Indo European Perspective* (Eds.) Girija Pande and Jan af Geijerstam, Nainital: PAHAR Parikrama. pp. 39-46.

Tripathi, V. 1985. From copper to iron – a transition. *Puratattva* 15.

Tripathi, V. 2001. *The Age of Iron in South Asia: Legacy and Tradition*. New Delhi: Aryan Books International. pp. 91-110.

Tripathi, V. 2007. *A Comprehensive History of Iron in India*. Delhi: Rupa & Co. and Infinity Foundation.

Twinning. T. 1893. *Travels in India A Hundred Years Ago*. London. p. 187, p. 217.

Tylecote, R.F. 1962. *Metallurgy in Archaeology*. London: British Museum. p. 27.

Tylecote, R.F. 1979. *A History of Metallurgy*. London: The Metals Society. p. 4.

Ubranski, T. 1985. *Chemistry and Technology of Explosives*. Vol. 3, Oxford: Pergamon Press.

Verhoeven, J.D. 1975. *Fundamentals of Physical Metallurgy*. New York: John Wiley.

Verhoeven, J.D. 1987. Damascus steel, Part 1: Indian Wootz steel. *Materials Characterization* 20: 145-151.

Verhoeven, J.D. 2000. A review of microsegregation induced banding phenomena in steels. *Journal of Materials Engineering Performance* 9: 286-296.

Verhoeven, J.D. 2001. The mystery of Damascus blades. *Scientific American* January 2001. pp. 74-79.

Verhoeven, J.D., H.H. Baker, D.T. Peterson, H.F. Clark and W.M. Yates. 1990. Damascus steel: Part III. The Wadsworth-Sherby mechanism. *Material Characterization* 24: 205-227.

Verhoeven, J.D. and L.L. Jones. 1987. Damascus steel: Part II. Origin of the damask pattern. *Metallography* 20: 153-180.

Verhoeven, J.D. and A.H. Pendray. 1992. Experiments to produce the pattern on Damascus steel blades. *Materials Characterization* 29: 195-212.

Verhoeven, J.D. and A.J. Pendray. 1993. Studies of Damascus steel blades: Part I—experiments on reconstructed blades. *Materials Characterization* 30: 175-186.

Verhoeven, J.D. and A.H. Pendray. 2001. On the origin of the Damask pattern of Damascus steels. *Materials Characterization* 47: 79

Verhoeven, J.D., A.H. Pendray and P.M. Berge. 1993. Studies of Damascus steel blades: part II. Destruction and reformation of the pattern. *Materials Characterization* 30: 187–200.

Verhoeven, J.D., A.H. Pendray and W.E. Dauksch. 1998. The key role of impurities in ancient Damascus steel blades. *JOM* 50(9): 58-64.

Verhoeven, J.D., A. Pendray and E.D. Gibson. 1996. Wootz Damascus steel blades. *Materials Characterization* 37: 9-22.

Verhoeven, J.D. and D.T. Peterson. 1992. What is Damascus steel? *Materials Characterization* 29: 335-41.

Voight, A.F.G. and A. Abu-Samra. 1965. Analysis of a Damscus steel by neutron activation. In *Proceedings of Conference on Modern Trends in Activation Analysis*. 1965.

Voysey, H.W. 1832. Description of native manufacture of steel in South India. *Journal of Asiatic Society of Bengal* I: 245-7; II: 402.

Wadsworth, J. and D.R. Lesuer. 2000. *Materials Characterization* 45: 289-313.

Wadsworth, J. and O.D. Sherby. 1980. On the Bulat – Dasmascus steels revisited. *Progress in Materials Science* 25: 36-68.

Wadsworth, J. and O.D. Sherby. 1985. *Scientific American* 252: 94.

Wadsworth, J. and O.D. Sherby, 1992. Comments on "Damascus Steel, Part III: The Wadswrth-Sherby Mechanism by Verhoeven et. al. *Materials Characterization* 29: 165-172.

Wadsworth, J. and O.D. Sherby, 2001. *Materials Characterization* 47: 163-165.

Wagner, D.B. 2000. Chinese monumental iron castings. *Journal of East Asian Archaeology* 2: 200-224.

Wayman, M. and G. Juleff. 1999. Crucible steel making in Sri Lanka. *Historical Metallurgy* 33: 26-42.

Williams, A. 1997. Ottoman military technology: the metallurgy of Turkish armour, In *War and Society in the Eastern Mediterranean 7th-15th centuries* (Ed.) Y. Lev. Leiden: Brill. pp. 363-398.

Wilson, C.R. 1897. *Catalogue of Antiquities in the Asiatic Society of Bengal.* Kolkata: Asiatic Society.

Wranglen, G. 1970. The rustless Iron Pillar at Delhi. *Corrosion Science* 10: 761-770.

Wulff, J. 1966. *Traditional Crafts of Persia; Their Development, Technology and Infuence on Eastern and Western Civilizations.* Cambridge. pp 8-9.

Xu, L. 1989. *Zhongguo Gudai Huopao Shi* ("The history of cannons in ancient China"). Renmin Chubanshe. Shanghai.

Yamashita, M., H. Miyuki, Y. Matsuda, H. Nagano and T. Misawa. 1994. The long term growth of the protective rust layer formed on weathering steel by atmospheric corrosion during a quarter of a century. *Corrosion Science* 36: 283-299.

Yater, Y.M. 1983. *THAR* 11(4): 2.

Yater, Y.M. 1983-84. The legendary steel of Damascus. In *The Anvils Ring.* (Spring 1982): 1-8; (Summer 1983): 3-13; (Winter 1983-4): 3-17.

Yazdani, G. 1947. *Bidar: Its History and Monuments.* London: Oxford University Press. pp. 35-43 and 85.

Zschokke, B. 1924. Du Dumasse et des Lames de Damas. *Revue du Metallurgie* (Paris) Part I. 21: 535-669.

INDEX